Gottfried Mergner
Social Limits to Learning

Gottfried Mergner
SOCIAL LIMITS TO LEARNING

Essays on the Archeology of Domination, Resistance, and Experience

Edited with an introduction by
Marcel van der Linden

Translated by
William Templer

Berghahn Books
NEW YORK • OXFORD

First published in 2005 by

Berghahn Books

www.BerghahnBooks.com

© 2005 Marcel van der Linden

Library of Congress Cataloging-in-Publication Data

Mergner, Gottfried.
  Social limits to learning : Essays on the archeology of domination, resistance, and
experience / Gottfried Mergner ; edited with an introduction by Marcel van der Linden ;
translated by William Templer.
    p. cm.
  Includes bibliographical references and index.
  ISBN 1-84545-004-3 (alk. paper)
   1. Social history. 2. Social change. 3. Learning-Social aspects. I. Title: Essays on the
archeology of domination, resistance, and experience. II. Title.

HN8.M39 2004
303.3'2–dc22   2004062285

British Library Cataloguing in Publication Data
A catalogue record for this book is available
from the British Library.

Printed in the United States on acid-free paper.

ISBN 1–57181–546–5 (hardback)

CONTENTS

1 Gottfried Mergner
Marcel van der Linden   1

2 The Theory of Social Limits to Learning:
On Social History as a Method   20

3 The "National Heritage" of German Colonialism   32

4 "Solidarity With the Savages?"
German Social Democracy and the African Resistance
Struggle in the Former German Colonies   46

5 Death and Social Democracy   63

6 "Faithful Fatalism":
On the Concept of "Total War" in the History
of Mentality   88

7 Social Change Without Social Actors?
The Continuing Legacy of the Philosophy of History   101

8 Racism as a Distinctively European Species
of Xenophobia   113

9 Inculcated Normality and Exclusion:
Six Theses on the History of European Xenophobia   123

10 Solidarity in a World of Growing Interconnectivity   131

11 Compulsive and Coerced Identities:
   Once More on the Theory of Social Limits
   to Learning   139

Acknowledgements   155

Index   157

Gottfried Mergner

Chapter 1

Gottfried Mergner

Marcel van der Linden

Introduction

At the heart of the historical and social sciences lies the remarkable gray area of learning processes. "Learning" is usually perceived as individual childhood development at home and at school and has been written about extensively. At this time, little is known about learning processes outside primary and secondary socialization (i.e., outside home and school environments), for example through collective action, although virtually everybody agrees that socialization is "never total and never finished."[1]

We are continuously involved in learning processes in all kinds of fields and through a great many institutions. Overall insight into these learning processes appears indispensable for understanding social changes or the lack thereof. The following example illustrates this point. Social revolutions have often been mentioned as causing the revival of pre-revolutionary behavior patterns after a while. Over a century and a half ago, for example, Alexis de Tocqueville noted that in post-revolutionary France all kinds of laws and customs from the old regime were restored after a relatively brief interruption. He attributed this pattern both to the fact that some "old" institutions had indeed suited modern needs and to the fact that they were never truly eliminated, "as some rivers flow into the earth to reappear further on, taking the same rivers along new river banks."[2] Reflecting on a similar pattern during the Soviet experience, Moshe Lewin postulated his tentative maxim: "The quicker you break and change, the more of the old you recreate," as "Institutions and methods which seemed to be entirely new, after deep insight show the often quite astonishing re-emergence of many old traits and forms."[3]

Such forms of historical repetition seem to indicate incomplete learning processes: new social relations arrived so quickly that people were unprepared

---

Notes for this section begin on page 15.

and—in their quest for what was trusted and familiar—resorted to established institutions. Problems such as these, however, are rarely discussed in such terms. In most cases, it is merely *noted* that the old was miraculously restored, but the subjective foundation of the pattern is not explored or is explored in insufficient depth. Learning processes are thus visualized exclusively through their outcome. Questions as to *how* and *why* people learn or do not learn generally remain unanswered.

In his short lifetime, Gottfried Mergner made a considerable effort to compensate for this shortcoming. Since the 1970s, he has tried through historical and current case studies, philosophical reflections, and critical commentaries to devise a "theory of social limits to learning" intended to explain not only why people accept or reject structures of domination, but also why people trying to emancipate themselves nonetheless form and accept new structures of domination. He presents an intelligent combination of analyses of primary, secondary, and tertiary socialization. Mergner's work has yet to become known outside German-speaking areas. This anthology serves to change this situation.

Autobiographical inspiration

Because Mergner used his own life experiences as an important "ingredient" for his theoretical efforts, some biographical details are in order. Mergner's youth was colored by the Third Reich and its consequences. Born on 4 May 1940 in Würzburg in the South of Germany, he was raised in a family that associated fascism with religious devotion. Both his parents were ardent National Socialists and had worked in Tanganyika as missionary doctors. His

mother had returned to Germany a few months before his birth, while his father remained behind and was later interned by the British. When his father joined the family a few years after the end of the war, he was a stranger, and Gottfried had difficulty growing accustomed to him. Gottfried's father firmly believed that individual will needed to be broken, on the ground that only fully humbled individuals could serve as a *tabula rasa* for God. As his son refused to submit, however, the two became entangled in a persistent conflict of wills. The young Mergner was involved in a second, parallel struggle as well. Because he had a heart condition and suffered from dyslexia, he was a poor student. One teacher mentioned regarding his "case" that "the Nazis would have dealt differently with this problem." Gottfried Mergner was forced to leave the gymnasium school he attended before graduation and supported himself for a while as a casual laborer. He later sat for his final exams as an extension student and went on to attend several university programs.[4]

Mergner's childhood experiences had a lasting impact on him. Convinced of the importance of having a mind of one's own, he developed a deeply rooted aversion to authoritarianism and traditional pedagogical approaches. Another fairly logical consequence of these experiences was that Mergner became involved in politics, like many others of his generation in the 1960s. Locally, he served for a few years as a social-democratic city council member in the village of Katzwang near Nuremberg and was active in the radical Sozialistischer Deutscher Studentenbund (SDS) from 1967 until the organization was disbanded in 1970.

The first radical thinkers who inspired him included philosophers from the Frankfurter Schule, such as Theodor Adorno and Max Horkheimer, as well as the leftist legal scholar and historian Wolfgang Abendroth.[5] Within the SDS, Mergner soon became fascinated with Hans-Jürgen Krahl (1944-1970), a doctoral student of Adorno, who was regarded as the most important theoretician of the student movement. Krahl represented the third generation of the Frankfurter Schule.[6] He advocated an anti-authoritarian practice that was neither spontaneist nor Leninist. Krahl formulated his view as follows:

> No highly industrialized country has had a successful revolution thus far. I attribute this to the failure to acknowledge during the first stage of both Internationals that the crisis situation arising from material misery does not intrinsically instigate revolution. It was not understood that the masses needed to be educated for a long time beforehand, as Marx had told the Willich-Schapper faction: you will need to wage civil war for fifty or sixty years, not to change relationships but to change yourselves and the awareness of the workers. This consciousness raising, which absolutely must occur in conjunction with actions, will take far longer in this day and age. Rather than a primary power struggle for political control of the state, the objective is to set in motion a long-term enlightenment process.[7]

Krahl aimed to combine critical theory with a broadly based learning process based on the people's own experiences. Mergner fully agreed with this view and was guided by it for the rest of his life. Mergner aimed to be an educator along the lines of Marx's third Feuerbach thesis, according to which "the educator must himself be educated", as "*revolutionary practice*" is attainable only through "the coincidence of the changing of circumstances and of human activity or self-change."[8]

This approach was already apparent in Mergner's first publication, which was an article he wrote in 1968 together with the historian Hartmut Mehringer for the Parisian radical journal *Partisans*. Here, Mergner raised the question: "how will the masses learn to emancipate?" The answer was that "self-organization of the masses" required a new educational practice, devoid of student elitism or moralizing appeals. The vanguard would need to encourage learning "by establishing and maintaining communication—and discussion—among these collectives of organized resistance that would be the foundation for formulating strategy."[9] During these years, Mergner hoped to connect the struggle of students and workers via the "long-term enlightenment process" advocated by Krahl.

In addition to tremendous patience, such a learning process demands extensive knowledge of the history of social movements, especially of labor movements.[10] Accordingly, Mergner started his theoretical activities with various historical studies concerning the problematic relationship between workers and outspoken members of the intelligentsia—based on the perspective of the intelligentsia. He initially focused on revolutionary European intellectuals at the end of World War I and the two decades that followed. He published about the Dutch council communists (Herman Gorter and Anton Pannekoek) and about the Russian Workers' Opposition (Alexandra Kollontai and others).[11] He was most fascinated, though, by Otto Rühle (1874-1943), a German and originally a social-democratic schoolteacher, who gradually embraced radicalism and was active in the politics of the far left during the 1920s and 30s. After editing a few of Rühle's writings in 1971,[12] Mergner completed his doctoral thesis "Workers' movement and ideological learning: on the political pedagogy of Otto Rühle" the next year.[13]

Mergner's decision to write his doctoral thesis on Rühle was highly indicative of his subsequent development. After all, from the mid-1920s, Rühle had been the first and foremost advocate of what we might refer to as pedagogical Marxism. Reflecting on the abortive German revolution of 1918-1919, Rühle concluded that its failure was attributable more to the mentality of the working class than to shortcomings in this or another revolutionary organization. Revolution would only be possible in industrialized countries when the working class had enough self-confidence and the will to take control of the real loci of power, the companies, and put them in the hands of Unity Organizations in which political and economic power were united. The fact that the working class had not done so in 1918-1919 was the result of its subaltern mentality. Rühle wrote in 1925:

> What is needed most today is the gradual dismantling of authority within people themselves, in their mode of psychic activity, in the general, daily practice of life in society. Dismantling authority in the organizational apparatus is important. Dismantling it in the theory and tactics of class struggle is more important. But most important of all is *dismantling authority in the human soul,* because without that it is impossible to abolish authority in either organization or tactics and theory.[14]

Rühle thus advocated a broad, revolutionary-pedagogical approach. Mergner was convinced of the current relevance of Rühle's theory but argued that it needed to be extracted from "the trappings of dated emotions" to be applicable.[15] Mergner's study, which continues to be regarded as a major contribution to research on Rühle,[16] did not cover the later period from the 1920s onward but addressed the learning process that had preceded it:

The present work aims to present a learning process. During his decades of involvement with the organized labor movement, the primary school teacher Otto Rühle learned that workers' emancipation can materialize only through their own activities in production. As an educationalist, Rühle uses his own experiences to extrapolate theoretical consequences for a socialist social pedagogy and for the avant-garde problem in the socialist movement. That is why his learning process merits consideration.[17]

The dissertation is not a biographical study in the conventional sense. Rather than minutely reconstructing the details of Rühle's life, it conveys the highlights of his development. Mergner engages in *analytical* historiography by asking history questions that he considers to be of central political importance.

Mergner reveals how Rühle drifted ever further from traditional social democracy. Whenever the leadership of an organization grew autocratic, Rühle joined the movements and groups that defended and promoted autonomous actions and ideas. At the same time, Rühle observed consistently that the working class made insufficient use of the learning opportunities available during the struggle for emancipation.[18] Rühle therefore came to view the classical working-class organizations, with their division of labor between union and party, as products of historical underdevelopment and set his sights increasingly on proletarian self-liberation.[19]

Origins of the Theory of Social Limits to Learning

While Mergner made frequent reference to learning processes in his earliest publications, he still interpreted these processes in linear terms. Rühle and the other intellectuals studied appeared to experience cumulative development, with each new insight elaborating previous ones. This linear perception of learning processes started to be challenged in 1974-1975, when Mergner obtained an appointment at the university of Oldenburg, where he met Richard Pippert (1939-1993). Together with Pippert, whose primary interest was the history of education, Mergner drafted a basic outline for the Theory of Social Limits to Learning.[20] The two wrote a voluminous, unpublished manuscript about "Educational strategies and learning prospects: introduction to the social history of education." In this text, they argued that reality consisted on the one hand of the "drive or compulsion to learn" and on the other hand of the "limit to learning."[21] Subjects would overcome limits on learning through practice, i.e., through knowledge-mediated activity. Each practice, however, would necessarily give rise to new limits on learning, which might once again be overcome through practice.

People learn, but—and here I use a sentence from Marx—they learn not "out of free choice but through circumstances encountered." Practical involvement with reality is constitutive for those learning. The circumstances encountered, under which people learn, are their reality, and these people are part of this reality. The learning subjects, who must conform to their reality and be part of it for practical reasons, juxtapose themselves against this reality through such learning, while this reality is at the same time juxtaposed against them.[22]

Mergner regarded the purpose of learning as "complete and undivided development of all living productive forces."[23]

The working class operates within social contexts that serve as an experiential horizon, which is "the framework of external conditions for the subjective attitudes, actions, orientations of those concerned," while "the organizations, types of movements, expressions and manifestations" offer "opportunities for learning and circumscribing action" within this framework, "with which these experiences achieve a collective formulation." From this perspective, "the diversity of the labor movement" is an expression of "manifold experience structures." Amid this diversity, unity may be attained solely through "experience with the class struggle" and not through "intellectual insight or enlightenment."[24]

Mergner elaborated this principle in a few subsequent publications. In a programmatic text from 1976, he formulated the central questions of the Theory of the Social Limits to Learning as follows:

(1) How do people accommodate the form and substance of the laws of capitalist production and social hierarchy in their actions—and as distinct individuals?

(2) How does individual action determine how individuals relate to reality as a whole, and do conscious expressions convey this relationship?

(3) Where and under which conditions do learning processes emerge that transcend system-adequate operations, make such action sensitive to limits and consequently make it possible to transcend them?[25]

These questions arise from the idea derived from Marx, Lukács, Korsch and others that capitalism is a society based essentially on competition that individualizes wageworkers and deprives them of the awareness that they reproduce capitalism themselves every day. "They may be controlled and integrated in the system, as long as they distinctively see only the importance of their own individual reproduction in their labor. Under these circumstances, they fail to understand that together they control social production and consequently social reality through their labor." Wageworkers therefore focus on their own wages and "experience their fear individually."[26]

The central issue is how to overcome this mystifying reification. How can workers learn to regard themselves as historical subjects? The first step is for them to organize "as carriers of the same interests" within capitalism, if only in rudimentary respects, such as in a workers' sports association or a trade union.[27] Such organizations in turn have a reifying effect and block ongoing learning processes. In the event of such an obstacle, the outcome will not be self-awareness. Instead, these disrupted learning processes will "engender generalized individual fear of the consequences of individual learning."[28] Overcoming such learning obstacles is therefore essential. To this end, labor organizations from past and present should be perceived as embodying a contradiction "between anti-capitalist experience (learning opportunities) and capital-appropriate limits."[29]

The discovery of ambivalence as a core category

Despite Mergner's major theoretical advances in the 1970s, his studies remained highly diagrammatic in this period. The workers ultimately concerned lacked an identity and were in fact merely the surroundings for the learning transpiring in the intellectual arena. The intellectuals described remained largely one-dimensional as well: they were "political creatures" without a love life, fears, or nonpolitical desires.

All this changed thanks to Mergner's personal development. He experienced a severe crisis between 1976 and 1979 and attributed "the unresolved problem of his existence" to the missing "unity of life and thought": "I mistrust my knowledge—like an intrinsically logical brickwork that I have built around my fears." He observed: "The ability we have acquired to think is consistently the effort to find the shortest possible lines between two points."[30] Mergner overcame his depression without a psychiatrist through a kind of autonomous psychoanalysis. He emerged with a remarkably enhanced vision of social history. Henceforth, individuals in his view were not "character masks" in the Marxian sense but layered personalities engaged in a continuous quest.

The ambivalence concept became essential in Mergner's work. Mergner argued that many of our experiences have several meanings at once and are therefore ambivalent.[31] In his analysis of human behavior, he started to focus far more on contradictions and repression. He was deeply influenced by two works. First, he found the literary scholar Hans Mayer's magnum opus *Aussenseiter* (1975) very compelling.[32] Mayer claimed "that the bourgeois Enlightenment has failed."[33] After all, the standards of the Enlightenment apply universally in equal measure, with respect to "normal" cases and outsiders alike. The universal applicability of these standards violates "the special existential quality" of these outsiders (e.g., women, homosexuals, Jews). The equality postulates of the Enlightenment are abstract. They are "universally" applicable but should in fact protect the rights of the specific individuals. "A mindset that looks down on any hint of personification and exclusively acknowledges collectivities, the quantitatively significant normal cases, rather than the qualitative individual cases, promotes fetishism and consequently inhuman practices."[34] Mayer therefore believed that enlightened humanist thought needed to be radicalized.[35] Mergner interpreted Mayer's argument as confirmation of his deep-seated suspicion of all abstract equalizing.

Sartre's great Flaubert study *L'Idiot de la famille* deeply influenced Mergner as well.[36] Sartre presented the case of the writer Gustave Flaubert to demonstrate that choice and fate are always separated by a gray area, no matter how small. That is why every historical situation comprises freedom, even when the room to maneuver is minimal. Subjectivity may therefore be regarded as *décalage*, as the difference between internalization and externalization. Mergner read this work as an in-depth analysis of the rise of resistance.

Mergner explored the complexities of the new approach in several essays. One of his first attempts was the study he wrote in the late 1970s about Johannes Knief (1880-1919), a leading leftist radical in Bremen during the German revolution of 1918-1919. Mergner tried to reveal in his analysis how Knief "depended increasingly on and succeeded in projecting his desires, his ideals, his conceptions, his fears on the movements of Bremen workers by acquiring an identity through his role and function in the labor movement and by generalizing his experiences into principles of the labor movement."[37] Mergner describes Knief's radicalization as successive identification with various "father figures, on whom he focuses, engages in close confrontations with, and subsequently breaks away from, usually vehemently rejecting them." Knief was surrounded by "largely male groups of workers, who accepted and even worshipped him as a figure of identification and leadership."[38]

In his essay "Death and Social Democracy," which he wrote with Petra Schwarzer, Mergner took issue with the view of death in the German labor movement in the late nineteenth century. Mergner and Schwarzer argued that the social-democratic outlook on death reflected the authoritarian structure of the movement. The social-democratic faith that progress was inevitable had become a spiritual doctrine of salvation, which—like the Christian churches— sacrificed individuality for a higher cause: "The 'inexorable' forward march of the organization seemed to bestow on the individual's life a meaning beyond death."[39] Funerals of comrades (and especially of leaders) became sites for "the creation of meaning in Social Democratic culture, the celebration of the transcendence of individual existence."[40] At the same time, the leaders fossilized into monuments became pillars of the political hierarchy, protecting the organization "from any unruliness and rebelliousness."[41] World War I, in which many Social Democrats sacrificed their own lives for the Fatherland, was thus a small step. Because radical workers had learned to suppress their personal fear of death for the sake of an abstract willingness to sacrifice, they could be manipulated into sacrifices for causes other than the original ones.

In a study he published with other scholars in the late 1980s, Mergner elaborated the ambivalence idea very explicitly through an analysis of over two thousand primarily German children's books issued since the eighteenth century. He defended the view—based in part on comparisons with African and Turkish children's books—that as childcare becomes exclusively the mother's domain, the relationship between children and their mothers becomes increasingly difficult and neurotic. Mothers come to embody love *and* almighty power and thus acquire a dual nature. They are both tender, loving, protective "good" mothers and merciless, cold, cruel, and evil "bad" mothers.[42]

The African turn

Along with his discovery of ambivalence, Mergner took a second major step. He increasingly replaced his European orientation with a focus on Africa, the continent he had heard so much about in his parental home. This geographical shift was a political transition as well. After all, protest movements in the advanced capitalist countries had stagnated since the mid-1970s, and Mergner had given up hope of sweeping changes in this part of the world in the near future.[43] This was part of the reason why he became especially interested in the practice of European cultural dominance in former and current colonies. This awareness first surfaced in his 1982 essay "Mission at Kilimanjaro: Education between tradition and geometrization of faith."[44] In this relatively static text, he reconstructed the efforts of German evangelist missionaries to teach the local population to adapt to the foreign rule through order, discipline, and forceful regimentation.

In a research project conducted shortly thereafter about Africans in German books for children and young adults until 1945, which gave rise to a traveling exhibition and a published monograph, Mergner tried to demonstrate the relationship between disciplining German youth (socializing boys to become soldiers and girls to become mothers) on the one hand and stereotyping the Africans, who consisted primarily of "horrific enemies or ridiculous caricatures," on the other hand. Devaluing the "captured cultures and peoples" enabled the "folk community" in the homeland to consolidate.[45]

Mergner made sporadic efforts to associate his old interest in labor and working-class history with his new African orientation, such as in his 1985 essay "Solidarity with the Savages?" In this study, Mergner examined the attitude among German social-democratic workers toward the colonial population in "German South-West Africa" (Namibia) around 1900. Based on sources such as the *Norddeutsches Volksblatt*, a regional social-democratic newspaper, Mergner revealed that the progressive workers could not imagine that they might "have anything in common with the 'uncivilized' savages" in the colonies.[46] Mergner attributed this to the adaptation of the working class "to the dominant social reality under the press of political constraints." The workers "attempted to achieve political and cultural identity and self-worth through autonomous organization" and elevated their self-respect via "the downgrading and exclusion of those on the margins of the industrial-capitalist frame of exploitation: the unemployed, minorities, children, women and colonized peoples."[47] Though based on a very limited range of sources, this essay nonetheless extended horizons, as historical studies on colonial attitudes among average workers remain few and far between.

A synthesis in the making

From the late 1980s, the different lines converged in increasing measure: the early theory of the Social Limits to Learning is integrated with the ambivalence idea and the African turn. Mergner derived great inspiration from the work of Ernest Jouhy (1913-1988), a theoretician whom he only truly "discovered" shortly after Jouhy's death, and who had been intellectually involved in the same field but in his essays had shifted his exploration from one aspect to another of the general field of learning processes.[48] Like

Otto Rühle, whom Mergner had studied so intensively, Jouhy had been a follower of Alfred Adler's *Individualpsychologie*. Jouhy's work led Mergner to abandon definitively the dialectical approach he had supported since the 1960s.[49] According to dialectics, conscious action "reveals only what is actually already inherent in embryonic form in creation (society, history), a kind of midwifery."[50] From this perspective, individuals degenerate to "more or less erring functionaries of a historical collective will."[51] The concept of ambivalence, on the other hand, does greater justice to human opportunities for choice.

> the concept of *ambivalence* is a tool for describing the relations between the open possibilities for decision and the diverse interests and motivations of human actors in historical situations. It arises in the tension between the non-predefined and nonetheless real possibilities *and* the contradictory concepts, hopes and ways of seeing of the human actors involved. Research on ambivalence explores the tensions and contradictions between possible action and conceptualized reality, between the contradictory motives and diverse ideas of those involved.[52]

From the ambivalence perspective, resistance by those opposed to "progress" acquires a value and significance of which the dialectical model appears to deprive them:

> According to the dialectical model, history is a one-way street. The resolution of social contradictions ... leads perforce to social solutions at an ever-higher "stage of development." This also means though that all previous and future human attempts, blueprints, concepts and models that are (or will be) defeated in this linear historical process were (and will be) *justifiably* eliminated and surmounted, because they were outdated and erroneous. The triumphal procession of history carries these past or disappearing curiosities along in its surging current as the spoils of victory.
>
> Ambivalent thinking is open to grief over defeated and shattered human chances and possibilities; it harbors a readiness to recall the "messianic moments" in the past, human hopes, resistance and ethical endeavor. The model of ambivalence does not exclude the hope in deliverance and an end to present and past suffering. Yet the basis for liberation does not lie in a future that finally cancels, redeems and dissolves all previous contradictions. Rather it is rooted in the *past*: in past history, even defeat, the "perspective for human redemption" was repeatedly revealed in the form of an ambivalence melded of conformity and resistance.[53]

Mergner's results: a rough summary

On 6 June 1999, a few weeks after he turned 59, Gottfried Mergner died of the effects of a stroke.[54] Had he not died so young, his restless spirit would undoubtedly have continued to revise and elaborate the Theory of Social Limits to Learning. Even if he had lived far longer, however, his work would definitely have remained fragmented, since he was always suspicious of apparently consistent theoretical syntheses. Accordingly, I will summarize what I consider to be the most important elements, although I am well aware that such a summary fails to convey the wealth and complexity of Mergner's oeuvre.

1. Young children possess exceptional elasticity and are able to master the cultural intricacies of any culture. "Anybody can be born into any culture."[55] Every culture, however, is a selective order of reality and is therefore based in part on exclusion and coercion. Socialization means incorporating a certain identity in a culture, which obviously implies mastering the dividing lines between "native" and "foreign," "normal" and "deviant," "established" and "outsiders." *All* people are therefore "culturally restricted" and must learn to deal as best they can with "foreigners" and "deviants."

2. In the culture of Europe (the capitalist core countries), fear of the alien acquires a special meaning.[56] In a society of generalized commodity production, where both labor products and nature and human labor power have become market commodities, social life is imbued with competition. "Individuals experience the limitations on their ego abstractly and anonymously via the marketplace, especially the labor market and the educational institutions that imitate it. The upshot is that individuals are ultimately isolated in their conflicts on the boundaries and their attempts to assert themselves."[57] The consequence is a thoroughly neurotic culture of solitary individuals who must try to be "normal." After all, those who are *not* normal risk exclusion. "Early on we learn that those classified as 'useless,' 'worthless,' 'not worthy to live' have no basic rights. As adults, we then go about propagating the neurotic world view engendered by these early experiences, styling it as a general and valid rationality, the conventional wisdom."[58]

3. Fear of the alien is largely the outcome of classical projection. We learn to suppress "evil" desires within us and subsequently attribute these characteristics to outsiders. "They" are lazy, profligate, sexually uninhibited and so on, whereas "we" have an understanding of "civilization" and self-control. "Inherent in this form of hatred for what is alien and Other is an element of *self*-rejection, the self-hatred with which we have been inoculated. In downgrading and rejecting the Other, we struggle against our own defeats, our own weaknesses, our lack of non-conformism, drilled out of us at an early age, our loneliness, our sense of inferiority mediated by the marketplace."[59]

4. The ambivalent disposition toward the Other has a collective dimension as well. The fundamental social isolation resulting from individualization gives rise—especially in times of crisis and rifts—to a quest for surrogate security in imagined communities, such as "fatherland," "race," religion, "culture." "The manipulable obsession with feelings of identity and tribal solidarity is but the flipside of modern individualization, isolation and cultural insecurity."[60] Every imagined community defines itself through exclusion. "Via the false 'solidarity' of a fictive 'shared organic community' of the 'truly' useful and usable citizenry, the vital interests of those 'inside' are played off against everything categorized as foreign and 'external.' The ideological boundaries fossilize into rigid dogmatic truths; in this ossified form, they are then defended, using any means necessary, as the protective sheath of one's own imagined identity."[61] Hatred of the "alien" and "deviant" articulated through imagined communities is essentially the outcome of collective projection.

5. If we do not aim to drive away or liquidate the Others, we will need to educate them. This holds true both for the nonconformists in our own societies and for the "uncivilized" in the South. "The repressed wishes and emotions seem increasingly alien to the civilized person and are shunted off into the devalued margins of civilization. Just as workers could imagine only the same education for their children that they had suffered through, they also believed a cruel and repressive process was necessary to 'civilize' the 'savages.'"[62] We need to discipline them, so that they will become like us.

6. The Others are disciplining us at the same time. Within the modern school system and outside, we continuously submit to abstract standards (as a reflection of abstract social relationships) via the deeply rooted fear of being punished through exclusion. "The industrial systems of socialization and education require readily available, submissive and obedient individuals within the system's perimeters—and groups that are readily stigmatized outside the ambit of utility to be exploited as a useful foil. Via this duality, the boundary between 'them' and 'us' is demonstrated and, if need be, is forcibly enforced."[63]

7. Our discipline, however, comes about not only through fear but also through hope. After all, the ambivalent Other also represents the desires that we no longer admit: "the outsider transformed into scapegoat is always marked by an element of hope for resistance, a strain of unruliness. The witches *also* embodied the hope for liberating *all* senses (not just those useful to the authorities); the Jews were *also* the expression of the unfulfilled promise of bourgeois society for social equality on the basis of intellectual and material riches."[64] We cannot, however, admit the hope embodied by the Other without mediation, as this would render our repression efforts futile. The hope of another life needs to become abstract to remain manageable. "Isolated individuals have various means to bridge the intolerable contradiction between their subjective, concrete expectations for happiness and the abstract, internalized social laws of exploitation that have been forced upon them: consumption, day-dreaming, addiction, utopias and ideologies. They strive for conditions, conceptions, dreams and images in which subjectivity and objectivity are congruent."[65]

8. Collectively, abstract hope is expressed through Utopias. "By their nature, the utopian systems necessarily negate current human beings and their ambivalent reality of thought and action in favor of an ideal future purged of subject-linked ambivalences. They supplant the analysis of concrete human beings in their ambivalent life-situations by conceptions of idealized persons, leached of their living contradictions, their often irksome vitality."[66] The emerging utopias "tend to negate concrete human beings in all their ambivalence, holding out the utopian harmony of an identity of subject/object. To this end, they mobilize images of the enemy, produce adversaries and identify ever new culprits to blame for the evil and awful disharmony that persists."[67]

9. Our lives turn into compromises between desire and reality in an objectified world. These compromises are often the tedious outcome of extended "battles" with our immediate surroundings and social powers.

They tend to seem like "bogus generality and counterfeit graphicness" and consequently isolate themselves from "experience, inspection and rationality."[68] Accordingly, they constitute "social limits to learning that lock wishes into historical boundaries."[69]

10. "Political commonalities are based on conscious and articulated needs and openly articulated shared interests."[70] Politics based on "cultural identities" are reprehensible: "Under the conditions of abstract dominance, rigid collective bonds often turn for the oppressed into apartheid, the oppressors become fascists and resistance degenerates into counter-terror." This is why Mergner is doubtful about the concept of a multicultural society, "at least if what is meant is a situation where numerous individually distinguishable and separate 'cultures' are supposed to exist side by side and thrive under the umbrella of a common shared polity. Language communities are not cultural communities, just as classes, 'races,' and religions cannot be easily compartmentalized within narrow, individually definable and segregated domains of life, nor should they be. The right to blend and mix, to participate in transcultural learning processes, is at least just as fundamental as the right of the individual (if he or she so wishes) to retreat into a rigid community of identity."[71]

11. Consolidated ideologies tend to negate ambivalences and consequently to block learning processes. "Nationalism, fascism, even Marxism and the faith in science are all ideologies (systems of thought) that arose from the matrix of these tensions. They are secularized *systems of belief.* They serve to eliminate the contradictions and ambivalences of bourgeois-capitalist economy and politics on the individual level, and to integrate these on the social plane. Where they thematize individual desperation, they generate hope, harmony or utopianism. Like other social movements, the workers' movements failed to develop any politically workable emancipatory alternatives to the bourgeois crisis of the subject. Yet for reasons of power politics and an opportune forced collectivity, they negated the unresolved question of the subject and subjectivity via the faith in a paradisical future purged of contradiction."[72] This is why their claims to emancipation degenerated into a politics of representationalism, a "camp mentality" and hierarchical division of labor.[73]

12. Learning means trying to transcend the limits of learning and overcome personal obstacles. Insight into the society at large is possible only through critical analysis of personal development ("the politicization of our own needs"[74]). After all, this is where the fears and desires are isolated that both encourage and complicate such learning. "It is thus the particular and pressing task of analytical thought to disclose the kernel of hope in the shell of despair, the will to life in the longing for death, the myriad array of ambivalences in the dominant 'clear consensus.'"[75] Understanding the Others requires "conscious recollection of the injuries, deformations and experiences of violence we endured as children in our own society."[76] Learning in this sense is a social process, based largely on communication with kindred spirits. Such learning is not necessarily theoretical and can be political or artistic as well.

13. The driving force behind this learning process is not the Utopia but "the principle of hope" (Ernst Bloch), which "derives its strengths and hopes from memory-work. Via the agency of the past, it discovers the concrete, hopeful political perspectives animating the real persons present here and now. It penetrates through the systematic characteristics imposed upon humans to the core of their hidden but concrete fundamental desires, their yearnings for freedom. Despite the capacity for human beings in history to be misled and seduced by 'perverted utopias,' the 'principle of hope' discloses human desires for a better life, scarcely realizable under the given present conditions: the desire for personal dignity, security in solidarity and an environment full of exuberance for life."[77]

14. The more ambivalent the position of individuals, the sooner they can challenge the limits on learning. People labeled as outsiders in one or several respects by the dominant culture tend to have fewer thresholds to overcome.[78]

15. Overcoming the limits on learning by no means indicates that learning will continue unimpeded from that point onward. Time and again we find that both individuals and social groups impose new limits on learning for fear of straying too far from what is familiar to them. Otto Rühle, for example, was unable to acknowledge his own ambivalences. He fell repeatedly "into the trap of dichotomous thinking. His lifelong learning process was marked by a repeated tendency to believe he had found security and 'the answers' in a certain position, only then to be disturbed by the real lack of consequence of the given conception or organization—and to stumble on to the subsequent 'consequence.'"[79] Likewise, throughout the student revolt from the 1960s onward, "our efforts were transformed again and again into concrete realities that had less and less in common with what was originally intended."[80]

This anthology

The recurring core theme in Mergner's work is that people can organize their experiences in two different ways: abstract or critical. Abstract or dogmatic is a classification of the experience based on an external idea and concerns, in the words of Lucio Colletti, "the assumption that knowledge is already *given*" and thus "the affirmative statement that the *content* itself of knowledge is independent of experience." Having an order of experience that can question itself based on those experiences and can "scrutinize both its own contents, preventing them from imposing themselves surreptitiously or '*sub rosa*,' and also scrutinize itself at work," however, is critical.[81] Power that does not derive exclusively from violence is consistently based on experiences interpreted in abstract terms as well.[82] In turn, liberation is based largely on critical learning processes that continuously seek to transcend abstract limits on learning.

Mergner has elaborated and made concrete this general idea in many different ways. The essays collected in this work attest to this practice and are snapshots of a theoretical development. Mergner always intended his texts as provisional statements for additional discussion. He wanted his own ideas to be subjected to the critical approach he advocated. In his view, dissent was a necessary condition for the existence of every free society.[83]

Post scriptum: Editorial comments or additions are identified by square brackets ([...]) that surround them.

Notes

1. Peter Berger and Thomas Luckmann, *The Social Construction of Reality. A Treatise in the Sociology of Knowledge* (Harmondsworth: Penguin 1971), p. 157.
2. Alexis de Tocqueville, *L'Ancien Régime et la Révolution*. Second Edition (Paris: Michel Lévy Frères, 1856), pp. 341 and 11 (quotation).
3. Moshe Lewin, "The Social Background of Stalinism," in: Robert C. Tucker (ed.), *Stalinism. Essays in Historical Interpretation* (New York: W.W. Norton & Co., 1977), pp. 111-136, at 126.
4. The paragraph above is based on Volker Mergner, "Der Antagonismus und die Symbiose von Liebe und Gewalt," in: Wolfgang Nitsch *et al.* (eds.), *Statt Menschenliebe: Menschenrechte. Lernprozesse zwischen gesellschaftlicher Anpassungsgewalt und Widerstand. Zur Erinnerung an Gottfried Mergner (1940-1999)* (Frankfurt am Main: IKO — Verlag für Interkulturelle Kommunikation, 2002), pp. 32-36. Gottfried Mergner studied public law, political science, and East European and modern history in Erlangen-Nuremberg, Frankfurt, and Amsterdam.
5. Wolfgang Abendroth (1906-1985) is known outside German-speaking regions primarily for his book *A Short History of the European Working Class*. Trans. Nicholas Jacobs and Brian Trench (New York: Monthly Review Press, 1972).
6. The first generation of thinkers included Erich Fromm, Herbert Marcuse, and Leo Löwenthal, in addition to Adorno and Horkheimer. Jürgen Habermas was the most important representative of the second generation.

   On Krahl, see: Detlev Claussen, "Hans-Jürgen Krahl — ein philosophisch-politisches Profil" (1985), in: Wolfgang Kraushaar (ed.), *Frankfurter Schule und Studentenbewegung. Von der Flaschenpost zum Molotowcocktail 1946-1995* (Hamburg: Rogner & Bernhard bei Zweitausendeins, 1998), vol. 3, pp. 65-70, and the editorial introduction in Hans-Jürgen Krahl, *Konstitution und Klassenkampf: Zur historischen Dialektik von bürgerlicher Emanzipation und proletarischer Revolution. Schriften, Reden und Entwürfe aus den Jahren 1966-1970* (Frankfurt am Main: Verlag Neue Kritik, 1971).

   Very few of Krahl's writings have been translated into English. Nevertheless, see Hans-Jürgen Krahl, "Czechoslovakia: The Dialectic of the Reforms," *New Left Review*, no. 53 (January-February 1969), pp. 3-12; Idem, "The Political Contradictions in Adorno's Critical Theory," *Telos*, no. 21 (Fall 1974), pp. 164-167.
7. Hans-Jürgen Krahl, "Aus einer Diskussion über Horkheimers Kritische Theorie (Mai 1969)," in idem, *Konstitution und Klassenkampf*, pp. 230-241, at 238. Krahl's reference to "both Internationals" concerns the International Working Men's Association, which is also known as the First International (1864-76), and the social-democratic or Second International (1889-1914). The exact wording of the Marx passage quoted by Krahl is: "You have 15, 20, 50 years of civil war to go through in order to alter the situation and to train yourselves for the exercise of power." "[Meeting of the Central Authority, September

15, 1850]," in Karl Marx and Frederick Engels, *Collected Works*, vol. 10 (London: Lawrence & Wishart, 1978), pp. 625-629, at 626.

8. Karl Marx, "[Theses on Feuerbach]" (1845), in Karl Marx and Frederick Engels, *Collected Works*, vol. 5 (London: Lawrence & Wishart, 1976), pp. 3-5, at 4.

9. Hartmut Mehringer and Gottfried Mergner, "La nouvelle gauche allemande et Rosa Luxemburg," *Partisans*, no. 45 (December 1968 – January 1969), 67-82, here at 75 and 82.

10. Gottfried Mergner and Wulf Radtke, *Die VDS-Maschine. Kritischer Bericht über die Behandlung der Hochschule durch die verschiedenen sozialistischen Gruppierungen der BRD und Westberlins* (Bonn: Verlag Deutscher Studentenschaften, [1970]).

11. Gottfried Mergner (ed.), *Gruppe Internationale Kommunisten Hollands* (Reinbek bei Hamburg: Rowohlt, 1971); Idem (ed.), *Die russische Arbeiteropposition. Die Gewerkschaften in der Revolution* (Reinbek bei Hamburg: Rowohlt, 1972).

12. Otto Rühle, *Schriften. Perspektiven einer Revolution in hochindustrialisierten Ländern.* Edited by Gottfried Mergner (Reinbek bei Hamburg: Rowohlt, 1971).

13. Published as Gottfried Mergner, *Arbeiterbewegung und Intelligenz* (Starnberg: Werner Raith Verlag, 1973).

14. Otto Rühle, "Der autoritäre Mensch und die Revolution," in: Idem, *Zur Psychologie des proletarischen Kindes* (Frankfurt am Main: März, 1975), pp. 138-44, at 141. (Originally published in *Die Aktion*, 15 (1925), 555ff.) Partly due to the influence of his wife Alice Gerstel, Rühle saw a logical connection between the pedagogical Marxism he favored and Alfred Adler's *Individualpsychologie*, in which the quest for integral consciousness of the self was also central. Rühle devoted the rest of his life to elaborating this idea. See Wolfgang Kutz, *Der Erziehungsgedanke in der marxistischen Individualpsychologie. Pädagogik bei Manès Sperber, Otto Rühle und Alice Rühle-Gerstel* (Bochum: Ulrich Schallwig Verlag, 1991), and Elsbeth Würzer-Schoch, "Otto Rühle und Siegfried Bernfeld: Eine vergleichende Darstellung zweier Pädagogen, ihrer unterschiedlichen psychologischen und soziologischen Grundlegung und ihrer pädagogischen Relevanz," (Ph.D. thesis, Zurich University, 1995).

15. Gottfried Mergner, "Zum Verständnis der Texte," in: Rühle, *Schriften*, pp. 206-213, at 207.

16. Henry Jacoby and Ingrid Herbst, *Otto Rühle zur Einführung* (Hamburg: Junius Verlag, 1985). Published almost simultaneously with Mergner's doctoral thesis: Friedrich Georg Herrmann, "Otto Rühle als politischer Theoretiker," *Internationale wissenschaftliche Korrespondenz zur Geschichte der deutschen Arbeiterbewegung*, no. 17 (December 1972), pp. 16-60 and no. 18 (April 1973), pp. 23-50.

17. Mergner, *Arbeiterbewegung und Intelligenz*, p. 7.

18. Ibid., p. 16.

19. Mergner agreed with Rühle that the division of labor between an economic organization (the trade union) and a political organization (the party) revealed that workers' economic power was insufficiently advanced. The greater such economic power became, the more it would overlap with political power. Ibid., p. 97.

20. At the time Mergner met Pippert, Pippert had published *Idealistische Sozialkritik und "Deutscher Weltberuf." Paul Natorps Pestalozzirezeption in seiner ersten und letzten Interpretation* (Weinheim [etc.]: Beltz, 1969), as well as a scholarly edition of Paul Natorp's *Sozialpädagogik* from 1898 (Paderborn: Ferdinand Schöningh, 1974). From 1975 until his death, Pippert was a professor of social history of education at Philipps University in Marburg.

21. Mergner and Pippert, "Erziehungsstrategien und Lernperspektiven: Einführung in die Sozialgeschichte der Erziehung," Ms., p. 7. Mergner described Pippert as the progenitor of this theory. This volume, p. 30. Mergner and Pippert's manuscript comprises the following parts: (1) "Introduction" (Mergner and Pippert, pp. 1-17); (2) "Fundamental principles of bourgeois revolution doctrine" (Pippert, pp. 18-111); (3) "The workers' movement as a cause and object of bourgeois educational strategies" (Mergner, pp. 112-246a); (4) "Social history as theory of learning. Perspectives" (Mergner and Pippert, pp. 247-268); and (5) "Bibliography" (Pippert, pp. 269-306).

22. Ibid., p. 248. The English translation of Marx's own words reads: "Men make their own history, but they do not make it just as they please in circumstances they choose for themselves; rather they make it in present circumstances, given and inherited." Karl Marx, "The Eighteenth Brumaire of Louis Bonaparte," in: Marx, *Later Political Writings*. Edited and translated by Terrel Carver (Cambridge [etc.]: Cambridge University Press, 1996), p. 32.

23. Mergner and Pippert, "Erziehungsstrategien und Lernperspektiven," p. 248.

24. Ibid., p. 144.

25. Gottfried Mergner and Marcel van der Linden, "De opheffing van de `marxistiese´ socialisatietheorieën; de theorie van de sociale leergrenzen," *Paradogma: tijdschrift voor socialistische theorie en politiek*, 7, 2 (July 1976), pp. 19-47, at 22. The article was the final outcome of a debate between Mergner and myself on socialization theories, in which our positions gradually grew closer together. See Mergner, "Inleiding tot de marxistiese socialisatietheorie," *Paradogma*, 1974/2, pp. 25-32; van der Linden, "Elementen van een marxistiese socialisatietheorie," *Paradogma*, 1974/2, pp. 33-42; Mergner, "Marxistiese socialisatietheorie — voortzetting van een diskussie," *Paradogma*, 1974/4, pp. 78-84.

26. Mergner and van der Linden, "De opheffing," p. 42.

27. Ibid.

28. Ibid., p. 43.

29. Ibid., p. 45.

30. Mergner to van der Linden, November 1977.

31. Zygmunt Bauman aptly described ambivalence as "the possibility of assigning an object or an event to more than one category." Bauman, *Modernity and Ambivalence* (Cambridge: Polity Press, 1991), p. 1.

32. Hans Mayer, *Aussenseiter* (Frankfurt am Main: Suhrkamp, 1975); American edition: *Outsiders. A Study of Life and Letters* (Cambridge, MA: MIT Press, 1982). Mergner identified with Mayer not only because they both saw themselves as outsiders (Mayer was a Jewish homosexual), but also because they shared a leftist radical past. See Olaf Ihlau, *Die Roten Kämpfer. Ein Beitrag zur Geschichte der Arbeiterbewegung in der Weimarer Republik und im Dritten Reich* (Meisenheim im Glan: Hain, 1969), pp. 173-174; Hans Mayer, *Ein Deutscher auf Widerruf: Erinnerungen*, Vol. 1 (Frankfurt am Main: Suhrkamp, 1982), pp. 122-139. Mergner wrote a few passages about Mayer in his essay "Politik und Moral," in: Heribert Baumann, Francis Bulhof and Gottfried Mergner (eds.), *Anarchismus in Kunst und Politik. Zum 85. Geburtstag von Arthur Lehning mit Beiträgen aus dem Symposion vom 24.-26. Mai 1984 in Oldenburg* (Oldenburg: Bibliotheks- und Informationssystem der Universität Oldenburg, 1984), pp. 140-149, at 140-141.

33. Mayer, *Aussenseiter*, pp. 9 and 459.

34. Ibid., p. 464.

35. See also the review essay by Egon Schwarz and Russell Berman, "Women, Homosexuals and Jews — Stepchildren of the Enlightenment," *New German Critique*, no. 9 (Fall 1976), pp. 175-179.

36. Jean-Paul Sartre, *L'Idiot de la famille. Gustave Flaubert de 1821 à 1857*. 3 volumes (Paris: Gallimard, 1971-72); published in English as *The Family Idiot. Gustave Flaubert, 1821-1857*. Trans. Carol Cosman. 5 volumes (Chicago: Chicago University Press, 1981-1993).

37. Gottfried Mergner, "Johannes Knief und seine Region," (parts I and II) *Archiv für die Geschichte des Widerstandes und der Arbeit*, No. 1 (1979), pp. 85-117; No. 2-3 (1980), pp. 45-89, here at 45.

38. Ibid., Part I, p. 87.

39. "Death and Social Democracy," in this volume, p. 68.

40. Ibid., p. 68.

41. Ibid., p. 78.

42. Gottfried Mergner and Peter Gottwald (eds.), *Liebe Mutter — Böse Mutter. Angstmachende Mutterbilder im Kinder- und Jugendbuch* (Oldenburg: Bibliotheks- und Informationssystem der Universität Oldenburg, 1989).

43. As early as 24 February 1976 Mergner wrote to me: "Learning requires consciously processed experience as well. But that does not yet constitute practice or change of social

reality. I am growing increasingly convinced that such change is generated in the Third World, especially in Africa!"

44. Gottfried Mergner, "Mission am Kilimandscharo — Erziehung zwischen Tradition und Geometrisierung des Glaubens," in: Jos Gerwin, Gottfried Mergner and Jos Koetsier (eds.), *Alltäglichkeit und Kolonialisierung. Zur Geschichte der Ausbreitung Europas auf die übrige Welt (II)* (Oldenburg: Bibliotheks- und Informationssystem der Universität Oldenburg, 1983), pp. 65-85.

45. Gottfried Mergner, "Der Afrikaner als Erziehungsmittel im deutschen Kinderbuch," in: Ansgar Häfner and Gottfried Mergner (eds.), *Der Afrikaner im deutschen Kinder- und Jugendbuch bis 1945. Untersuchungen zur rassistischen Stereotypenbildung im deutschen Kinder- und Jugendbuch von der Aufklärung bis zum Nationalsozialismus* (Oldenburg: Bibliotheks- und Informationssystem der Universität Oldenburg, 1985). pp. 151-160, at 155.

46. "Solidarity with the Savages? German Social Democracy and the African Resistance Struggle in the Former German Colonies," in this volume. The text was written in honor of the fiftieth anniversary of the International Institute of Social History in Amsterdam.

47. Ibid., p. 47.

48. His collected essays have been published as *Klärungsprozesse. Gesammelte Schriften*. Edited by Robert Jungk, 4 volumes (Frankfurt am Main: Athenäum, 1988). Jouhy was born Ernst Jablonski into a Jewish family in Berlin and was expelled from the university for communist activities in 1933. He fled to France, where he joined the Resistance as Jouhy. He continued to go by this name for the rest of his life. Jouhy also established the chair for Education: Third World at the university of Frankfurt am Main in 1976.

49. Jouhy never took this step himself and consistently regarded himself as a dialectician.

50. Gottfried Mergner, "Zur Aktualität des Erziehungswissenschaftlers Ernest Jouhy," in: Gottfried Mergner and Ursula von Pape (eds.), *Pädagogik zwischen den Kulturen: Ernest Jouhy. Zur Aktualität des Erziehungswissenschaftlers [Jahrbuch "Pädagogik: Dritte Welt"]* (Frankfurt am Main: IKO-Verlag, 1995), pp. 135-160, at 156.

51. Ibid.

52. Ibid.

53. Ibid., p. 157.

54. On Mergner, see also the commemorative volume Nitsch *et al.*, *Statt Menschenliebe: Menschenrechte*.

55. Gottfried Mergner, "Compulsive and Coerced Identities. On the Theory of Social Limits to Learning," in this volume, p. 141.

56. While Mergner consistently refers to "Europe," this concept is not to be interpreted in purely geographical terms.

57. Mergner, "Compulsive and Coerced Identities," p. 144.

58. "Inculcated Normality and Exclusion. Six Theses on the History of European Xenophobia," in this volume, p. 125.

59. Ibid., p. 128.

60. Gottfried Mergner, "Kulturelle Identität, Eurozentrismus und Ausländerfeindlichkeit," in: *Ausgewählte Schriften*, Vol. 1: *Dominanz, Gewalt und Widerstand. Fragmente und Brüche europäischer Mentalitätsgeschichte* (Berlin [etc.]: Das Argument, 1998), pp. 35-44, at 37. See also Mergner, "Ernst Bloch und der Glaube," in: *Ausgewählte schriften*, Vol. 2, pp. 194-206, at 201: "Already in 1924, and thus shortly after Hitler's November 1923 Beer Hall Putsch in Munich, Bloch understood that fascism's strength lay in its capacity to seize upon and bind wishes and longings. One example can serve to illustrate this: modern capitalist society is increasingly shaped by competition, the struggle of all against all. This engenders individualism. But the wish for community lingers on. The fascists were able to occupy and reverse this wish for community using the concept of the folk community."

61. Mergner, "Compulsive and Coerced Identities," p. 145.

62. Mergner, "Solidarity with the Savages?," p. 48.

63. Mergner, "Compulsive and Coerced Identities," p. 145.

64. Gottfried Mergner, "Thesen zur politischen Theorie Peter Brückners," *Psychologie und Gesellschaftskritik*, Sonderheft 1 (1980), pp. 75-91, at 79.

65. Gottfried Mergner, "Über Notwendigkeit und Gefahren von Utopien und Visionen," in *Ausgewählte Schriften*, Vol. 1, pp. 74-83, at 81.

66. Ibid., pp. 81-82.

67. Ibid., p. 81.

68. "Racism as a Distinctively European Species of Xenophobia," in this volume, p. 118.

69. "Compulsive and Coerced Identities," p. 150.

70. Mergner, "Kulturelle Identität," p. 37.

71. Ibid., p. 38. Mergner defended this view in 1991. Later, Slavoj Žižek argued along roughly the same lines in "Multiculturalism, or, the Cultural Logic of Multinational Capitalism," *New Left Review*, no. 225 (September-October 1997), pp. 28-51.

72. Gottfried Mergner, "Der Politiker als Dichter: Herman Gorter. Die Marxismusrezeption in der Dichtung Herman Gorters," in: Marcel van der Linden (ed.), *Die Rezeption der Marxschen Theorie in den Niederlanden* (Trier: Karl-Marx-Haus, 1992), pp. 124-149, at 136.

73. Ibid. "In their fear of ambivalence and unsoluble contradictions in subjectivity, Marxists too allowed theory to atrophy into dogma. Where they were unable to eliminate the contradictions theoretically, they were liquidated with the help of organizational splits, exclusions, power struggles, and the manufacture of images of the enemy." Ibid., p. 114. The "camp mentality concept" ties in with Oskar Negt and Alexander Kluge's work *Öffentlichkeit und Erfahrung. Zur Organisationsanalyse von bürgerlicher und proletarischer Öffentlichkeit* (Frankfurt am Main: Suhrkamp, 1972); American edition: *Public Sphere and Experience. Toward an Analysis of the Bourgeois and Proletarian Public Sphere.* Trans. Peter Labanyi, Jamie Owen Daniel, and Assenka Oksiloff (Minneapolis: University of Minnesota Press, 1993). The concept refers to parties in the labor movement that organize proletarian experiences in abstract terms without doing justice to contradictions and ambivalences.

74. "Inculcated Normality and Exclusion," p. 128.

75. Gottfried Mergner, "Rechtsradikalismus, Ausländerfeindlichkeit, Rassismus," in *Ausgewählte Schriften*, Vol. 1, pp. 55-59, at 57.

76. "Inculcated Normality and Exclusion," p. 127.

77. Mergner, "Über Notwendigkeit und Gefahren," p. 82. Also: Mergner, "Ernst Bloch und der Glaube."

78. While Mergner defended this thesis orally on several occasions, he never recorded it in writing to my knowledge. It ties in with Mayer's book *Aussenseiter*. See, however, Gottfried Mergner, "Politik und Moral," in: Heribert Baumann, Francis Bulhof, and Gottfried Mergner (eds.), *Anarchismus in Kunst und Politik. Arthur Lehning zum 85. Geburtstag* (Oldenburg: Bibliotheks- und Informationssystem der Universität Oldenburg, 1984), pp. 140-149, especially 140-142.

79. Gottfried Mergner, "Zwischen Erziehung und Politik. Kritische Reflexionen und Parteilichkeit im Denken und Handeln Otto Rühles," in: Mergner, *Ausgewählte Schriften*, Vol. 2, pp. 189-193, at 190.

80. Mergner, "Thesen zur politischen Theorie Peter Brückners," p. 88.

81. Lucio Colletti, *Marxism and Hegel* (London: Verso, 1979), p. 90.

82. Mario Erdheim rightly states that: "Wherever individuals are unable to resolve internal conflicts, these may turn into potential support bases of rule." See his *Die gesellschaftliche Produktion von Unbewusstheit. Eine Einführung in den ethnopsychoanalytischen Prozess* (Frankfurt am Main: Suhrkamp, 1982), p. 417.

83. Gottfried Mergner, "Paulo Freire: Zur Vernunft der Solidarität," in: Nitsch *et al.*, *Statt Menschenliebe: Menschenrechte*, pp. 100-108, at 103.

CHAPTER 2

THE THEORY OF SOCIAL LIMITS TO LEARNING
On Social History as a Method

Human beings make their own history, but they do not make it just as they please in circumstances they choose for themselves; rather they make it in present circumstances, given and inherited. Tradition from all the dead generations weighs like a nightmare on the brain of the living.

— Karl Marx[1]

Reflection shows us that our image of happiness is thoroughly colored by the time to which the course of our own existence has assigned us. The kind of happiness that could arouse envy in us exists only in the air we have breathed, among people we could have talked to, women who could have given themselves to us. In other words, our image of happiness is indissolubly bound up with the image of redemption. ... The past carries with it a temporal index by which it is referred to redemption. There is a secret agreement between past generations and the present one. Our coming was expected on earth. Like every generation that preceded us, we have been endowed with a *weak* Messianic power, a power to which the past has a claim.

— Walter Benjamin[2]

The theory of social limits to learning is a powerful tool in social history. It can be used to interrogate learners' thought and action in the contradiction-ridden terrain between their objective situation and their subjective everyday practice, between new historical perspectives and the past residues of dominant force, between resistance and conformity. It seeks to explain how and why people in their individual and collective practice remain bound by shackles, both cultural and political, to existing structures of rule and domination. Why, both within social resistance movements and outside them, do individuals work against themselves, contributing to the making of new structures

---

Notes for this section begin on page 31.

of domination? Why do they build their own walls to learning or capitulate in the face of such barriers?

Yet the theory of social limits to learning goes a step further. It explores where existing limits on learning are broken down and how they can be surmounted. Methodologically, that step pries open an aperture in the compulsive character of existing social relations. A method that confronts and interrogates the "material" can accomplish a double task: first, it becomes possible to make a meaningful systematic classification of the totalizing dynamic of historical sequences and the contradictory relations of dominance and oppression that they contain, relating these to acting subjects in line with their respective forms of social life and organization.[3] Second, building on this, the method can disclose potentials for emancipation that humans can achieve by their own action. As a result, history sheds the deterministic character often ascribed to it either in the form of functionalist systems and their straitjacketing logic or in the unceasing "progressivity" of the capitalist logic of progress.[4] Fresh perspectives are opened up by the new possibilities for meaningful action that arise within definable boundaries. They ultimately make it possible to forge a concept of progress that is emancipatory in thrust and content, enlightening and humane.

The history of bourgeois culture will be used here to exemplify the theory of social limits to learning based on concrete historical material. However, that focus is no arbitrary example: rather, it constitutes the historical point of departure for the central blueprint for society today. Without a knowledge of that design and its concrete historical unfolding, present-day societies cannot be understood. Through the prism of the theory of social limits to learning, the history of bourgeois culture can be described as an era of limitations on learning; during this epoch, important revolutionary and indeed emancipatory inventions were transformed into structures of domination and oppression. Historically, this transformation of resistance into rule marks the transition from feudal to bourgeois society: i.e., the bourgeoisie proves successful in jockeying for a new position within the social hierarchy. However, that success was also due in no small measure to an effort by those in power to constrict and control an embracive resistance with emancipatory potential. In the tradition of resistance movements, this pattern of constriction stands as a decisive rupture. Manifested in it are new relations of dominance, coupled with relations of force. It now marks the altered boundaries on the social turf of the bourgeois-dominated societies. The establishment of the "new order" coerces individuals here too to accept conformity and change, forces a "new order" and "new orientation" in the array of sites for social action. The latter can be characterized as loci of resistance due to the emancipatory energies channeled into them.[5]

The theory of social limits to learning locates these ruptures on the social map and describes their impact. However, the boundaries of social resistance in the organized labor movement and anticolonial liberation struggles are not defined here solely from the perspective of power, but are perceived in their ambivalence; i.e., they are also conceived as a form of *self-imposed* limitation by accommodating to bourgeois and pre-bourgeois forms of dominance that have not yet been overcome. It is important to recognize that ambivalent dimension, because only from this perspective can human action be meaningfully integrated into the historical framework. Otherwise it degenerates into empty phraseology, cynicism or ideology. Through the prism of this theory, the respective steps in and limitations on learning can be correlated with their historical agents in this historical era. For example, initially the popular masses in motion at the outset of the bourgeois revolution[6] (in France, the *sansculottes*) pursued only their own social interests. Acting together with the bourgeoisie, they shattered the order of feudal-absolutist society. In their revolutionary fervor, they identified their immediate interests with the general "good of the republic."

Since they remained restricted in thought and action to the compass of their historical experiences, they achieved *both* more *and* less than what they had originally bargained for. Though their victories did not eventuate in what they considered an "ideal" society, they did lead to the historical breakthrough of bourgeois forms of rule. They were thus able to create the prerequisites for an enormous unfolding of productive forces. Since the latter was ultimately realized in the form of the development of bourgeois property (the real political-economic content of the bourgeois revolution), the mobilized popular masses created the necessary social conditions for new modern forms of exploitation. The acting masses of bourgeois revolutions are the proletariat in the stage of genesis.

Yet this constriction of resistant action and focus on the political-economic content by dint of which the bourgeoisie assumed power was unable to eradicate from history's memory the emancipatory potential articulated in revolution. Quite the contrary: after their ascent to power, the ruling burghers found themselves confronted with a difficult choice. They could either give all those under their yoke—other subjugated peoples, the lower classes, their own wives and children—a share of the power (thus forfeiting their political and economic interests) or they could be overrun and submerged by the expectations of the dominated.

In a bid to salvage their dominance, they "devised" the masking ideology of the nation-state, in whose superordinate interests they now ostensibly continued to function while concealing their own economic and political interests behind the facade of its demands. The social contradictions were bridged over with the aid of this ideology contra those outside the walls (colonies and hostile countries) and within.[7] As developments in the German Empire after 1871 illustrate, the ideology of the national (folkish-ethnic) community of fate[8] became the unifying cohesive force. It helped the ruling class consolidate internal social tranquillity; yet at the same time, under the banner of imperialism, it drove a process of constant expansion that ultimately culminated in a massive conflagration engulfing Europe and the globe.

The bourgeois class expanded public force in the domestic and foreign arena using national legislation and a rationally organized state and company administration. It secured its economic and political dominance by means of the police, a force "invented" during the period of absolutism, and the aid of the military. The public school system inculcated the new, general "conventional wisdom" of the nation-state in the heads and hearts of its controlled citizenry. State violence and administration became institutionalized, systematic, ideological, its scope thus increasingly "unlimited." In order to maintain power—which under the conditions of profit maximization was possible only by means of a permanent expansion of power—it constantly increased the levels of political and economic force within and without under the pressure of competition. Bloody suppression of social unrest and rebellion, colonialism, wars, expansion of the potential to threaten other states, the global exploitation of nature and the human race are stages in the intensification of a lethal threat via the capitalist development of the forces of production.

By contrast, freedom, equality, property and progress are the utopian ideas that gave the transition from the feudal to bourgeois form of rule the semblance of being an emancipation of "all humankind." In particular, the organized workers' movements in Europe arose from the contradictions of the bourgeois revolutions. Those revolutions loudly proclaimed the freedom and solidarity of all; in actual fact, they sought to accord these only to a male, property-owning middle class. The class interests of the incipient proletarian social movements and the anticolonial liberation movements[9] differed from the new social relations that had been achieved as a result of the dramatic events of the bourgeois revolutions—although those revolutions were possible only with the agency of proletarian mass action. These differences in interests forced the bourgeois nation-states into an abiding and insoluble contradiction: the plebian demands went beyond the "gut issues" of food and shelter to include the *general* human demands that the bourgeoisie had promised to fulfill.

By a huge ideological effort, bourgeois rule and capitalist economy tried to paper over the fact that the implementation of these general promises would mean the end of their dominance. They employed every means at their disposal to prevent their realization. In order to enlist the allegiance of the plebian classes, the revolutionary bourgeois class had propagated the passion of general human emancipation; however, right from the start, their practical political wisdom remained confined to the ambit of their own political and economic interests. Yet "after the battle's end," the victorious burghers could no longer silence the voice of these general promises among their former comrades in the struggle (and now their subjects) or eliminate them from collective memory—this despite great efforts to promote reaction and counter-enlightenment. The contradiction between the classes was thus established as a critical idea, in its content and utopian contours providing a blueprint for future conflict.

With the development of the proletarian base and organizational structures, which can be regarded as a partial success of the working class within the bourgeois state in the nineteenth century, the bourgeoisie gradually shed its social inhibitions and political innocence. Most ideologies of the bourgeois class in all cultural domains (art, science, religion, and education) now finally degenerated into a mere justification of their interests in domination and control, and were brutally opposed to all social interests and goals that contradicted those interests. The times had thus become ripe for racism, dictatorship, and totalitarian forms of rule that were established in order to maintain property and power.

Yet this did not just involve a dynamic to centralize institutions and prerogatives in a bid to safeguard power and dominance. These ideologies and measures were also always a response to movements for social emancipation and to threatened and real resistance. Even the most brutal suppressive measure was thus likewise invariably a reaction to an emergent wish for freedom, a concrete conception of emancipation or a strategy for social resistance. Here lies the manifest, material basis of hope as the potentiality of power that can be realized solely by means of acting subjects—a form of power that can, under the circumstances of dominance, be welded into a counterforce, thus posing a threat to oppressive systems of rule.

In conflicts over national constitutions in the nineteenth and twentieth centuries, the oppressed and exploited subjects were likewise always concerned with trying to legitimate various intermediate goals on the path to realizing their longings for freedom and genuine equality by anchoring them in law. On the other hand, the bourgeois class endeavored to establish and consolidate bourgeois property as a freely available capacity for production. Yet the contours of those contrasts repeatedly blurred as a result of the seemingly superordinate interests of the nation-state, and were neutralized in ideologies of communality. The constraints of the market turned these ideologies of community into a virulent reality, always at the expense of the competition or the excluded enemies. However, the contrasts remained, resurfacing again and again. If propaganda failed, the remedy against such differences were the "inventions" adopted from absolutism's arsenal of control, namely the police and military.

The initial methodological conclusion we can draw from this is that most historical events in Europe and vast areas of the world controlled by Europe can be analyzed within the frame of the tension between revolutionary utopia, capitalist exploitation, resistance, and state violence. Yet in such analysis, historical events remain within the straitjacket of abstract systematizations, that always contain a certain admixture of generalization diluting their power of explanation. This contradiction cannot be eliminated, it is an integral part of human existence (see also below). Here we also encounter a "boundary" for scientific inquiry once it is overstepped and an attempt is made to eliminate existing contradictions theoretically: their findings become exploitable, functionally useful for the furtherance of interests of domination.

Yet despite this limitation, the bond between theory and practice can be welded discursively, because that contradiction can be thematized utilizing the theory of social limits to learning. The theory *also* makes it possible to raise the question of the subjects' ability to take meaningful action—*despite* social contradictions, political oppression, and economic exploitation. Since social limitations on learning always contain options for their own elimination in the form of the wasted, unrealized possibilities they incorporate, by thematizing and analyzing these limitations, it is possible methodologically to analyze and break down the generalizations mediated by theoretical abstractions. As far as the relations of rule and dominance in the bourgeois state are concerned, this means that the theory of social limits to learning describes the political and social confrontations in the bourgeois state as possibilities for and limits on learning under the conditions of contradictory social interests manifested in this state, no matter how confused and opaque the configuration.

On the history and dialectic of bourgeois education

The theory of the social limits to learning is above all also a theory of education. Consequently, an important focus for its application is in the investigation of the system of public and private education. Here the dialectic of learning and the hindering of learning is organized; this is the site where the desired attitudes are reproduced. Here too, the focus is on bourgeois society and its enthroning of particular forms of education.

In their ideological polemics against feudal theological ideas that looked to the world after death, and whose "methodological principle" was a deductive method oriented to the hierarchical structure of propositions, the Enlightenment philosophers pursued an approach that was systematic, mediated by theory, and geared to experience. Systematic thinking supplanted a scholasticism oriented to hierarchical logic. The progressive feature of that approach was that individuals were now able to comprehend themselves, at least philosophically, as the *subjects* of history. In philosophy and bourgeois economics, they began to distance themselves systematically from their environment—so as to appropriate that environment productively. Philosophically, they no longer viewed themselves solely as onlookers watching events unfolding on the world stage, but as *participants* in their world, human actors. However, this new freedom in thought and action continued to remain confined within narrow class boundaries, generating differential conceptions and images of the future. From the very outset, the ruling bourgeoisie was alarmed: it feared that this philosophy could become a guideline for action by wage earners, colonized peoples and even their own wives and children, and thus took steps to prevent this from occurring. Their critical representatives realized that the new world view in fact already presupposed the idea of the emancipated subject as a concept of equality.

Thus, on its logical-systematic plane, Enlightenment thought and its pedagogy already linked the emancipatory utopia of universal human rights with a justification of the oppressive real presence of bourgeois-capitalist politics. It united the dominant purposeful rationality of the maximization of profit with the general promises for the "pursuit of happiness" held out by the bourgeois revolution. Before the emergence of the proletariat, the early pioneers of bourgeois educational thought subscribed to the general principles of freedom for all: equality, fraternity and the right to property. (Only slaves, imbeciles, and primitives, among which they soon included their own wives and children, were excluded from these rights.) After the victory of bourgeois class rule, these same ideologues justified restricting human rights to a smaller and smaller circle by individualizing the claim to equality and limiting it in terms of class. Every person, by dint of the development of his or her own individual natural capacities, could participate in general bourgeois rights. Yet there were numerous reasons "due to the nature of things" that many were called but only few chosen. Education conceived in this way served to promote the privileging of a small select few and the stigmatizing of the rest.

Critical thinkers (within the bourgeois intelligentsia as well) attempted to link the question of the individual and collective ability to act with the question of emancipation of humanity. Siegfried Bernfeld has given this pointed formulation.[10] In his eyes, education as a discipline is centered on exploring the conditions and forms of the transition from one generation to the next. Thus, social traditions and forms of rule are reproduced via public and private education, and the continuity of rule can only be explained and described in this way. At the same time, however, education also helps pass on to succeeding generations the experiences of social contradictions and strategies for dealing with them. Consequently, strategies to change society must grapple with the legacy of the ruling generation. Intrinsic to this unavoidable linkage to existing circumstances are the limits on strategies for change. Only from this perspective can we understand why change is always heavily bound up with what has been already achieved. However, it becomes possible to examine and assess promise vs. reality in the debates and struggles over the content and aims of education in modern public educational systems. There are two principal goals involved here:

1   The subjective component "human being" is to be made generally available for the purposes of the economy and the state. It should be possible to subsume the individual, in his or her capacity as an agent of special moral values, general and technical abilities and skills, under bourgeois property, the freely available capacity for production.
2   Education's role is to prevent individuals (who embody the commodity human labor power) from resisting the social roles that have been assigned them. Or, to formulate it more positively: its task is to guarantee that subjects identify with the given status quo, or at least resign themselves to its constraints.

The bourgeois class, which initially indeed wished to renounce the arbitrary force and terror of absolutism, attempted at first to put their social principles into practice. They tried to anchor them in society and thus reproduce them by means of a system of public, general and systematic education. Bourgeois society defined education as educational policy, making it a public, general task. It served to secure public (bourgeois) interests within individuals, to put state norms and values into practice in private domains. Education thus serves to make the subjective factor (i.e., human beings) utilizable and adapt it for functions in the political and economic system. In its educational concepts (and thus in the educational institutions set up by the state), the above-described contradiction between interests of dominance and utopia reappears in psychological, didactic, and philosophical educational ideology.

The once-revolutionary demands for linking theory and practice, education and work, the private and the public realms, individual and society—in short, private interests and the public system—are ultimately realized in capitalism only in the arena of the labor power or commodity market. It is transformed here into the coercion to conceive of own's own labor as a commodity. That view must be seeded and nurtured in the general school system. As a result, a democracy based on solidarity and democratic education is conceptually impossible. The public democratic school system of bourgeois society serves ideologically to underpin the inequality of all citizens. The school system becomes one huge machinery for social integration and role assignment. Bourgeois education also entails systematic exclusion from the curriculum of any questioning of private property; it enchains pupils by inculcating in them the ideology of the national community of fate. In this way, limits on learning are established in the public school system which then have a recurrent lifelong impact on the behavior of individuals so schooled. The proper functioning of the capitalist commodity and labor market is based on the success of this educational enterprise.

However, education in bourgeois society, precisely because it is general and in its prime contents abstract, always remains "ambiguous": on the one hand, it serves to reproduce bourgeois society; on the other, it *simultaneously* imparts knowledge and insight. This other dimension of systematic education in modern times becomes evident in the analysis of social practice and thinking using the prism of the theory of social limits to learning. The aims of modern education can only be reached by imparting *general* knowledge and competencies. Yet this very knowledge likewise always enables learners to grasp their own situations and the possibilities and perspectives for action open to them. Via the ability to think abstractly, they concomitantly acquire the capacity to link up their experiences and interests with social conditions and possibilities. They learn a language and concepts by which they can communicate with "peers" and others, stepping out over and beyond the given boundaries. Via a quantitative understanding of reality, they also learn to examine it critically.

Enlightenment, both as an historical era and a principle of thought, cannot be properly characterized without this dialectic of limitations on and possibilities for learning. Even the anticolonial freedom fighters, who in their success also demonstrate the possibility of the social organization of power against domination in modern times, learned "all that was needed" for their resistance in the Catholic mission schools and the racist universities of their colonial masters.

The cognitive value of the theory of social limits to learning for a critical history of education now becomes evident: the goals propagated in the pedagogical conceptions of bourgeois revolution aimed in both theory and practice at liberating individuals from the ideological shackles of feudal rule; they were weapons against traditional prejudice and inculcated superstition. Yet at the same time, their implementation and systematization in society, again both theoretically and in practice, led to new social limits to learning. The systematic separation between education and production implemented by the bourgeois revolution, the "misappropriation" of important historical educational content and the ideology of the national unity of interests repeatedly served systematically to erect new socially effective barriers to learning. In addition, this education propped up the existing structure of domination by a mystification of the contradictory everyday experiences of the oppressed. On the other hand, however, this system of education also imparts general skills, knowledge and abilities; these can be mobilized and utilized as one wishes, and thus can also serve an individual's own learning interests.

The concepts of the subject and action as the core of the theory of social limits on learning

It is possible to explore the broad array of concrete human activities—whether abstract, conceptual or concretely practical—by means of the theory of social limits to learning. This theory conceptualizes learning as a consciously transformative process of influencing one's own historical reality. It differentiates between the acquisition of skills and knowledge and the more embracive concept of learning. Learning can be cautiously experimental, hesitatingly half-hearted, or sacrificingly rigorous and consistent. The ability of human beings to take their history into their own hands is revealed in the practical capacity to learn. Any and all learning is shaped *and* limited by one's own ideas and the forms of communication acquired. Learning thus presupposes the communicative dissolution of one's own ossified past (and that of society) in the interest of the individual's own knowledge. The aim of all learning is to recognize the objects, arrangements, and institutions handed down from the past in their human constructedness and to appropriate them anew in one's own interest. One can then utilize them to communicate with others in order to be able to change them, again in one's own interest. If learning is to lead to resistance against the dominant relations, it is useful to reconnect with the messianic[11] traces in the past and the diversity of the present-day (global) practice of resistance.

In the quotations that stand as an epigraph to this chapter, Marx and Benjamin seem to contradict one another on one point: for Marx, the legacy of the past is nothing but a shackle, a burden, a source of oppression. For Benjamin, the largely hidden efforts by the oppressed in the past to find happiness, survive, and resist point to a future liberation of humankind from the "triumphal procession of the victors." Both agree that a critical historiography should investigate the living activities of the oppressed within the web of contradictions between resigned or opportunistic conformity and a resistance eager to learn. The theory of social limits to learning seeks to weld the contradiction between these two approaches: it views the contradiction anchored in the acting subject, oscillating between the given conditions and the open possibilities, between insight into reality and the courage to face life, between hope and utopia, everyday cunning and the dignity of resistance. The conceptual pairs "freedom and necessity," "practice and theory," "experience and reflection" point up these tensions in the acting subject.

Human beings think and act in the field of tension between the past, present, and future. Any action is a compromise between the desired possibility and the constraints experienced, between success and failure, between seeing and blindness. Here lie the reasons why human action, in order to be comprehended, must be referenced to its respective contradictory historical reality. The point of departure for any knowledge (and thus any action) is one's own body and brain. My journey of exploration into other times and places begins with an investigation of my own self, the "strange and alien" areas of my own wishes and longings, my suppressed sufferings, an exploratory voyage to the sites of memory of my own repressed and suppressed resistance.

Our ideas, thoughts, and wishes take on concrete form under the respective historical conditions in which we live. They assume objective form via our activity, transforming into things, institutions, arrangements, and meanings. These "cultural goods" accumulate in an immense and immeasurable storeroom, the collective memory. Here these residua of past and present times are "archived," stored away in a disordered and disjointed manner. In order to bolster the system of rule, this human diversity is constantly being reordered anew, defined and hierarchized by the meaning-creating megamachinery of the state and social organizations by means of national, ethnic or even "racial" limitations and exclusions. In this way, it is processed into cultural orderings.[12] Networks of communication are created by knitting together meanings, by using rituals and nets of meaning. People never belong to such networks completely voluntarily, though their cultural identity is formed by linking up and interlocking with them.

Today new mighty megamachines global in their impact appear to be emerging alongside internal systems of order within societies and the nationstate; these megamachines forge unity while eliminating unruliness. This is why a more decentralized, regionally secured ability to learn is becoming more and more important. But learning can only lead to hardy and resistant forms of resistance if a person's perspective is not bogged down in the narrowness of local region and one's own limited interests. There has as yet been no successful amalgam of regionalism and openness to the world as a binding and durable historical model. So it must remain an open question as to whether meaningful relations and communities of identity—free of domination and geared to genuine communication—can be created in a durable and binding form between equals. Walter Benjamin sees the "monads of resistance" as the primal forms of an emancipated culture. Ernst Bloch assumed that the longing for "home"—the place where we haven't as yet arrived—contained the inherent possibility of such a culture from below. Yet collective identities, as evinced in the Chinese Cultural Revolution, the anticolonial liberation movements in Africa, and the various small groups of the global youth revolts during the late 60s and early 70s, tend rather to point up the difficulties involved in trying to fuse political resistance and collective identity humanely into a "culture from below."

However, in our close and familiar personal relations, there are signs that we are indeed able to choose social traditions and life-affirming orders from the immeasurable variety of possible significations and cultural options. This capacity for cultural creativity in a clear and comprehensible frame remains a source of hope. We can learn that ability via intimate communication at the precise locus where we also learn subjugation and how to conform to the dominant definitions and limitations: i.e., via socialization as children in the family. With the help of affection, nurture and care, through intimacy and regard, especially as children, we learn to live "identically" with our inner selves. The family (or a family-like relation) acts as a filter: it limits the unbounded desire and curiosity of the young to the respective social frame-work into which they were born, while simultaneously making it possible to experiment with new possibilities. Here the young acquire patterns of behavior for later orientation in life. In times of crisis, due to factors both internal and external, these inculcated patterns are thrown into disarray. In part, they succeed in grasping the new situation and "inventing" new solutions by communicating with others. In part, they prevent people from thinking and acting; in part, they promote conformity to new realities of oppression or encourage identification with past forms of oppression that have been passed down to the present.

The proper object of study for education as a science lies in these changing, ambivalent social conditions: the social relation of education or, to phrase it differently, the clarification of the question as to how the "new" generation is to be "introduced" into society as a given historically evolved configuration—and how they can themselves internalize that configuration, to whose constraints they are inescapably subject.

The theory of the social limits to learning is a method geared to social history; it does not analyze humans in terms of their technical functionality, qua systemic components, or as "role players." Rather, they are viewed through its binocular as acting subjects, and the theory seeks to apply this perspective on education methodologically as well. It makes use of the investigation of limits on and options for learning as an analytical tool, probing into hindrances to learning and the overstepping of boundaries as an educational experience. Yet it remains oriented at all times to progress; this orientation to a necessarily critical concept of progress, one committed to promoting a more humane world, must therefore be constantly reformulated. Without that commitment to humanity, enlightenment becomes farcical; the proponents of a science of education oriented to the model of the natural sciences float weightless in space, available when needed as ready instruments of social domination.

Post scriptum: This essay is dedicated in lasting gratitude to the memory of the founder of the theory of social limits to learning, my friend Richard Pippert, who unfortunately died far too young.

Notes

1. "The Eighteenth Brumaire of Louis Bonaparte [1852]," in: Marx, *Later Political Writings*. Trans. Terrell Carver (Cambridge [etc.]: Cambridge University Press, 1996), pp. 31-127, at 32.
2. Walter Benjamin, "Theses on the Philosophy of History," in: Benjamin, *Illuminations*, edited with an introduction by Hannah Arendt (New York: Schocken Books, 1969), pp. 253-4 (Thesis II).
3. Ernest Jouhy has developed a systematic scheme for the ordering of the relations between social "units."
4. Since the conceptions of real existing socialism as developed since the October 1917 Revolution were ultimately destroyed by the violent system of rule they built up, a form of force doctrinairely implanted by them in their blueprints for socialist society, they are excluded from this initial enumeration.
5. Resistance is understood here as an emancipatory action directed against existing relations of rule and force. By contrast, resistant action can also be understood in terms of concepts of misled or inverted utopias, as in Rainer Rotermundt's critical work. [See "Compulsive and Coerced Identities," in this volume.]
6. I understand "bourgeois revolutions" to mean the social, political, and economic movements for emancipation and revolution since the crisis of feudalism, an upheaval that culminated in the French Revolution as well as in the expansion of Europe across the globe.
7. In the colonial liberation movements, a kindred contradiction was repeated: for example, although liberation from postcolonial rule in Zimbabwe would have been impossible without the active participation of women fighters in the ranks, the victorious men pressed them back into their old, subservient social roles. The corresponding ideological construct for this was so-called African cultural identity.
8. Space does not permit me to explore the ideology of the nation-state, i.e., nationalism, any further here. There is a voluminous literature on the subject, and nationalism has moved ever more into the center of attention among social and political scientists, especially since the 1980s. Let me point out here only that despite controversy on many issues, there appears to be general unanimity in regard to one point (though of course with exceptions): namely that nationalism is a phenomenon closely bound up with the emergence of modern states, i.e., with the bourgeois form of rule.
9. It is important to stress that anticolonial liberation movements have been in existence practically since the beginning of colonialism, although attention is often focused only on the "successful" liberation movements after World War II.
10. Siegfried Bernfeld, *Sisyphus. Or The Limits of Education*. Trans. Frederic Lilge. Foreword Anna Freud. Preface Peter Paret (Berkeley: University of California Press, 1973).
11. Walter Benjamin regards "messianic moments," or monads as memories of a possibility for alternative action partially experienced early on that flare up during moments of danger.
12. Benjamin calls this the "triumphal procession in which the present rulers step over those who are lying prostrate." *Illuminations*, p. 256 (Thesis VII).

CHAPTER 3

THE "NATIONAL HERITAGE" OF GERMAN COLONIALISM

The continuing presence of the colonial past in Germany

The German Empire had colonies for "only" about fifty years, most of them in Africa. Yet this short period of direct participation in the "white man's burden" is deceptive: it blinds us to the longstanding presence and impact of colonialist discourse in German history. The present paper is an exploratory attempt to provide some answers to the following: what attitudes, views, and perspectives had to be on tap or newly constructed in Europe in order to keep the machinery of European expansionism fed with human fuel, with both victims and victimizers? Did the deeds of earlier generations of Germans leave traces in our contemporary ways of looking at the world? Do critical, engaged Germans today still have any links with the darker undersides of the history of German expansion? Is that history of colonialism not dead and buried now, since we are so hard put today to recall even its vaguest contours?

The sense of relief that our inability to remember provides is an illusion. Specifically because we lack a capacity for remembering it, the past lingers on. We inherit the legacy of what our ancestors did, the deep traces these acts have left in our lives. We profit from the pilfered riches, the violent experience of our superiority imposed by force over others, our birthright of dominance. The seemingly natural way we deal with human rights and champion their spread, our confident reliance on the freedom of thought we claim for ourselves, our claims to mobility for the individual and a ready range of consumer goods from coffee to computers—all this is rooted in the patrimony of Europe's history of expansive force. Our internalized certitude that we are history's grand winners, the champs and not its losers, is most sensitively perceived by the generations after, the victims' descendants. Our collective self-esteem is bolstered by the matter-of-factness with which we universalize our thought patterns into a conventional global wisdom spanning time and place, by our implicit trust in *our* ways of thought and living—and our ability, even in self-criticism, to fall back self-assuredly on a tradition of homebred heroes, saints, yes even dissenters.

One small illustration: some years ago, Lydia Potts and a group of women published a book on journeys by women around the world from 1785 on. In her introduction, the editor places these "female travelers" in the context of European expansionism: "the ordinary garden variety of Eurocentrism or racism of their time often appears in these travelers' writings.... In principle, each and every one of the female travelers presented here benefitted personally from colonialism and imperialism, directly or indirectly, consciously or unawares."[1] But then, in a remarkable intellectual somersault, the author reverses herself: "This meant that precisely when they were not travelling and thus participating in power, they led lives beset by contradiction, though as a rule that went unarticulated."[2] What the author means to say is that specifically because they participated in (masculine) power without bearing any personal accountability, they could indulge in the luxury of "escape and adventure."

In the eyes of the Others, we thus become the envied members of a seemingly successful, powerful culture. European culture is a culture grounded on the unabated power of definition over nature and human beings. It is so violent precisely because it partakes of the experience of limitless power and the ostensibly unlimited scope for action, finding ever new means and modes for its perpetuation. The history of European expansionism can be read from our world images and their global reception. Past ways of seeing are objectified in our symbols and metaphors, they stamp our gestures and character, structure our perceptions.

One recent example from my own city: a progressive group of activists associated with the Third World Shop in Oldenburg was preparing a show for children. It was to feature two African clowns. A poster was drafted, the artist indulged in associations. The upshot was that the African clown became an ape-man: with an apelike nose, long ears, the round head and eyes of a child. The group liked this "funny" poster and started to prepare it for printing. Then one of the members noticed to his horror that all of the colonial stereotypes of the Africans had crept into the draft for the poster. On closer examination, the "funny" image was a degrading caricature, with pictorial elements drawn from an ostensibly repressed colonial past.

I remain leery about the concept of culture, since it generally serves as a concept for exclusion, a means to draw lines. Yet it is shortsighted and distorting to view the concept of culture solely as an ideological construct. In our childhood, we fall heir to and imbibe historically evolved world images, collective ways of looking at the world transmitted via the network of adults in our early environment. Such modes of looking at the world *pre*order, *pre*interpret and *pre*select our individual perceptions.[3] These ways of viewing existence are bridges between the generations, they structure communication between yesterday and today. Both perception's wealth and poverty are founded on them, the contradiction between adaptive compulsion (education) and the ability to learn (subjectivity).

These images of the world are culturally circumscribed, since as children we maintain contacts with only a limited number of individuals. As a result of biographical experiences confirming or relativizing these images, they consolidate in our minds and are incorporated into our subjectivity. They only lose their absolute power of definition over us as a result of work on consciousness and grieving, the concious grasping of our experience. This is why we cannot dodge ethnocentrism. We have to confront it head-on, face up to its history in us.

Superiority and self-righteousness: pity with the victims accompanied the crimes of our fathers and mothers

In his book on xenology, Munasi Duala-M'bedy has shown that in the history of European ideology, alterity served as a screen on which to project our own unresolved problems.[4] The Other helps to strengthen the Europeans' belief that they are tops and stand at the pinnacle of human evolution. Armed with this certainty, the European can thus venture abroad into strange and foreign parts, pigeonholing the remainder of the world as an extended anomaly. And "if possible, they can heal its wounds."[5] Based on the expanding capitalist production of goods, this culturally acquired ability to view oneself as the norm and the Others as abnormal leads to a relentless passion to improve the world morally in one's own interest, before going on to exploit it. In this process, officially staged pity had a legitimating, regulating, and dynamizing function. It welded the emotions of the individual to the armature of aggressive imperialist logic and rationality.

However, the poverty-stricken have to earn this pity. They have to become worthy of it by their attitude, to appear to us as objects suitable for pity. That status as an object of pity blocks us from developing our own views about them. The churches in particular have sought again and again to try to prevent needs from being represented as social rights or developing into political opposition. The dependent gratitude of their clientele still masks the way the colonial process degraded them into powerless dependents, stripping them of their adulthood. Even today, pity for the poor is still publicly staged and politically misused.

Public pity staged by the state and the church: the antislavery movement in the late 1880s

Mustering historical examples as evidence, I intend to show that the effects and traces of historical events have been engraved in our collective consciousness, conserved in specific sets of meanings.

Soon after its advent, German colonialism was beset already in 1888 by a major crisis. Large capital was chary about investing in the territories of German influence in Africa, since the German state had failed to build an adequate infrastructure there. The brutal methods of exploitation implemented

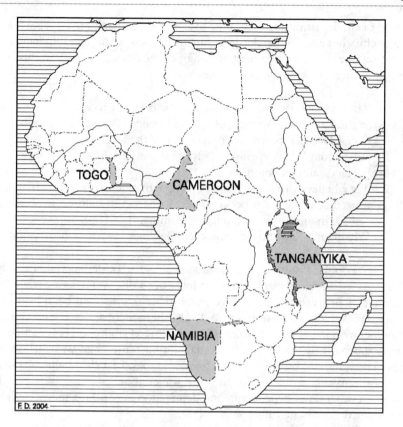

by smaller-scale capital as organized in the German East Africa Association resulted in unrest, leading to uprisings in the so-called protectorates.[6] This placed Bismarck's policy of "protectorates" (private ownership of colonies without direct state administration and control) in doubt. At the Congo Conference in 1884-1885, the German Reich had been granted colonial possessions; it was deemed important now, for geopolitical reasons, to utilize these territories.[7] However, the Catholic Zentrum party (in contrast with influential sections of the Catholic Church), the Social Democrats and "free-thinking" Liberals were opposed to state involvement in the colonial territories and voted against financing by the government.[8]

Yet within parts of both the Catholic and Protestant churches, a need arose for the state to provide guarantees for "fields for missionary activity" in the colonies. Church initiatives there were in urgent need of government safeguards for their security. Moreover, the Roman Catholic Church wanted, by means of a national affirmation of loyalty, to overcome the consequences of the *Kulturkampf* (Law on Jesuits, prohibition on German missionary orders, etc.).[9] Meanwhile, nationalist elements inside the Protestant church sought to create a German missionary movement on a double front: against the Catholic Church and Islam. Although competing one against the other, the churches nonetheless outdid one another in their opportunism vis-à-vis the authoritarian, imperialist state. Moreover, both were united by a common bond of enmity toward their Islamic rival.[10] It thus seemed reasonable for the large churches and Bismarck's government to close ranks and join hands in a joint political campaign to further an aggressive colonial policy. In this common venture, they pursued two aims:

1. They wished for public pressure to be brought to bear on elements in the Reichstag skeptical of colonial policy (Catholics, Liberals, Social Democrats) in order to convince them to accept the anticipated large expenditures for financing the transition from protectorates to colonies.
2. They believed that the military campaign against the influential Arab resistance to German occupation, planned even before the political campaign and under the military command of Hermann von Wissmann,[11] should be reinforced ideologically in public opinion.

The "Popular Campaign Against the Arab Slave Trade" served both aims. Trafficking in African chattel had suddenly been discovered as a new evil. As a result of British policy, the slave trade in East Africa had been in decline since 1850. Nonetheless, down to 1918, there were slaves in the German colonies working as porters, domestics, and forced laborers. This practice had been approved by the German colonial administration and was anchored in law. The system of buying a slave's freedom (a law of 1904) helped to shape a long transition from slavery to "free wage labor" at the lowest possible wages, a situation of dependency and deprivation in which former slaves were still denied their basic rights.[12]

So despite the fact that neither the churches nor the government was ever seriously concerned about the fate of the East African slaves, a vocal, well-coordinated antislavery movement came into being in the German Empire around 1888. The intellectual leader of this antislavery initiative in the autumn of 1888 was Friedrich Fabri (1824-1891), the former director of missions in the largest and most important German missionary society, the Lutheran Rheinische Mission.[13] In October 1886, Fabri sent Bismarck a memo:

> After the shock of the *Kulturkampf* ... associated with a hardening of the differences on both sides between the churches in recent years, it is extremely important to find a practical object that has direct popular appeal and general human interest: one to which both the Protestant and Roman Catholic population might equally turn their attention. If the matter at hand [the antislavery conference, G.M.] is taken up in the sense I have described above, and penetrates into the broadest segments of the population, then the Zentrum will also be resolute, even enthusiastic in its support for the idea of an African expedition.[14]

At the beginning of 1887, Bismarck gave the green light for Fabri's project. Now a central office sought to mobilize the Protestant and Roman Catholic mass membership organizations, along with the parochial press and parish priests. All these institutions and persons addressed the topic of Arab slavery and appealed to a Christian sense of responsibility for the "poor

Negro heathens." Yet it did not stop there: writers of literature for young people, brochures distributed at children's religious services, and religious instruction were all enlisted in the campaign. They provided them with horror stories about the cruel, sly, and cunning Arab slave traders and slave hunters. Bismarck himself had suggested that it should be possible to unearth horrible details about atrocities. Polygamy and the Islamic faith were also attacked and vilified as part of the campaign. Priests, vicars, and Christian journalists vaunted the fabricated products of a xenophobic fantasy as truth and incited the masses to embark on a "crusade."

The high point of the campaign was the large mass meeting in Cologne's Gürzenich Hall held in October 1888, with prominent personalities from the government, the two main churches, and the colonial policy elite in attendance, along with a carefully selected segment of the common "people." This was followed in November by a number of similar gatherings throughout Germany. At the meeting in Cologne, the Catholic agitator Hespers painted the plight of enslaved women and children in lurid and bloody detail. Lt. Wissmann, who later led the expedition, reported about his own experiences in Africa; Fabri spoke on "The African Question and Germany's Role in its Solution." The so-called Gürzenich Resolution incorporated the main points of his address. The central government was called upon to intervene militarily against the Arabs: "Should such a move enjoy the unanimous endorsement of the German people irrespective of religious and political affiliation, we are confident the Reichstag in Berlin will also provide active support." And indeed, the Zentrum party introduced just such a resolution on 14 December 1888. This marked the party's final break with its critical stance toward colonialism. In its resolution, it stated: "In order to win over Africa to Christian ideals, it is first necessary to combat traffic in Negro slaves and hunting for slaves." Measures by the government to further this would receive the support of the party's parliamentary group.[15]

On 2 January 1889, the so-called East African bill of the government was passed with the support of the Zentrum representatives (Liberals and Social Democrats voting against it), and the government was granted two million Reichsmark for its implementation. Wissmann was appointed Imperial Commissioner; he stated publicly in Parliament that the purpose of the operation was to "subdue the natives." Wissmann then marched with a mercenary army through East Africa, castigating the population with fire and sword, murdering at will. All African peoples that did not enter into voluntary cooperation with Wissmann were declared friends of the Arabs—and thus enemies of the German Reich. His campaign concluded victoriously in May 1890. Friedrich Fabri summed up its success: it had "awakened in the broad masses an understanding and awareness of African colonial policy," had "brought the two churches closer together," and had "helped gain more public recognition for missionary work in Africa." Finally, it had also had a "political" impact.

Klaus J. Bade has noted: "Over the short term, it seemed possible to achieve national integration by means of a demagogic exclusion of a colonial minority vilified socioculturally, religiously and in racial terms."[16] Its success was based on "negative integration," whose object was "*the* Arabs." This "technique of negative integration" was to rear its head again and again.[17] On the basis of an "image of the enemy," it also proved possible to generate a shared sense of unopposed national unity and solidarity utilizing this shared, abstract feeling of national compassion for the distant, "unfortunate Negro slaves." In a large-scale experiment, the joint government and church propaganda had proven that national consensus could be manufactured on the basis of a sense of moral superiority.

Now it was possible to launch new campaigns of commiseration mobilizing virtually arbitrary images of the enemy. Only a short time later, for example, after 1905, all the atrocious attributes that had been fancifully ascribed to the Arabs in the antislavery movement were transferred to the rebelling Africans themselves now engaged in the Southern African wars of resistance. The discursive tables were turned: now the victims for commiseration were the wives and children of the German settlers and the murdered missionaries and mission nurses.

Stereotyping the image of the "Negro"

Als unsere Kolonien vor Jahren noch unentdeckt und schutzlos waren schuf dort dem Volk an jedem Tage die Langeweile grosse Plage denn von Natur ist nichts wohl träger als ein so faultierhafter Neger. Dort hat die Faulheit, das steht fest gewütet fast wie eine Pest. Seit aber in den Kolonien das Volk wir zur Kultur erziehen Und ihm gesunde Arbeit geben herrscht dort ein munteres reges Leben. Seht hier im Bild den Negerhaufen froh kommen die herbeigelaufen weil heute mit dem Kapitän sie kühn auf Löwenjagden gehn ... (poem for children, 1910)[18]	When years ago our colonies still lay undiscovered and unprotected boredom was a great nuisance for the people day in, day out 'cause nothing is by nature more lethargic than a slothful Negro. Laziness raged there, it sure did almost like a pestilence. Yet since we've started to teach the people in the colonies culture and give them healthy, wholesome work the place is full of merriment and activity. Look here in the picture: the boisterous crowd of Negroes is rushing over joyful they're going out today on a lion-hunt a bold expedition with the captain ...

The image of the "Negro" often crops up in the immense variety of children's literature, but always in a strange, stereotypical simplicity: thick lips, grass skirts, nose-rings, childishly flat and dull facial features. Never a hero, he or she is always relegated to play a marginal figure. His most beautiful clothing is the colorful dress of a manservant from the feudal period, as sported today by the "Sarotti Negro" in ads for chocolate. Yet he is mobilized as an object to demonstrate the principles of a consistent and harsh middle-class education. Using the example of the "Negro," the youngest whites were inculcated with an object lesson: that whoever becomes a "Negro" in our society forfeits the right to their own life.[19]

Sarotti Negro

However, stereotypes do not just fall out of the blue, they have a history. By the turn of the century, the stereotyping of the Africans in connection with colonialism had been simplified and reduced to a highly distorted and negative "image of the Negro." It has remained essentially the same down to today, activated in the most diverse situations. The history of the image of the Negro can also be taken up to show the general conditions underlying social discrimination in industrial societies.[20] Right from the start, the image of the African involved a peculiar contradiction, still operative in the stereotypic denigration of the Other: every disparaging image also contains positive discrimination and one's own repressed wishes.

Thus, empirical surveys of travel agents have revealed that the dream destination of most Germans would be Africa—if it weren't so dangerous there. A girl contestant asked in the TV program *Wortschätzchen* about paradise, indicated, rather typically, that it must be somewhere in the African jungle. On the other hand, surveys of pupils in Berlin vocational schools in 1985 indicated they categorized Africans as being "uncivilized," "underdeveloped," and "primitive."

These stereotypes reflect the historical development of the European image of Africa. Down to the seventeenth century, Africa was the "dark continent"—where myth long since banished from Europe was still alive. In the eighteenth and early nineteenth century, it was the continent of the "noble savage" who had developed in harmony with nature. Later on, when aggression by the nation-state, political and cultural reaction and authoritarian rationality emerged victorious in Europe, the primitive could no longer be permitted any nobility: he was made into the "Negro."

The European image of the Negro contains the first and most lasting expression of the legend of the superiority of the white "race" and culture, the absolute right of modern civilization over the rights of other peoples, cultures, and individuals, and contempt for everything that rejects or is incompatible with "modern" development. The uniformity in the perception of the African down to today is due to the *uniform* aims for their utilization: the "Negro" was perceived in line with practical needs. Or, to put it differently, people perceived in the African only what was useful, exploitable, or (in negative reversal) what was categorized as useless. Such stereotypy also goes hand in hand with a uniform self-image: we bear responsibility (the "white man's burden"), we are adult, self-possessed, self-contained, just, stern and exacting. In 1905, a banner strung across a street in the German colonial town Windhoek (today the capital of Namibia) proudly proclaimed in learned and ominous Latin: "suum cuique," i.e., "to each his own."

That was also reflected early on in children's literature. Moreover, the concept of the "Negro" is closely bound up with that of childhood in bourgeois society. Because it was possible to treat the Negro, "half beast, half child," both as beast and child: blacks were perceived in precisely the same way as children are by their bourgeois educators. Namely, as creatures of nature who require civilizing and have to be educated to be useful. As long as children—like "Negroes"—had not proven their bourgeois utility (always predefined), they remained beings devoid of any power of their own to define situations, bereft of any right to self-determination. Their lack of rights includes the possible threat of liquidating what is deemed worthless.[21] Yet the bourgeois child and the "Negro" differ in this ideology of rule in respect to one important point: by dint of birth, the bourgeois child is predestined for the highest levels of development—by contrast, the "Negro," apparently for genetic reasons alone, is relegated to the lowest level of utility and serviceability. The respective strategies for their education also differ in line with this distinction.

The denigration of what is feminine took on historical clarity in the image of the "Negress." Down to the end of the eighteenth century, black women had a positive function in literature for girls: they were examples of female devotion and paragons of the motherly virtues. Then for a time they completely disappeared from authors' horizons during much of the nineteenth century. Only after the problem of "miscegenation" and the question of the citizenship of children from mixed unions was discussed in the Parliament in Berlin in 1905 did Negro women reappear in literature for young readers. The Women's League of the German Colonial Society then launched a campaign with the aim of providing colonists with German wives in order to combat their "niggerization." In connection with this initiative, numerous books for girls were published describing life in the colonies as harsh and full of privation—but for enterprising girls at the side of a faithful husband a lofty and liberating goal.

The national and natural cultural task of these women is made clear to them: over against the danger posed by the sensuously attractive but otherwise bestial "Negress," they should learn to rule over the land and its inhabitants, standing at the side of their husbands as mistresses called to rule. In this literature, the "Negress" was now depicted as more devious, filthy, and loathsome than her male counterpart. She was represented as devoid of all motherly virtues. Nonetheless, white women were to try to educate the "female Negroes." In actuality, this constituted a quite tempting offer to German girls who had been denied any independence and autonomy back home in Germany during the Imperial period.[22]

After the racist imagery had been sketched and introduced, the continuing marginal figure of the "Negro" remained on tap as a pedagogical tool. It reveals the cruelty with which the imperialistic European first treated his own children—and then everyone else across the planet—in order to process them for service to his own interests. Woe to the weak and dispossessed! Woe to those who have to let themselves be disciplined in order to be exploited. But there is another important message here to "those down at the bottom": whoever is poor and wretched, a slave and "Negro," is there as a result of their own lack of natural endowment. They have only their own innate negative traits to blame. Though each is useful in whatever rung they occupy, there are natural boundaries and differences between human beings, peoples and cultures. The respective pedagogical methods and measures should thus be in accord with the various abilities, talents, and natural worth levels of those to be educated. In the everyday praxis of European education, the African was ascribed the status of an ever-present example illustrating and embodying the lack of culture and worth, an archetype of brute instinctuality. His fate served to demonstrate what happened to those who stand outside the dominant norms of civilization.

From the numerous examples that could be mustered to illustrate this concretely, I would like to concentrate on one children's book: H. Oswalt's *Unterm Märchenbaum/Under the Fairytale Tree*, illustrated by Eugen Klimsch (1877). It contains the following tale:

Erzählen will ich noch geschwind gleich von einem anderen Kind, das auch sich nicht mehr waschen liess.	I want to tell a quick tale about another child it also did not want to be washed.

The educational situation is crystal-clear: civilization means being clean, but children don't always like that. So that they have to be threatened with punishment. In our story, the child who is afraid of water is transformed into a "Negro," a so-called *Mohr*. It is then identifiable as an outsider in a civilized world.

Da bleiben alle Leute stehn; die Kinder kamen all' geschwind und riefen: Seht das Mohrenkind! Juchheisassa! Juchheisassa! Ein schwarzes Mohrenkind ist da!	Then everyone stood still The children came a-scampering Shouting: Look at the Negro! Hurray, hurrah! A little black sambo!

As a "Negro," the child is ostracised from civilized society and exposed to general ridicule. This has an immediate pedagogical effect. The child now wishes to be washed and wants to behave properly once again. But in this tale there is no way back. Whoever has been revealed to be a Negro must remain so permanently. It doesn't rub off.

Allein zu spät! ... Man rieb und rieb, man wusch und wusch, das Kind,—es blieb so schwarz und schmutzig wie zuvor,— es blieb sein Leben lang ein Mohr!	But it was too late! ... They scrubbed and rubbed, they washed and swashed, but the child was as black and dirty as before once a Negro, a Negro for life!

The good-for-nothing remains identifiable in this way. The educative purpose of the figure of the "Negro" largely lies in serving as a vessel to inculcate into the European child at a young age that you have no rights if you're "black."

The flipside: the European's repressed secret wishes are alive and well in Africa

Die ganze Welt.	The whole world.
Wo hängt der grösste Bilderbogen?	Where's the world's biggest show?
Beim Kaufmann, Kinder, ungelogen!	At the store, kids, no kidding!
Man braucht nur draussen stehenbleiben,	All you gotta do is stop outside
guckt einfach durch die Fensterscheiben,	and take a look through the windowpane. There
da sieht man ohne alles Geld	you can see the whole wide world without paying
die ganze Welt.	a red cent.
Man sieht die braunen Kaffeebohnen,	You see the brown coffee beans,
die wachsen, wo die Affen wohnen.	they grow where the apes live.
Man sieht auf Waschblau, Reis und Mandeln,	Rice and almonds, on a blue background,
Kamele unter Palmen wandeln	Camels walking beneath the palms
und einen Ochsen ganz bepackt	and an ox loaded down
mit Fleischextrakt.	with meat extract.
Man sieht auch Zimt und Apfelsinen	You can see cinnammon and oranges
und Zuckerhüte zwischen ihnen.	sugar loaves in between.
Man sieht auf rotlackierten Blechen	On red-lacquered tin cans
Chinesen mit Matrosen sprechen,	Chinamen are talking with sailors
und manchmal steht ein bunter Mohr,	And sometimes there's a brightly colored Negro
der lacht, davor.[23]	out there in front, laughing.

By contrast, back home in Europe:

Lern Deine Leidenschaft besiegen,	Learn to conquer your passion
Es schafft Dir Ruhe und Vergnügen.[24]	It'll give you peace and pleasure.

One of the most popular advertising icons in Germany today is the Sarotti Negro, a figure you can see decked out in fanciful feudal costume in ads for a popular chocolate. In considering the denigration of the African into "Negro" in children's books, it is initially rather astonishing that African icons continue to play an important role in advertising. Thus, for example, there is a kind of chocolate-covered marshmallow in Germany called "Negro kiss / *Negerkuss*." In the alternative scene, I have repeatedly come across the name Lumumba for a drink that is a mixture of rum and chocolate. Patrice Lumumba was one of the few African leaders with his own convincing conceptions of politics, and was murdered with the help of the CIA.

The job of the "Negro" as a figure in ads and on the screen of fantasy points up a feature often overlooked in the analysis of literary imagery.[25] The

"Negro" is denigrated as a primitive and, analogous to nature itself, degraded into a mere object. In this way he forfeits his human rights and in the constructed scale of value, is placed on a plane far beneath that of the civilized white. Whites derive their right to rule over nature—and thus over the African as well, and to exploit Africans for their own purposes—in part from the fact that by dint of their education and innate talents, they believe they stand on a lofty rung far above nature, instinct, and their own childish, uncivilized wishes and desires.

Yet nonetheless, those instincts, wishes, and desires still continue to exist. They have been repressed into the soul's basement by the process of education and the demands of competition in the industrial labor market. Mediated by advertising, ethnological museums, circuses, fairs, picture books, and colonial novels, they now take on an exotic and distant habitation: the continent of sub-Saharan Africa. Africans are despised and envied because Europeans attribute to them all the sensual freedoms and pleasures that they themselves have stifled. One's own hidden, forbidden instinctual drives, desires, and longings live on in the "savage Other." Those emotions are shifted by fantasy and projected into distant Africa, transferred to races that are naked, despised and primitive. Driven by a sense of aggression, envy and longing, these emotions are devalued and denigrated—together with the "Negro" who embodies them. Here looms a repressed realm of hot wet dreams and ecstasy, rank with wild debauchery, raw nudity, adventure, independence, intoxication, laziness, and the idle life of leisure.

This double loading in racist stereotypy also points up why it is so easy to shift from negative to positive discrimination. But it must be clear to us that not only the despised African, but all maligned and vilified Others—and denigrated alterity as such—can take on the functions described here. Indeed, must assume those roles.[26]

Notes

1. Lydia Potts, "Einleitung: Reisendinnen überschreiten die Grenzen Europas — eine Spurensuche," in: Lydia Potts et al., *Aufbruch und Abenteuer. Frauen-Reisen um die Welt ab 1785* (Berlin: Orlanda-Frauenverlag, 1988), pp. 8-19, at 13-14.
2. Ibid.
3. Umberto Eco, *A Theory of Semiotics* (Bloomington: Indiana University Press, 1976).
4. Munasi Duala M'bedy, *Xenologie. Die Wissenschaft vom Fremden und die Verdrängung der Humanität in der Anthropologie* (Freiburg and Munich: Alber, 1977).
5. Ibid., p. 115.
6. The concept *Schutzgebiet* (protectorate) was coined by Bismarck in order to avoid having to call the overseas territories "colonies." See Horst Gründer, *Geschichte der deutschen Kolonien* (Paderborn [etc.]: Schöningh, 1985), p. 58.
7. "They met in Berlin in 1884 and declared: 'Why should we fight one against the other? They're just animals — let's divide them up amongst ourselves. As civilized human beings,

why should we fight and die because of these primitives? Let's simply divide them among ourselves.' Then they took a map of Europe and divided us up. They drew lines where they wanted to. That's how we were divided up." [The source of this quotation could not be found.]

8. [Zentrum (1870-1933): political party of the German Catholics, established following the German unification. The name refers to the position of the Catholic faction in the Prussian House of Delegates in the years 1852-1867.]

9. [*Kulturkampf*: Political struggle between the Prussian state and the Catholic Church, 1872-1887.] The periodicals *Gott will es*, and its successor from 1893 on, *Kreuz und Schwert*, espoused the idea down into the early years of this century that politics and missionary work should go hand in hand with the aim of educating the Negro into a Christian subject (*Labora et ora*). Beginning in 1897, *Kreuz und Schwert* had a new icon on the title page: on the left a missionary performing a baptism, on the right a soldier of the colonial army brandishing a flag and sword. In 1895, *Kreuz und Schwert* had some 10,000 subscribers. The importance of the periodical and of the entire battery of Catholic missionary propaganda for spreading bloodthirsty and cloying cliches about Africans, Arabs, and white missionaries was considerable.

10. See Horst Gründer, "Gott will es. Eine Kreuzzugsbewegung am Ende des 19. Jahrhunderts," *Geschichte in Wissenschaft und Unterricht*, 2 (1977), pp. 210-224; Klaus J. Bade, "Antisklavereibewegung in Deutschland und Kolonialkrieg in Deutsch-Ostafrika 1888-1890: Bismarck und Friedrich Fabri," *Geschichte und Gesellschaft*, 3 (1977), pp. 31-58.

11. [Hermann von Wissmann (1853-1905), German "explorer" in Africa. As German commissioner (1889-1892) he supressed an Arab revolt in German East Africa.]

12. In particular, the Catholic Benedictine mission in East Africa profited from the quasi-indentured servants it acquired by buying the freedom of former slaves (especially children). If an indentured servant ran away before paying off his or her debt (and it was usually impossible to pay that off even by working all one's life), then the colonial troops assisted in finding the fugitive.

13. The propagandistic activity of Fabri and others, such as Ittameyer in Bavaria, led in the subsequent period to an ever closer link in Germany and the colonies between missionary work and colonial policy, as reflected in a statement by Bismarck's successor Caprivi in the Reichstag on 12 May 1890: "First of all, we have to set up a number of stations in the interior which both the missionary and merchant can utilize as a base; the rifle and the Bible have to join forces in their efforts here."

14. Bade, "Antisklavereibewegung," p. 44.

15. Ibid., pp. 52-53.

16. Ibid., p. 53.

17. Ibid.

18. The poem appears in a picture book by Max Möller with the suggestive title *Die grosse Kiste oder: Was uns die Kolonien bringen/The Large Chest or What the Colonies Provide Us*, illustrated by O.H.W. Hadank (Charlottenburg: Schiller Buchhandlung, 1910).

19. On traces of this propaganda and colonial propaganda more generally, see Gottfried Mergner and Ansgar Häfner (eds.), *Der Afrikaner im deutschen Kinder- und Jugendbuch. Untersuchungen zur rassistischen Stereotypenbildung im deutschen Kinder- und Jugendbuch von der Aufklärung bis zum Nationalsozialismus*. Second, revised edition (Hamburg: Ergebnisse, 1985).

20. See Gottfried Mergner, "Die Berufung zur Besserung der Welt: Zur Geschichte von deutscher Erziehung im Kolonialismus," in: Klaus von Freyhold and Rainer Tetzlaff (eds.), *Die "afrikanische Krise" und die Krise der Entwicklungspolitik* (Münster and Hamburg: Lit Verlag, 1991), pp. 67-101.

21. See Alice Miller, *For Your Own Good. Hidden Cruelty in Child-Rearing and the Roots of Violence*. Trans. Hildegarde and Hunter Hannum (New York: Farrar, Straus and Giroux, 2002).

22. See Petra Schwarzer, "'Negerweiber' und weisse Frauen in der Kolonialliteratur für die weibliche Jugend von der Jahrhundertwende bis zum ersten Weltkrieg," in: Mergner and Häfner, *Der Afrikaner im deutschen Kinder- und Jugendbuch*, pp. 105-112; Simone Prodolliet, *Wider die Schamlosigkeit und das Elend der heidnischen Weiber. Die Basler*

Frauenkommission und der Export des europäischen Frauenideals in die Kolonien (Zürich: Limmat Verlag, 1987); Martha Mamozai, *Herrenmenschen. Frauen im deutschen Kolonialismus* (Reinbek bei Hamburg: Rowohlt, 1982).

23. From Fried Wittber, *Allerhand Sachen zum Lesen und Lachen* (Leipzig: Dürr'sche Buchhandlung, 1927), pp. 36f.

24. Ibid.

25. See Amadou Booker Sadji, *Das Bild des Negro-Afrikaners in der Deutschen Kolonialliteratur (1884-1945). Ein Beitrag zur literarischen Imagologie Schwarzafrikas* (Berlin: Reimer, 1985). This study is marred by a certain tendency to downplay the importance of colonial and postcolonial racist perceptions in Germany. See also Martin Steins, *Das Bild des Schwarzen in der europäischen Kolonialliteratur 1870-1918. Ein Beitrag zur literarischen Imagologie* (Frankfurt am Main: Thesen-Verlag, 1972).

26. [The final section of this chapter has been deleted since it overlaps considerably with a section of the next chapter.]

CHAPTER 4

"SOLIDARITY WITH THE SAVAGES?"

German Social Democracy and the African Resistance Struggle in the Former German Colonies

Beginning in the 1960s in East Germany and in the 70s in the Federal Republic, a number of studies have appeared that deal critically with a long repressed topic: German colonial history and its effects on domestic policy and politics.[1] On the 100th anniversary of the Berlin Conference (1884-1885)[2], various scholarly conferences and numerous publications explored further aspects of the German colonial past.[3] There are also well-documented and diverse investigations on the question of the relation of the organized German workers' movement to colonialism.[4]

Building on this, I wish here to address what seems to me an aspect of this question that has not been sufficiently investigated: is there a connection between the process of "civilizing" the workers into loyal "citizens of the national community" (*Volksgenossen*),[5] as was successfully done in the two world wars, and the ways in which Social Democrats perceived the "rebellious savages" during the colonial wars fought by imperialist Germany? I think this question is not in any sense bizarre or misplaced. We should recall that both at the time of the violent imperialist penetration of the periphery as well as during the wars waged by the Kaiserreich and Nazi Germany, the organized workers' movement proved neither an unsurmountable impediment to policy nor much of a troublemaker. On the contrary: when it came to the crunch, German imperialism was always able to count on the national solidarity of the organized workers.

On the other side, until the formation of the Third International, the African resistance fighters did not look to the workers' organizations in Europe. They did not attempt to contact their leadership nor did they seek assistance. For a long period, the African resistance remained limited to the region and was largely tribal in orientation.[6] Mutual knowledge was scant and was mediated via the culture of the colonial rulers. Even Bebel[7] expressed his satisfaction in the Reichstag about the fact that he had never been "tempted" to inform himself directly on the spot in the colonies. There were no Social Democratic correspondents in the colonies, until 1912 no systematic collecting and evaluation of information. Africans and Social Democrats remained strangers.[8]

Caution is advised in trying to establish the presence of any bond of solidarity between the indigenous population in the colonies and the population in the Social Democratic homeland. Partisan research is too quick to come up with generalizing projections of its own expectations onto social movements around the globe. Such projections are often based on the specious construct of a uniform worldwide social movement, claiming that the liberation movements in the periphery were sweeping aside the last filthy remnants of bourgeois civilization. And that the workers' movements in the metropolitan centers had a double task: latent preparedness for revolution and active international solidarity.

Though Marx's concept of class does point to the latent possibility of workers' resistance as a response to oppression, it is certainly false to cast the industrial proletariat as the sole basis and agent of socialist redemption.[9] Erhard Lucas points out that on the one hand, there was always a significant readiness in the working class to resist, and the memory of concretely experienced utopia is an integral part of the cultural and political legacy of the social movement among the workers. On the other, however, when it came to overcoming and eliminating oppression, the concept of the workers' movement in Germany (and elsewhere) was inseparably linked with the notion of "failure."[10]

In approaching this whole complex, I proceed from three fundamental theses:

1. The industrial revolution in Europe constitutes the high point in a process of internal colonization, the domestication of a traditionally agrarian or artisan population into a functioning army of industrial workers.

2. To the extent they were interested in utilizing their labor power for the purposes of industrial capitalism, the bourgeoisie and its intellectual retinue degraded the social worth of the workers. At the same time, there was a mounting fear of the threat or reality of resistance by certain segments of the working class.

3. As the workers succeeded in organizing against their economic devaluation, they adapted to the dominant social reality under the press of political constraints. Within that context, they attempted to achieve political and cultural identity and self-worth through autonomous organization. In this they were successful, utilizing the agency of their own organizations and a strategy of constant, "quietistic" growth. Without pausing to reflect, they contributed to the downgrading and exclusion of those on the margins of the industrial-capitalist frame of exploitation: the unemployed, minorities, children, women, and colonized peoples.

Recent studies of working-class autobiographical materials also corroborate the thesis put forward by Norbert Elias: namely, that adaptation to hyperorganized, bureaucratic industrial society is associated with internalized repression and the pains of accommodation for each and every individual, entailing a voluntary repression of affect.[11] The repressed wishes and emotions seem increasingly alien to the civilized person and are shunted off into the devalued margins of civilization. Just as workers could imagine only the same education for their children that they had suffered through, they also believed a cruel and repressive process was necessary to "civilize" the "savages." It was most comfortable for them to talk about their own experiences and feelings with male comrades who thought and felt the same way.[12] That is why Social Democratic political culture was gendered masculine.[13] They developed few needs to communicate with women and children, or with the "uncivilized" territories on the periphery. They fostered solidarity only with their "own kind." The concrete might of capital, expanding untrammeled, profited from this constriction.

Yet the middle classes had an increasingly contradictory attitude toward the Social Democratic workers. On the one hand, bourgeois eyes viewed the workers as unpredictable, potentially vicious, and even brute savages. Such discourse stressed their instinctual nature, capriciousness, unruliness, and rebelliousness, and they were hated because of this. The brutal outrages of the Freikorps in 1919-1920 revealed their sadistic fear of what was "base and primitive" in civilization.[14] On the other hand, progressive caucuses in Parliament tried to foster the integration of "decent and proper" workers into the German imperialist folk community.[15]

In this connection, Klaus-Michael Bogdal has analyzed the image of the industrial proletariat as depicted in the works of German naturalist writers. Like the image of the Black African in colonial literature after 1900, the perception of the workers oscillated between benevolence toward the faithful servant and fear of the constant threat of his brutishness.[16] A representative description from a naturalist novel of the time points up this anxiety:

> Alas, she was similar to a gigantic torso with tiny, crippled sense organs. With an eye protruding on a rigid stalk, capable of looking only in one direction, unaware of what is happening to the right or left. With a brain unable to distinguish between good and evil, true and false. With limbs that obey only the stimulus of the nerves, the accustomed external reflex, and not the free, self-determining thought of one's own mind.[17]

Ernst Haeckel, who had a great influence on the Social Democratic monistic movement, described the aims of Social Democracy in this vein in 1892 as a "relapse into barbarism, into the bestial primitive state of the brute primitives."[18]

The proletarian "savage"
and his social democratic acculturation

Our mayor was somewhat taken aback once when a glassmaker who had newly moved into the neighborhood came to register. Asked about his address, the man replied: "yeah, well it's over in Cameroon, No. 4." Cameroon is the popular name for the area formed by the two new streets.[19]

There were many similar place names after colonies. In Osternburg, an industrial settlement near the city of Oldenburg, which had a section nicknamed "Cameroon," another neighborhood was called "Zanzibar." Such designations can also be found in the Ruhr and in other parts of northern Germany around the turn of the century, the period when German colonies were established in Africa and the South Pacific. I have a suspicion this bespoke a self-ironizing identification by workers with the lack of rights in the colonies and their lowly discriminated status—based on their own experience of being without rights and despised members of society. After the abrogation of the Law on Socialists[20] it became ever clearer that Social Democracy was making enormous efforts to shed its negative image and to achieve auto-emancipation, lifting itself from the status of a "Negro" to that of a citizen with equal rights. An article from the periodical of a professional craft union can serve to document the growing orientation on the part of workers to the dominant values:

Certain opponents have spoken of the materialistic workers' movement, that only wishes to serve the stomach's needs while neglecting and brutalizing the spirit and soul. Now what is the actual situation? ... It is not only the workers' right, it is their highest moral duty to provide for the well-being and health of their families and to enlist all their energies in the furtherance of such demands. ... But we have other goals as well. ... Our longing does not halt at the stewpans on the kitchen stove. ... Life's garden is immense. And we know that there is more there than just nourishing apples hanging from the trees. Roses bloom, larks and nightingales sing, to the delight of human hearts and ears. ... What joy we have now is a mere morsel handed to beggars. But true joy—we know that is not the phoney pleasures people have to make do with today, in this present state of affairs. And by true joy, we don't mean oysters and edible birds' nests. In fact, it doesn't refer to mere physical pleasures at all. What we have in mind are the most excellent presentations from the world of *science* and *art*, realms ordinarily closed for us. Our highest aim must be to make these the common possession of the entire nation.[21]

Brigitte Emig has shown that this quote can be considered typical for the thinking of the socialist movement at the time. The effort to compete with the middle class in the field of culture was augmented by a strong desire for their recognition. Workers lived "second-hand ... constantly hobbling on behind bourgeois culture."[22] As workers developed the pride to be more diligent, proper, and community-oriented than segments of the parasitic bourgeoisie, they also brought up their children to be respectable, obedient, and industrious workers.

I do not wish to discuss the link between authoritarian education for children and the politics of the workers' movement in any detail. But we should recall in this context the work of the Social Democratic educator Otto Rühle, one of the first to call attention to the connection between proletarian education and authoritarian attitudes on the basis of his own experiences in the workers' movement; it was Rühle, for example, who initiated a campaign against corporal punishment.[23]

In this context, it was only natural that the attitude toward international solidarity also incorporated bourgeois features. That can be nicely illustrated by a few extracts from a lecture given on 16 February 1902 by Paul Müller, national representative of the seamen's union. Responding to the charge that the workers were unpatriotic and "had no fatherland," Müller commented:

> Workers who in times past were still opposed to internationalism now think just the opposite, because they are learning this from the diplomats. They, after all, like the sailors, have to communicate with the world abroad. Just take the postal services, for example: they've held various international postal conferences. ... Or in China: as everyone knows, Germany played first fiddle there, when troops from all the countries cooperated to put down what's called the "Boxer rebellion." Princes also pay one another visits.[24]

In summary then, the socialist movements achieved two effects with their publications, meetings and organizations:

1. Immense efforts were invested by their own organizations in countering discrimination and intentional political and economic downgrading of the workers in Imperial Germany.
2. These organizations themselves served as a transmission belt for so-called progressive industrial values and middle-class ideals of culture, i.e., they became compensatory institutions of education.

The contradictory attitudes of the social democratic caucus toward German colonial policy

In a study that has unfortunately not been given the attention it deserves, Willfried Spohn has demonstrated the existence of two economic developments important for our topic here:

1. At the turn of the century, Germany was able to maintain its position quite well in the face of competition from the world market, despite economic fluctuations. The reason lay in the stable growth rates in advanced industrial branches (electronics, chemistry, machine engineering) and in industrial concentration, which was being promoted by the government and the banks. This ravaged the manual trades, increasing social tensions in this sphere. Yet until the 1907 crisis, agriculture, heavy industry, and shipyards were able to maintain their position to some degree thanks to the policy of protective tariffs and rearmament, even though they showed smaller rates of growth.

2. During this period of development, German colonial policy had the function of providing a long-term, global policy for infrastructure. In the context of mounting competition between nation-states and global flows of capital, colonial policy and rearmament served over the longer term to improve investment conditions and reduce production costs.[25]

Additionally, it is important to note that on the level of nation-states, heightened competition for venture capital and an ever more aggressive colonial policy by all European colonial powers led to a dramatic increase in the threat of international conflicts. Based on these economic trends in the frame of globally intensified competition, one can understand the arguments advanced by the pragmatic political wing within the organized workers' movement, the heightened influence enjoyed by the top echelons of the workers' associations, and the centralization of decision-making. One can also explain the growing orientation among large segments of the working class toward the nation-state. If we look today at the resolutions of the Second International in the context of these developments and the danger of war they harbored, they appear quite naive and impotent.

They also failed to see the long-term strategic importance of colonial policy. In the debates in the Reichstag, the most important speakers on the colonial question, Ledebour[26] and Bebel, argued citing the negative profitability of the colonies and relatively high state expenditures they required. The speeches in the Reichstag took on a special importance along with party and International conference resolutions; and that importance increased as the organized workers' movement became more nationally centralized. Most Social Democratic daily papers published key extracts from the Reichstag speeches of Social Democratic representatives, contrasting these with the views of the opposition. Particularly at election time, statements from the center formed the basis for the speeches and comments in parliamentary debates. They helped defend and delineate Social Democratic political identity vis-à-vis the opposition.

In addition, the colonial debates demonstrated that the previously insignificant financial and formative power of the Reichstag was on the rise. This helps to explain the professionally well-equipped colonial lobby, and the growing involvement of the Catholic Zentrum in this question.[27] It is still necessary to investigate the minutes of Reichstag proceedings in regard to the ways in which they were shaped by imperialist conditions. Probably taking a cue from the Catholic Zentrum, the position of the Social Democratic party (SPD) on the colonial question begins to shift slowly after 1906: from basic rejection because of the unacceptable costs and the misfortune that colonization visits on the "natives" to an effort to expose scandals in the colonies, such as the sadistic abuse of the "Negroes," instances of corruption, and surplus profits of monopolies obtained by fraud. By such an approach, dealing with individual concrete cases, they protected themselves against the charge that they were doing fundamental damage to German interests and made it possible to negotiate on possible reforms in colonial policy. Noske, who replaced Ledebour after 1909 as colonial expert in the SPD parliamentary group, had a perfect command of this discourse.[28] He argued that colonization, with the requisite rigor and severity, could "civilize the Negro" and bring profit to the Reich without all the Junkers and other adventurers, without speculators and sadistic punishments, without injustice. After delivering such a speech, it was easy then to state that capitalism in its present form was unable to eliminate these wrongs and abuses.

Noske justifiably viewed himself as standing firmly within the continuity of the Social Democratic caucus in the Reichstag. That is clear from the somewhat contradictory speech given by Bebel on 19 January 1904 to explain why Social Democracy had abstained. The matter at issue was the approval of a supplementary budget for the colonial troops. The funding was needed to put down the uprising in German Southwest Africa. Bebel complained about how poorly informed the Reichstag was about what was happening in the colonies:

> We hear so extraordinarily little that we are really very distant from everything there. We know nothing about what is really happening. If someone from time to time does not find the courage to be "indiscreet" and speak openly about what is taking place there, we learn nothing about the reality.[29]

We may wonder why the party was unable to remedy this lack of information by its own activity, why it sufficed with information passed on by the state bureaucracy, the bourgeois press and its correspondents in the field, along with occasional letters from missionaries, colonial soldiers and settlers. Bebel commented on the problems of the uprising:

> The head of the Colonial Office has stated that no European colonizing power has to date been spared colonial uprisings. That unfortunately is true. However, these rebellions are not connected with colonization as such. Rather, they are bound up very closely with the way in which colonization is being carried out. These are the consequences of the treatment meted out to uncultivated peoples by the so-called advanced nations.[30]

Moreover, this false approach to colonization was proving very costly for the German Reich and the German taxpayer. The uprising, an "extremely daring and dangerous undertaking," had also been brought about as a result of the "arbitrary dispossession of the Negroes." Bebel now drew a parallel with the "ancient Germanic tribes in their struggle against the Romans," and concluded:

> That is why I now wish to put forward the urgent plea that if it comes to a violent struggle—and as it looks from the situation, this cannot be avoided—that struggle should be carried out with the utmost of humanity. And there should be no acts of revenge afterward that would be unworthy of our people.[31]

The lack of knowledge about the real situation there on the ground and the interest of the nation lead to an explanation as to why the Social Democrats abstained on a motion to grant funds for quelling the liberation struggle. "Since we are still unclear about the causes that have led to this uprising, we have decided to abstain from voting on an approval for these demands." For Social Democrats in the Reichstag at that juncture, to abstain was the maximum possible means to express support. Abstention sent a message to the Reichstag "to end the rebellion as soon as possible and if feasible, to rescue the colonists who have settled there trusting in the promises and assurances of the government."[32] Thus, national common interest, the community of the civilized, had priority over the insight in Social Democracy that for the ruling class, the opponent was always the one who clashed with its interests: first it had constructed the "yellow beast," then the "black beast," and now finally the "proletarian beast" as adversary.[33]

The image of the African "savage" in the provinces

Let us return to the German provinces. I will deal here with the regional sphere of media influence enjoyed at the time by the *Norddeutsches Volksblatt*, a Social Democratic daily for the region of East Frisia, Wilhelmshaven, and Oldenburg in northwest Germany. The area was a region of industrial development with a small amount of industry geared to export. There were shipyards in Wilhelmshaven and a woolen mill and glass factory in Oldenburg. The workers in these plants were largely Social Democratic; one exception perhaps was the spinning mill with its mainly unskilled workforce. There was a diversified Social Democratic cultural life in the region.[34]

Particularly the glass workers in northern Germany had had good experiences with international solidarity. That was reflected, for example, in a report in their craft-union paper on 11 May 1901:

> There is ever more visible international solidarity by foreign glass workers with the strike in Nienburg-Schauenstein [near Hanover]. Contributions are pouring in from America, Australia, Denmark, England, Holland, Italy, Austria, Switzerland, etc., so that there is no basis to fears expressed by the shield-bearers of *Kommerzienrath* Heye that the strikers are in terrible distress.[35]

Even though there was a trend at this time for strike assistance to be more and more confined within national boundaries, this quote indicates that active international solidarity was able to surmount both language barriers and great distances. Solidarity was organized via the trade associations and resulted in concrete support for strikes, mutual information and defense against strike-breakers. However, these experiences did not lead either to antimilitaristic or anticolonial defense struggles or to any attempts to change the brutal system of exploitation of black labor in the colonies by development aid supplied via the trade unions. It was impossible for workers even to imagine they could have anything in common with the "uncivilized" savages in the colonies. They were "not considered acting subjects in the history of that system they had been drawn into."[36]

The *Norddeutsches Volksblatt*, oriented to the line of the party mainstream (Bebel, Kautsky),[37] reflected this perception. The so-called "Hottentot elections" were held at the end of 1907, after the early dissolution of the Reichstag in the wake of a defeat of the government in a vote on the supplementary budget for the colonial troops. The election campaign rolled on for a month. No Social Democratic candidate was victorious in the area of the *Volksblatt*'s readership. Although it had a slight rise in total votes, the SPD lost nearly half of its seats on the basis of the division of polling districts. Aided by the bourgeois media, the government was able to wage the campaign completely in terms of the issue of existing colonial policy, pro and contra. For its part, Social Democratic arguments in the campaign tried to link the colonial question to the real rise in the cost of living and the threat of an impending increase in indirect taxes. Which is why Social Democratic leaders were denounced as "men without a fatherland."

Concomitant with the ongoing election campaign, the paper reported extensively on the colonial question, publishing several editorials on the issue. This allows a comparison of their daily colonial reporting with its politicized form on the editorial page. The *Norddeutsches Volksblatt* reported on supraregional events under three regularly recurrent rubrics: (a) "International News" (which gathered together reports from the "civilized industrial nations"), (b) "From the German Reich" and (c) "From the German Colonial Territories."

This distinction was evident in reportage. Below are two examples from category (c) by way of illustration. On 5 January 1906, the paper ran a story about Cameroon:

> Sad tidings from Cameroon. The news that Lt. Foertsch was seriously wounded while on an expedition in Cameroon has recently focused attention on this area of the German colonial territories. Now a report from the south of the protectorate[38] reveals that the insurgent movements among the natives unfortunately extend across a far larger area than is generally assumed by the German public. ... Its size exceeds that of the Kingdom of Saxony and contains some 10,000 able-bodied Negroes. These are countered in the field by a force consisting only of two companies of the German colonial troops and a few smaller units.

Given such an "objective" style of reporting attuned to German interests, it is not surprising that only "our own men" suffered losses in the clashes. Thus, the paper reported on 6 February 1906: "The most recent lists of casualties from Southwest Africa included five men dead, five wounded and one missing." Nor did this change when it became known during the course of that same year that General von Trotha bore responsibility for the massacre of 10,000 rebels after the defeat of the Herero at Waterberg (1904). The second report I wish to quote is dated 9 February 1906:

> Two "victories" over the Hottentots who stole cattle are reported from Southwest Africa. Total pacification seems to be on the horizon. Otherwise it is meaningless to continue to dispatch ever new contingents of troops to Southwest Africa. After

all, fifteen thousand men ought really to be able to keep 400 Hottentots pretty much in check, even if they cannot decapacitate them completely.

Sometimes there was also a sense of compassion for the "savages," backward but fearless. A story carried by the *Norddeutsches Volksblatt*, 12 January 1906:

> Uprising in Zululand. Reliable sources have informed the paper from Natal that there is dangerous ferment among the independent Basutos. This threatens to erupt in violent rebellion. As in German East Africa, the immediate cause is high taxes. The natives are especially bitter about the newly introduced poll tax. A white citizens' militia is being organized by the government. The Zulus put the Europeans to shame. They rise up valiantly when the load of taxes becomes too heavy. We, on the other hand, put up with the most terrible tax burden.

The association between increased taxes at home and unnecessary colonies abroad dominated colonial debate in the Reichstag and the SPD electoral campaign. The concept of "colonial blood taxes" thus does not refer to the burden placed on the indigenous population in Africa, but on the German taxpayer. On 29 November 1906, the *Norddeutsches Volksblatt* published the following figures:

> Every soldier in Southwest Africa costs 10,000 marks annually. Since the number of soldiers in the protectorates now exceeds 14,000, one can get some idea on this basis alone of the extraordinary expenditures required, along with the ordinary costs, for maintaining that misfortunate colony, which consists largely of sandy deserts.

In order to correctly assess this reduction of the colonial problem to a fiscal question, one should not only recall the genocide perpetrated by General von Trotha but also the fact that it had become necessary to constantly reinforce the troops in the southern African colonial territories due to the rather successful guerrilla insurgency led by the former mine worker and Nama leader Jacob Marenga (1885-1907). The electoral campaign propaganda of the colonial parties demonstrated this when it accused the Social Democrats of abandoning the German soldiers in the field to a vicious and brutal enemy. The government reiterated on several occasions that the country was in a virtual state of war, and that these operations were not merely police actions against rebels.

The defensive and falsifying content of the following SPD campaign appeal must be analyzed in this context:

> East Frisians, party comrades, fellow citizens, workers, voters in the Hanover First Precinct!
> Parliament has been dissolved because it finally wished to halt the squandering of funds in the totally useless and superfluous colonies. The Kaffir war[39] in Southwest Africa has cost 400 million, the supplementary budget for 1906 calls for another 29 million, and again 160 million more are asked for 1907. ... The only

reason for that sacrifice is to totally exterminate the poor savages, who have been brought to the point of desperation by the cruelty of their German tormenters. And to maneuver all their possessions into the hands of the favorites and offspring of the clan of Prussian officers and Junkers. The natives have been driven to revolt by the infamous, dastardly practices of dissolute individuals who were no longer able to maintain themselves socially and financially in Germany, and who were shunted off to Africa as the horrible brats of their highfalutin families. Natives whom they cheated out of their land and cattle and deprived of the very minimum for survival. ...

There is solid proof that the German rulers in Southwest Africa have wreaked more dreadful havoc than the pitiless barbarians. Shameful acts have been committed that beg description. And the working population is to be bled white for these colonial kicks and thrills of the ruling class. ... Working people must bear the entire brunt of the burden for the army, the navy and the colonies. ... This is the reason Social Democracy has joined hands with the Zentrum party in order to put an end to the senseless squandering of money in the colonies.[40]

This electoral campaign appeal shows that the contradictory policy of the party at the center regarding resistance in the colonies was likewise present at the provincial level; indeed, it was even stronger there due to the greater pressure to integrate into the dominant values emanating from the center.

Another facet of this provincial picture was the full-page ad placed in the *Norddeutsches Volksblatt* on 19 and 20 January 1907 by the coffee wholesaler Tengelmann on the occasion of the opening of a branch of his firm in Wilhelmshaven. The paper ran this ad, without commentary and with no later responses from the readership, at the very high point of the "anticolonial" election campaign. Under the heading "Tengelmann's Plantation Coffee," the advertisement proudly informs readers that the company owns stock in various coffee plantations, which is why it can keep its prices so low. The ad features a number of Negroes in silhouette, in racist stylization, all diligently hauling Tengelmann coffee sacks on their backs. A report in the paper on 23 January 1907 is part of this same complex. It notes without commentary that an expert has stated Southwest Africa could not become a colony for settlers since there is not enough fertile land there. And, naturally enough, the paper also simultaneously was running the racist novel in over 100 installments by Friedrich Gerstäcker, *Die Missionare. Ein Roman aus der Südsee/The Missionaries. A Novel from the South Pacific.*

A blocked learning process in the workers' movement: the linkage between completed internal colonization and continuing external colonization

Using the example of Portugal, Ronald Daus describes the reciprocal effects of colonial rule on Europeans' relations with one another. He notes that the "colonial experiments of several European states have given all Europeans a lasting and significant advantage in their sense of self-esteem." That also made it possible for the European underclasses to "experience themselves and the fate forced upon them as something special and uniquely valuable (although at times tragic), even when their rulers led them into catastrophe on a massive scale." However, identification with the colonial power and a blinkered attitude toward the peripheral objects of this power, their culture and resistance, acted to block one's own learning process leading to self-emancipation. In support of his thesis, he cites the Salazar regime, the conditions in France at the time of the war in Algeria, and those in Nazi Germany. If one listens to Daus's arguments, it becomes evident that historians have given far too little attention to date to the domestic political reflex of colonial policy abroad.[41]

The revolutionary passion of Social Democracy under Bebel's leadership still contained within itself the contradiction between radical critique of society and an increasing acceptance of the dominant circumstances. For that reason, it was at least able to show some compassion and sympathy for the suffering of the colonial peoples. That alone distinguished the party before 1914 positively from the attitudes of indifference and racist prefascism toward the indigenous population in the colonies prevalent at the time in broad circles of the German bourgeoisie.[42]

Only after the faction of pragmatic politicians (Ebert, David, Noske et al.) took over party leadership during World War I did the attitude described by Daus take hold in broad ranks of the party. Under the new condition, namely the inclusion of trade union and party leaders in state discussions, these *Realpolitiker* demonstrated the ability to forge a political link between the interests of imperialist Germany and those of the workers. In so doing, they laid the foundation for a new entitlement for workers within the imperialist polity: they became *Volksgenossen*, citizens in the national community. For Eduard David,[43] it was evident that this would be impossible without the oppression or exploitation of other peoples. His war diary clearly documents that perception. Already on 29 August 1914, he found himself in a discussion with other party comrades on German war aims, and espoused an old plan of the pan-Germans:

> Café Austria in the afternoon: Robert Schmidt, Schöpflin, Wels, Cohen (Reuss), Göhre. We discuss question France, Belgium. Are agreed: no territorial annexation. ... My position: no territorial annexation, but the Congo must be taken; formation of a large German colonial empire sweeping right across equatorial Africa. France would have to surrender all of the French Congo, poss[ibly] Tangiers as a base for the German fleet. Germany would thus get a field for its expansive forces. For France and Belgium, these losses do not constitute encroachment on the nation. The natives in the countries involved can only gain by being transferred to German administration. The others agree with me, also think that there will be no opposition to this from the large majority in the party.[44]

In declaring a transition from revolutionary passion to practical national politics, it is important to come up with approaches that try to forge analytical linkages between the daily experiences of politicized workers with the dominant system and the political decisions reached at institutional level in their own organizations. Even the most "bungling" leadership can only intensify the contradictions present in the concrete social movement, and exploit them to advance its agenda. The extent to which the new leaders had indeed succeeded in this during the course of the war is pointed up by the action of the German National Assembly on 1 March 1919: they issued a "vehement protest" against the dispossession of the German colonies proposed by President Wilson and demanded that "Germany's colonial rights be reinstated." The fact that the resolution was put forward jointly by the Social Democrats, the DDP, DVP, and DNVP[45] indicates the broad consensus in the German "revolutionary" camp on this question. Nonetheless, it is surprising that the resolution was passed with a staggering 414 in favor and only 7 opposed, which means that most of the USPD delegates on the far left also backed the resolution.[46]

The contradictory nature of Social Democratic position statements on internationalism and the colonial question in the prewar period was to leave traces in Noske's political agenda after the war. An editorial in the *Norddeutsches Volksblatt* on the Stuttgart Conference of the Second International in 1907 casts light on this strand of continuity. After severely criticizing the "tasteless attacks" of the French delegate and pacifist Hervé[47] on Bebel, the *Volksblatt* commentator reported on the retort of Georg von Vollmar,[48] correct but far too icy for the "sentiments of the German workers."

Among other things, Vollmar had stated: "Our love for humanity cannot prevent us for one second from being good Germans. As much as we recognize the common cultural interests, as much as we condemn and fight against the incitement of one nation against another, we cannot abandon ourselves to the illusions of utopian schemes." The commentator summed up by saying that German Social Democracy did not wish "any antimilitary agitation that can hamstring the struggle for emancipation or slow its victorious course." Commenting on colonial policy, he noted there had been discussions on whether positions could be worked out already now for a "provisional, and in this case unfortunately, still unforeseeable future":

> Indeed, it is impossible to foresee what the critique of capitalist colonial policy now can have to do with the question whether socialism at some future indeterminate time will pursue a civilized colonial policy. … And whether there can be a civilizing colonial policy by the time our grandchildren will be tossing our bones to knock apples from the trees is a question hardly worth speculating about today. Such utopian musing can be misused by the patrons of capitalist colonial policy to obscure all its atrociousness.[49]

I have attempted in this paper to lay out a few reasons why the idea never even occurred to the journalist here that free, independent, and sovereign nations might perhaps exist in the areas of the former colonial territories by the time of their grandchildren.

Notes

1. Examples from the German Democratic Republic: Manfred Nussbaum, *Vom Kolonialenthusiasmus zur Kolonialpolitik der Monopole* (Berlin [East]: Akademie-Verlag, 1962); Horst Drechsler, *Südwestafrika unter deutscher Kolonialherrschaft* (Berlin [East]: Akademie-Verlag, 1966); Kurt Büttner and Heinrich Loth (eds.), *Philosophie der Eroberer und koloniale Wirklichkeit. Ostafrika 1884-1918* (Berlin [East]: Akademie-Verlag, 1981). From the Federal Republic: Karin Hausen, *Deutsche Kolonialherrschaft in Afrika. Wirtschaftsinteressen und Kolonialverwaltung in Kamerun vor 1914* (Zürich and Freiburg: Atlantis-Verlag, 1970); Rainer Tetzlaff, *Koloniale Entwicklung und Ausbeutung. Wirtschafts- und Sozialgeschichte Deutsch-Ostafrikas* (Berlin: Duncker & Humblot, 1970); Klaus J. Bade (ed.), *Imperialismus und Kolonialmission. Kaiserliches Deutschland und koloniales Imperium* (Wiesbaden: Steiner, 1982); Martha Mamozai, *Herrenmenschen. Frauen im deutschen Kolonialismus* (Reinbek bei Hamburg: Rowohlt, 1982); Helmut Bley, *Kolonialherrschaft und Sozialstruktur in Deutsch-Südwestafrika 1894-1914* (Hamburg: Leibniz-Verlag, 1983); Horst Gründer, *Geschichte der deutschen Kolonien* (Paderborn [etc.]: Schöningh, 1985) — rich in factual material but analytically flawed.
2. [Berlin Conference: gathering of nearly all European potentates and the United States (15 November 1884 – 26 February 1885). It established the rules for the colonial powers to divide control of Africa and ushered in the scramble for this continent (1885-1904).]
3. In cinema: Egon Günther's "Morenga" (1985), and various TV productions, including Peter Heller, "Die Liebe zum Imperium" (1978); "Usambara — das Land wo Glauben Bäume versetzen soll" (1979); "Mbogos Ernte oder die Teilung der Welt" (1980); "Mandu Yenu — Schwarzer König zwischen Anpassung und Widerstand" (1984). Among conferences and scholarly projects: Manfred O. Hinz (ed.), "Namibia: Die Aktualität des kolonialen Verhältnisses. Beiträge aus dem Projekt Politische Landeskunde Namibias," in: *Diskurs. Bremer Beiträge zu Wissenschaft und Gesellschaft*, no. 6 (1982); Jos Gerwin and Gottfried Mergner (eds.), *Innere und äussere Kolonisation. Zur Geschichte der Ausbreitung Europas auf die übrige Welt, Internationales Symposium 1981* (Oldenburg: Bibliotheks- und Informationssystem der Universität Oldenburg, 1982); Jos Gerwin, Gottfried Mergner, and Jos Koetsier (eds.), *Alltäglichkeit und Kolonialisierung. Internationales Symposium 1982* (Oldenburg: Bibliotheks- und Informationssystem der Universität Oldenburg, 1983); Entwicklungspolitische Korrespondenz (ed.), *Deutscher Kolonialismus. Materialien zur Hundertjahrfeier 1984* (Hamburg, 1983); Henning Melber (ed.), *In Treue Fest, Südwest! Eine ideologiekritische Dokumentation* (Bonn: Edition Südliches Afrika, 1984); "Kolonialismus und Kolonialreiche (Referate des 5. Tübinger Gespräches, Mai 1984)," in: *Zeitschrift für Kulturaustausch*, nos. 3-4 (1984); Manfred O. Hinz et al. (eds.), *Weiss auf Schwarz. Hundert Jahre Einmischung in Afrika. Deutscher Kolonialismus und Widerstand* (Berlin: Elefantenpress, 1984); Evangelische Akademie Bad Boll (ed.), *Kolonialismus: zwischen Anpassung und Widerstand* (Bad Boll, 1985).
4. Günther Mager, "Die deutsche Sozialdemokratie und die Aufstände der Herero und Nama in Südwestafrika, 1904-1907," (PhD. diss., Halle, 1966) — based in part on local periodicals; Mager arrives at the same findings as mine, but draws completely different conclusions in evaluation and theory; Gerda Weinberger, "Die deutsche Sozialdemokratie und die Kolonialpolitik. Zu einigen Aspekten der sozialdemokratischen Haltung in der Kolonialen Frage in den letzten Jahrzehnten des 19. Jahrhunderts," *Zeitschrift für Geschichtswissenschaft*, 15 (1967), pp. 402-423; Günther Müller, "Sozialdemokratie und Kolonialpolitik vor 1914," *Aus Politik und Zeitgeschichte*, 13 March 1968, pp. 16-24; Hans-Christoph Schröder, *Sozialismus und Imperialismus. Die Auseinandersetzung der deutschen Sozialdemokratie mit dem Imperialismusproblem und der "Weltpolitik" vor 1914* (Bonn-Bad Godesberg: Verlag Neue Gesellschaft, 1975); Massao Nishikawa, "Zivilisierung der Kolonien oder Kolonisation der Zivilisation? Die Sozialisten und die Kolonialfrage im Zeitalter des Imperialismus," in: Joachim Radkau and Imanuel Geiss (eds.), *Imperialismus im 20. Jahrhundert. Gedenkschrift für Georg W.F. Hallgarten* (Munich: Beck, 1976), pp. 87-112; Hans-Christoph Schröder, *Gustav Noske und die Kolonialpolitik des Deutschen*

Kaiserreichs (Berlin and Bonn: Dietz, 1979); Roger Fletcher, *Revisionism and Empire. Socialist Imperialism in Germany 1897-1914* (London [etc.]: Allen & Unwin, 1984).

5. Regarding the legitimacy of this concept, note the theory of "state socialism" in Friedrich Naumann, *Mitteleuropa* (Berlin: Reimer, 1915). For the thesis that German Social Democracy was always "Prussian" in its discipline and quiet determination, see Oswald Spengler, *Preussentum und Sozialismus* (Munich: Beck, 1920).

6. Uwe Timm, *Morenga* (Munich: Verlag Autoren-Edition, 1978); Helgard Patemann, "Zum Beispiel Marengo," in: Hinz, *Weiss auf Schwarz*, p. 104; The various spellings (Morenga, Marengo) refer to the same person.

7. [August Bebel (1840-1913), cabinetmaker, cofounder of the German Social democratic Party. Party chairman from 1892. Reichstag member in the years 1867-1872, 1874-1881, and 1883-1913. His best-known book is *Die Frau und der Sozialismus* (1883).]

8. On 5 December 1905, sentences of from three to nine years' imprisonment in chains were handed down against several chiefs by a court in Duala (Cameroon). Their "crime" was that they had written directly to the Reichstag, bypassing the local governor. Naturally, the Reichstag had not replied. The Social Democratic caucus had not bothered to answer either. See *Norddeutsches Volksblatt*, 13 January 1906. Noske was the first Social Democrat to try to obtain solid knowledge about the colonial territories. [Gustav Noske (1868-1946), basket maker, social-democratic politician, Reichstag member in the years 1906-1918 and 1919-1920, Minister of War 1919-1920.]

9. See the introduction in Erhard Lucas, *Zwei Formen von Radikalismus in der deutschen Arbeiterbewegung* (Frankfurt am Main: Roter Stern, 1976).

10. Erhard Lucas, *Vom Scheitern der deutschen Arbeiterbewegung* (Basel and Frankfurt am Main: Stroemfeld-Roter Stern, 1983).

11. See Norbert Elias, "Towards a Theory of Social Processes," *British Journal of Sociology*, 48 (1997), pp. 355-383; Wolfgang Emmerich (ed.), *Proletarische Lebensläufe. Autobiographische Dokumente zur Entstehung der Zweiten Kultur in Deutschland*, 2 volumes (Reinbek bei Hamburg: Rowohlt, 1974, 1979); Georg Bollenbeck, *Zur Theorie und Geschichte der frühen Arbeiterlebenserinnerungen* (Kronberg: Scriptor Verlag, 1976); Michael Seyfarth-Stubenrauch, *Erziehung und Sozialisation in Arbeiterfamilien im Zeitraum 1870 bis 1914 in Deutschland*, 2 volumes (Frankfurt am Main [etc.]: Peter Lang, 1985).

12. For a later era, though also applicable to the years before 1914, see Oskar Negt and Alexander Kluge, *Public Sphere and Experience. Toward an Analysis of the Bourgeois and Proletarian Public Sphere*. Trans. Peter Labanyi, Jamie Owen Daniel, and Assenka Oksiloff (Minneapolis: University of Minnesota Press, 1993).

13. Anneliese Bergmann, "Geburtenrückgang — Gebärstreik. Zur Gebärstreikdebatte 1913 in Berlin," *Archiv für die Geschichte des Widerstandes und der Arbeit*, 4 (1981), pp. 7-55; Erhard Lucas, *Vom Scheitern*, pp. 45-46; Gerda Tornierporth, "Proletarisches Frauenleben und bürgerlicher Weiblichkeitsmythos," in: Barbara Schaeffel-Hegel et al. (eds.), *Mythos Frau. Projektionen und Inszenierungen im Patriarchat* (Berlin: Publica-Verlagsgesellschaft, 1984).

14. See the paradigmatic study by Klaus Theweleit, *Male Fantasies*. Foreword Barbara Ehrenreich. Trans. Stephen Conway in collaboration with Erica Carter and Chris Turner, 2 volumes (Minneapolis: University of Minnesota Press, 1987-1989).

15. See Gerhard A. Ritter, *Die Arbeiterbewegung im Wilhelminischen Reich. Die sozialdemokratische Partei und die freien Gewerkschaften 1890-1900* (Berlin: Colloquium Verlag, 1959), esp. chapters 7 and 8.

16. Klaus-Michael Bogdal, *"Schaurige Bilder." Der Arbeiter im Blick des Bürgers am Beispiel des Naturalismus* (Frankfurt am Main: Syndikat, 1978).

17. Conrad Alberti, *Wer ist der Stärkere? Ein sozialer Roman aus dem modernen Berlin*, 2 volumes (Leipzig: Friedrich, 1888), Vol. 2, p. 67.

18. Bogdal, *"Schaurige Bilder,"* p. 53. [Ernst Haeckel (1834-1919), German philosopher and biologist, Darwin supporter, formulated the discredited biogenetic law of recapitulation, which held that individual development is a repetition of the history of the entire species. His works, in which he argued vigorously against the Christian representation of God, were

internationally highly influential before World War II.]

19. *Der Osternburger*, 31 August 1891.

20. [Law on Socialists (*Sozialistengesetz*): the emergency law against German Social Democracy (1878-1890), forced through the legislature by Bismarck following attacks on Kaiser Wilhelm I, which allowed the police to dissolve associations and confiscate publications. The law was initially enacted for three years but was extended several times.]

21. *Der Fachgenosse. Organ der Glasarbeiter aller Branchen bzw. deren Verbände*, 28 April 1903.

22. Brigitte Emig, *Die Veredelung des Arbeiters. Sozialdemokratie als Kulturbewegung* (Frankfurt am Main and New York: Campus, 1980), p. 298; see also chap. 17, "Kultur als aussenpolitischer Wertmesser," pp. 214-228.

23. On Rühle's activities before World War I, see Gottfried Mergner, *Arbeiterbewegung und Intelligenz. Die politische Pädagogik Otto Rühles* (Starnberg: Werner Raith Verlag, 1973). The most important of Rühle's writings for this question is his work on the psychology of the proletarian child, see Otto Rühle, *Zur Psychologie des proletarischen Kindes* (Frankfurt am Main: März Verlag, 1975).

24. *Der Fachgenosse*, 1 March 1902.

25. Willfried Spohn, *Weltmarktkonkurrenz und Industrialisierung Deutschlands 1870-1914* (Berlin: Olle & Wolter, 1977).

26. [Georg Ledebour (1850-1947), merchant, journalist, Reichstag member in the years 1900-1918 and 1920-1924, first for the SPD and later for the USPD. Emigrated in 1933.]

27. Klaus Epstein, *Matthias Erzberger and the Dilemma of German Democracy* (Princeton, NJ: Princeton University Press, 1959), chapters III and IV.

28. Schröder, *Gustav Noske*, pp. 23-24.

29. Minutes, Deutscher Reichstag, 11th Leg., Vol. 1, pp. 366-68.

30. Ibid.

31. Ibid.

32. Ibid.

33. *Leipziger Volkszeitung*, 19 January 1905; see also Mager, "Die deutsche Sozialdemokratie," p. 138.

34. I rely here on the richly documented study by Detlev Rossmann, "Kulturelle Öffentlichkeit in Oldenburg-Osternburg 1918-1933. Kritische Untersuchungen zum Verhältnis von Arbeitsalltag und Politik der KPD" (PhD. diss., Oldenburg, 1979). In its first section, the dissertation deals in great detail with cultural life before the Great War.

35. *Der Fachgenosse*, 11 May 1901. [*Kommerzienrath* was an honorary title conferred on distinguished businessmen.]

36. Armando Córdova, "Rosa Luxemburg und die Dritte Welt," in: Claudio Pozzoli (ed.), *Rosa Luxemburg oder die Bestimmung des Sozialismus* (Frankfurt am Main: Suhrkamp, 1974), pp. 65-93, at 77. Mitschein has tried to offer an explanation for the fact mentioned by Córdova. He believes the cause lies in the opinion largely internalized by the workers that bourgeois society "only recognizes someone as a human being who is its member; and only considers those persons members who are active in exchange in the marketplace." This profoundly internalized identification with the capitalist economic system, and not the betrayal of some abstract principles, is what led to the growing integration of the organized workers into a global capitalist system based on nation-states. This system necessarily excluded the "savage" as "still uncivilized" — until that "savage" had successfully passed through the civilizing educational dictatorship of colonialization and become an emancipated exchange partner. See Thomas Mitschein, *Die Dritte Welt als Gegenstand gewerkschaftlicher Theorie und Praxis. Zur Analyse der internationalen Politik metropolitaner Gewerkschaften* (Frankfurt am Main and New York: Campus, 1981), pp. 51-60.

37. [Karl Kautsky (1854-1938), leading social-democratic theoretician before World War I, founder and editor of the theoretical journal *Die Neue Zeit*, 1883-1917.]

38. This totally unquestioning acceptance of the discourse of the imperialists is a clear indication of just how removed Social Democracy was from the interests of the colonized peoples in emancipation.

39. The term "Kaffir" was even then disparaging, like the name "Hottentot." This shows that the Social Democrats were not prepared to call the "savages" by their own names.

40. *Norddeutsches Volksblatt,* 20 December 1906.
41. Ronald Daus, *Die Erfindung des Kolonialismus* (Wuppertal: Hammer, 1983), p. 276.
42. See also Gottfried Mergner, "Die europäische Berufung zur Besserung der Welt," in: Klaus Hirsch (ed.), *Kolonialismus zwischen Anpassung und Widerstand* (Bad Boll: Protokolldienst Evangelische Akademie, 1985), pp. 31-54.
43. [Eduard David (1863-1930), teacher, editor of social-democratic party journals, party secretary for the Grand Duchy of Hessen since 1907. Reichstag member in the years 1903-1918 and 1919-1930.]
44. Susanne Miller with Erich Matthias (eds.), *Das Kriegstagebuch des Reichstagsabgeordneten Eduard David 1914 bis 1918* (Düsseldorf: Droste, 1966), p. 28.
45. [DDP: Deutsche Demokratische Partei (1918-1930), progressive-liberal party that arose from a merger between the freethinking liberals from the Fortschrittliche Volkspartei and other liberal groups. DNVP: Deutschnationale Volkspartei (1918-1933), conservative monarchist party, heavily influenced by sections of the Prussian major landowners and large industries. DVP: Deutsche Volkspartei (1918-1933), moderate conservative party.]
46. [USPD: Unabhängige Sozialdemokratische Partei Deutschlands (1917-1922), leftist party split off the German social-democratic party. In 1920 the majority joined the Communists. Two years later the remaining minority returned to the SPD.]
47. [Gustave Hervé (1871-1944), French teacher, lawyer, and journalist, who became known before 1914 as a radical antimilitarist. After the start of World War I, he became a fervent nationalist.]
48. [Georg von Vollmar (1850-1922): officer, civil servant, social democrat. Reichstag member in the years 1881-1887 and 1890-1918.]
49. *Norddeutsches Volksblatt,* 27 August 1907.

CHAPTER 5

DEATH AND SOCIAL DEMOCRACY[1]

A. Historical sources of the conceptions of death in Social Democracy

1. The death of the subject and collective resistance

Death as the expression of our earthly mundane nature, our creatureliness, cannot be comprehended by rational means; it eludes the grasp of instrumental reason and thus even today provides the occasion for diverse projections and speculations. We create images of death, the result of our wrestling with the fear of the unknown, what is uncontrollable and its repression in consciousness. These images and often contradictory extensions of social reality are reflected in the conceptions and imagery of life after death. We intend here to explore various projections of death associated with German Social Democracy before 1933.

In his book on the failure of the German workers' movement, Erhard Lucas criticizes Karl Marx, blaming him for the repression of subjective death in Social Democratic politics: "[so] what all participants cheat themselves out of is their life in the present. Or, phrased more precisely, they cheat themselves completely out of their life. In many respects then, even the churches are more attractive."[2] But Lucas argues here on the basis of a mistaken understanding of Marx. He refers to the often quoted sentence in the *Economic and Philosophic Manuscripts of 1844* where Marx states that the given individual is only a "specific representative of a genus," and consequently only mortal in that sense. But the genus for Marx is imperishable. From this Lucas reasons that Marx (and later Social Democracy) subordinated the individual to the development of the "genus."[3] Yet Lucas overlooks the fact that this particular passage in Marx deals with the more encompassing question of "private property and communism"; Marx notes there that the nexus between the life of the genus and that of the individual will only become recognizable in communism, since "at the present day *general* consciousness is an abstraction from real life and as such confronts it with hostility."[4] Thus,

Lucas shifts the critical content in Marx's statement into its very opposite. His critique of Marx is marked by a new one-sided view that has gained vogue in our time: restricting the dimension of resistance to the life of the individual, Lucas is unable to see the historical perspectives of *collective* resistance. By defining the active life of the individual in terms of the terminus of death, death becomes for Lucas decisive in determining the *meaning* of an individual's life—similar to ideas in the Christian church or, in secularized form, in Martin Heidegger.

Yet "death does not bestow meaning on life; rather it is the abrupt cancellation of any meaning. 'My' death doesn't exist, since death is only the external indeterminate negation of subjectivity."[5] This view of death opens a double perspective for my existence: my own life is solely an end for me personally. And it is so to its fullest extent only if my life is not secondarily or largely a means to achieve purposes that are alien and inimical to me, contrary to the unfolding of my own possibilities and prospects. If I have to live in a social reality that I regard as false for myself, *resistance* to these alien ends becomes my life's central meaning. This implies that it is also possible for me to determine the meaning of resistance *together* with others. That insight can prevent me from dying as a result of alien ends or squandering away my life for the sake of such ends. Yet insight is but the first step to overcoming necessity, its sublative *Aufhebung*. Necessity grasped conceptually is not yet freedom, not yet life. Because freedom "requires progress from theory to practice: actual conquest of those necessities which prevent or restrain the satisfaction of needs."[6] However—and here indeed is the absurdity of the conditions of power and domination that still exist—the prospect for an individual and his/her future can lie in risking that life in order to change prevailing social conditions: not to imbue one's life with meaning by death, but in order to resist the meaninglessness of a life forced upon an individual externally. Since death for me must spell the end of all meaningfulness, the meaning and aims of resistance must be communicable to me alone, and while I am still alive. This is what gives resistance its illuminating power and democratic perspective. Without being linked to my own concrete biography, resistance becomes meaningless in a personal context. Yet if my resistance fails to impinge upon the existing social relations of power, it also remains devoid of any personal meaning.

But the senselessness of death and the subjective side of resistance must be hidden from those who are also to be deprived of their subjectivity, their right to create personal meanings. Enlightenment is then replaced by transcendental hope, e. g., a belief in the mystic unity of a community—be it a political party, a folk-community, or even the community of all democrats. The individual is distracted from the fact of personal death, and is seduced by the desire for immortality into self-sacrifice for the sake of supraindividual goals. In modern times, domination requires a considerable degree of consent by the individuals under its sway. This is why modern ideologies of domination repudiate death's meaninglessness, mounting an unparalleled effort to persuade the dubious.

That misled the functionaries in the organized labor movement to respond with kindred attempts to secure their hierarchical authority by shoring it up with historicophilosophical ideologies. They appropriated for themselves the power to define joint resistance against repression and exploitation and then ennobled it to the level of some historical, supraindividual truth—one that can become concrete reality only in future generations. Nonetheless, those modern ideologies of rule differ in an essential point from their predecessors, such as in Imperial Germany: the dead in the worker's movement were to die like Moses, in sight of the promised paradise. By contrast, those who died for Imperial Germany did so stripped of any personal perspective; they perished for the sole benefit of a negative present cloaked in nationalist garb, and misrepresented as the moment's sole possible happiness.

2. The transition from ecclesiastical to enlightened notions of death

With the transition to the bourgeois age, a new philosophically enlightened conception of death arises on the basis of an advanced stage in the domination of nature, conceptualizing death as immanent in all life. By contrast, the Christian religions propagate an image of the afterlife which, through the prospect of the soul's survival, engenders hope in the perpetuation of the existence (albeit transformed) of the dead in the world to come. That image acts to mitigate the fear of death. During their earthly life, human beings can shape and design their lives with a view to the hierarchical heavens above; in so doing, they provide already here on earth for their final redemption. Yet beginning in the late medieval period, even within the official church, the terrifying aspect of death as a concrete event became ever more central in conceptions of death; that horrifying dimension appeared to relativize class differences in feudal society. This turn toward the equality of all in their fear of the hour of death was part of a general shift away from traditional feudal social order, a pyramid that had also been reflected in the hierarchical imagery and iconography of heaven. Once death was recognized as a harrowing common fate, the path was also open to its becoming a "natural" fact. Anxiety about the perils of the afterlife gradually gave way to enlightened fears regarding the dangers of life before death.[7] To the extent that death was viewed as a *natural* fact—i.e., amenable neither to divine nor human will—the conception took ever firmer root that the fear of dying could be surmounted by a rational analysis of the phenomenon of death. Every person had to be granted the possibility to die a *natural* death. The concept "natural" here denotes the final victory of the power of nature over the medical and social concern to prolong life, in contrast with "unnatural" death due to violence or adverse social circumstances. This also marked the beginning of modern rational discourse on the meaning of premature death in the service of a cause and the ideological transfiguration of death for the sake of the community.

3. The attitude toward death in the ideology of Social Democracy

In Feuerbach's critique of religion, divine power appears as the image and representation of human fantasies about perfection: "God is nothing but man's projection of himself. Thus, man is not dependent on God, as religion claims, but rather God on man."[8] Dreams that go beyond death allude to the deepset desire to see a change in the given conditions. Consequently, Feuerbach stresses the notion of man as a concrete-sensuous, living creature, not a mere spiritual entity. But human beings had deceived themselves in their fantasies of omnipotence, since they are creatures delimited in time, historically determined and thus mortal. Death as a natural event is ineluctable. "Nothing stands as finalistically as death does at the end, and nothing shatters the work of the subjects of historical purpose-setting so antifinalistically into fragments."[9] However, death took on its meaning and value by dint of the advancement of the genus Homo, in terms of whose benefit the individual transcends himself: an individual life flows on into nature, unlimited and eternal, and into the onward advance of the genus.

Marx, taking a cue from Feuerbach, stresses *activity* in this life, rejecting the mere abstraction, the projection:

> The *task of history*, therefore, once the *world beyond the truth* has disappeared, is to establish the *truth of this world*. The immediate *task of philosophy*, which is at the service of history, once the *holy form* of human self-estrangement has been unmasked, is to unmask self-estrangement in its *unholy forms*. Thus the criticism of heaven turns into the criticism of the earth, the *criticism of religion* into the *criticism of law* and the *criticism of theology* into the *criticism of politics*.[10]

This critique is the basis for the struggle for freedom from external control and determination, making possible, in Engels' formulation, "mankind's leap from the realm of necessity into that of freedom." Although death is transfigured in the light of an emancipated humanity, the creaturely fear of death felt by the individual stands in contradiction with that transfiguration. The radical worldliness of Feuerbach and Marx is transmuted in the ideology of Social Democracy, increasingly hierarchical in structure, into a "philosophy of history."[11] It appropriates the crude materialism of bourgeois ideologies of progress (such as Darwinism, monism), overlaying it with a brand of Marxism degenerated into quasi-religious dogma. More influential than Feuerbach or Marx in shaping the Social Democratic conceptions of death were Haeckel, Kautsky and Bebel in his military memoirs.

Let us look first at Haeckel's monistic theory. According to the so-called "law of substance" in monism, matter and energy (nature and spirit) form the world, the realm of substance, whose phenomena can be empirically grasped and traced back to their origins. "The sum of matter, which fills infinite space, is unchangeable. A body has merely changed its form, when it seems to have disappeared."[12] Human beings do not differ from animals qualitatively, but only quantitatively in terms of mental and physical characteristics; thus, there is no specifically human soul. There is only a higher degree of mental activity, a higher plane of development. It would be unscientific and illusory to assume the existence of a specifically human spiritual essence.

> Do we find a different state of things in the history of peoples, which man, in his anthropocentric presumption loves to call "the history of the world"? Do we find

in every phase of it a lofty moral principle or a wise ruler, guiding the destinies of nations? There can be but one answer in the present advanced stage of natural and human history: No. The fate of those branches of the human family, those nations and races which have struggled for existence and progress for thousands of years, is determined by the same "eternal, iron, big laws" as the history of the whole organic world which has peopled the earth for millions of years.[13]

Yet this line of reasoning also strips resistance against existing realities of its very warrant. Whatever exists is justified by the fact that it has come to be and prevailed over everything else (that no longer exists). Consequently, it has the right to exist if it can continue to maintain itself against the press of every-thing else. This is the grounding of the logic of nationalism, indeed of impe-rialism. It is thus only consistent that upon closer examination, Haeckel turns out to be an out-and-out racist.[14] Progress now is no longer "emancipa-tion," but rather the victory of "what is stronger, better, of greater worth." The fascination this theory exercised, even for the working class, was that such a conception of humankind progressing according to natural laws allowed them to harbor hopes for improvement: a bettering in their social condition without having to give much thought to the meaning and risk of individual or collective resistance. This is why they portrayed their own inter-ests as part of civilization's forward march and tended more and more to identify themselves unthinkingly with what was stronger, such as the domi-nant culture or the nation-state. Moreover, they were fascinated by the anti-clerical rejection of religious beliefs oriented to the world beyond, which had been supplanted by the secular worldliness of a transcendent trust in the community. This surrender of individuality shares an important feature with the church's perennial position. Religious morality gestured toward an eter-nal realm beyond the grave; the new morality of scientific socialism, degen-erated into a doctrine of salvation, held out the promise of *generic* salvation beyond one's own individual existence.

Consequently, the burial of party members, and most particularly of lead-ers, became a site for the creation of meaning in Social Democratic culture, the celebration of the transcendence of individual existence. It served to pre-vent the individual from pondering the absurdity that the dead no longer participate in their own ceremonial homage, but are now subject to the con-trol of others. The actual freedom to give one's own life a meaning could only exist while a person was still alive. But that presupposed collective forms of resistance in which the rank-and-file membership of the organiza-tion would have to take part, itself shaping such forms and imbuing them with meaning.

Our critique of authoritarian organization should be augmented by the following: in this period, a certain form of proletarian, individual self-deter-mination became ever more ubiquitous, namely the option of suicide. Around the turn of the century, many workers, even entire families, were driven to suicide as a result of poverty, destitution, and hopelessness. This manifested the bourgeois enlighteners' insight that "death was the great equalizer," likewise reflected in the murderous working and living conditions in modern industry, and the mass slaughter of modern warfare. This helps explain why Social Democracy was especially concerned to protect the general interests of the proletariat from collective threat, even utilizing the existing state if necessary. Such a bid presupposed acknowledging the state's monopoly on power. As long as the cause of death for most workers was not biological aging and they continued to die an *unnatural* premature death, Social Democracy's primary demand was for the state to introduce social policy that would protect the lives of its citizenry. Insofar as it was in the imperialist interests of the state, such demands were also incorporated into the government's social policy. These successes in turn strengthened the Social Democratic ideologies of community and the readiness on the part of workers to be integrated within the existing state. "The right to a natural death was formulated as a claim to equal consumption of medical services, rather than as a freedom from the evils of industrial work or as a new liberty and power for self-care."[15]

B. Death and Organization

For the believing member, the organization of Social Democracy became in time itself the locus for the hope of resurrection. The "inexorable" forward march of the organization seemed to bestow on the individual's life a meaning beyond death. This was the clear message enunciated at the graveside of rank-and-file members and the funerals of SPD functionaries and party ideologues. The organization itself was an expression of prevailing social contradictions, organizing them both politically and culturally. The party was geared primarily to enlightenment—a beneficiary to (and also prisoner of) the heritage of bourgeois Enlightenment. Yet in communicating between the rank-and-file and party functionaries, enormous quantities of paper and verbiage were always expended, over and beyond political instruction, in an effort to banish uncertainty and win over the membership's faith and hopes. This imbued Social Democracy with a burning passion for duty, an ardent ambition for what was higher and absolute—and that in turn totally excluded any lust for life or *joie de vivre*. Beneath the level of the funeral, it appeared that the official party could hardly make any public statement: everything spoken and written had to stand the test of evolution's eternal judgment. We will now explore more closely the relation between the rank-and-file membership and the SPD leaders in the period down to World War I by examining several questions relating to the intra-party culture of death.

1. *Social Democracy was committed to an anticlerical atheism, a belief centered fully on this world. What consequence did that have for the individual's fear of death, and how was that expressed?*

In 1925, the Bremen schoolteacher Carl Dantz published a popular children's book *Peter Stoll. Ein Kinderleben. Vom ihm selbst erzählt.*[16] Employing the stylistic technique of "child reporting," the book contained among other things a description of the death and burial of a seventeen-year-old worker. As the editors Johannes Merkel and Dieter Richter note in their afterword to the new edition, the book's author, Dantz, a leftwing Social Democrat, appears to have observed and described the life of his proletarian pupils very accurately.[17]

Hermann, the brother of the ten-year-old first-person narrator, gets a job working outside on the docks in Bremen, contracts pneumonia, and succumbs a few days later. He is treated by a doctor from the state medical scheme and dies in the hospital, but the authorities try to scrimp on the necessary medication. The deathbed scene expresses the proletarian family's cohesion. The dying young man is worried chiefly about the well-being of his family and asks his brothers and sisters to assume the burden of his duties at home. Yet his final wish is to die in a separate bed of his own in the hospital. Hermann's father reacts to his son's death with restrained fury: "He shouted at the mailman, the doctor, the dairywoman and the master workman who'd piled all that work on Hermann's back." Yet as a good Social Democrat, he has learned to recognize the "true" cause of this tragedy: "And the fat-assed factory bigwigs, look, those guys are the only ones who've got Hermann on their conscience."[18] That statement also appears to console and calm the bereaved father.

As was increasingly more common practice in Social Democratic families after 1919, the boy's remains are cremated.[19] Since Aunt Betti, who is a practising Christian, pays for the cremation, a Protestant minister speaks at the funeral in place of a representative of the "organization" (the party or trade union), as the family had wished. Members of the immediate family and several fellow workers of Hermann and his father are present at the ceremony. Naturally, the minister consoles them in his own way: "Blessed are the poor in spirit, the kingdom of Heaven is theirs. Hermann was one of them, he was too good for this earth."[20] Those words infuriate the workers, but they remain silent. Only after the ceremony is over do they comment: "You can't bring a dead man back to life with a snatch of singin' and prayin'." Turning to his father, the workers admonish, "Hang tough, Stoll, better times are a-comin'. Workers like us, well, we mustn't get disheartened, see. And machinists never should, 'cause otherwise there could be some accident."[21]

Hermann's father is grateful for these words of solace, they are in tune with his way of thinking and help him return to reality: "OK, you guys, get back to work. Day after tomorrow's pay-day, we're all gonna have to suffer again. The factory won't miss this chance, they're gonna deduct 80 pfennigs for every hour we knock off to mourn."[22] The story ends on an upbeat note: "It wasn't even two months later, and Hanna [another sister of the narrator] arrived. She started to holler and shout day and night, and livened up the place again."[23]

Many reports and workers' autobiographies[24] indicate that Dantz gave a pretty accurate description of everyday death and the way it was dealt with in the working-class milieu around World War I. After 1923, there was a slight improvement in medical care, and cremation became common practice in the larger cities, despite the Catholic church's futile opposition. The crematorium became a site for the successful implementation of Social Democratic communal policy. After the Great War, in cities such as Berlin, Hamburg, Bremen, and Vienna, crematoria were constructed with the active involvement of Social Democratic elected officials. There was defiant support for the right to have one's body cremated after death in a municipal facility, based on *rational* reasons—contra to church dogma and its avowed belief in physical resurrection. Not decay but cremation: clean, quick, and sensible; moreover, it was cheaper and a space-saver to boot. This was a public-health measure that reflected Social Democratic conceptions of public order. And it allowed the individual *after* death to declare publicly his or her adherence to a materialist *Weltanschauung*. However, even the idea of the crematorium could only be implemented with the help of middle-class allies. The indifference to death in the massive battles of attrition during the Great War was a factor that helped dissuade those from the bourgeois ranks from granting the Roman Catholic church any special consideration.

Poverty, simple and realistic mourning, and optimism about the future shaped the event of death and the subsequent funeral held in the circle of the immediate family and fellow workers. Death was integrated into life, experienced as a part of proletarian fate. Increasingly, savings to cover the cost of cremation were set aside in the death benefit funds, the so-called *Sterbekassen*, schemes that people joined for ideological reasons at a young age. These savings schemes were an integral component of Social Democratic culture after World War I. They were extolled as an achievement of the proletarian organization and a concrete expression of political dignity.[25] Another factor involved here was the wish to at least "have a decent burial."[26] Workers had learned, as part of "class consciousness," that under the existing working and living conditions, a "decent" life for them was not yet possible. But they hoped that at least in death, the family, fellow workers, or even the organization (and increasingly, the Social Democratic clubs) would give fitting tribute to their worth as conscientious comrades, their dignity as workers.

As achievements multiplied in government social policy and Social Democratic education, the forms of the middle-class way of death were imitated even in the burials of the simple rank-and-file, and were imbued with Social Democratic symbolism. Death and its celebration were a striking expression of the conviction that workers as a class would some day emerge victorious under the banner of these symbols—even if the individual's time was up and he or she had to exit from the stage of struggle. This presupposed expectations for the future that individuals on their own could no longer pursue and develop in times when they had politically to bide their time (quietism). Consequently, it was incumbent upon the Social Democratic organizations to represent this hope in symbolic form in their politics and culture.

2. *The organization based its authority on the claim that it was able to forecast the future correctly. As long as political progress remained something largely beyond the individual's experience, the common expectations for the future constituted the necessary bond linking the individual to the organization and its politics.*

In his *Die Frau und der Sozialismus/Woman and Socialism*, August Bebel formulated how the resisting individual subject was absorbed into the Social Democratic mass: "In the struggle for the progress of mankind, no power, not even the weakest, can be spared. The steady fall of drops will finally hollow the hardest stone. ... If all who feel called upon devote their whole strength to this struggle, the ultimate victory will be certain."[27] Two conceptions are conveyed in the image of the drop of water that hollows out the stone: what really matters is only the good will of all who believe they are summoned to the struggle; and the final goal can be long in coming. This gives rise to the maxim: victory "will be all the greater, the more eagerly and unselfishly each ones pursues the mapped out path. Doubts, whether the individual for all his sacrifices, toils and efforts, may still live to see the dawn of a new, more beautiful period of civilization, must not affect us, nor must they prevent us from pursuing the chosen path."[28] This transformation of concrete needs and subjective readiness to resist into an abstract and general sense of duty to support the common cause becomes an educational program for the worker:

> The dawn of a better day is drawing nigh. So let us struggle and strive onward, regardless of "where" and "when" the boundary-posts of a new and better age for mankind will be raised. If we should fail in the course of this great struggle for liberation, others will take our place. We will fall with the consciousness of having done our duty as human beings *and with the conviction that the goal will be attained, no matter how the powers hostile to humanity may oppose and resist the triumphal march of progress.*[29]

The hard and bitter life of the worker—if only the workers are buoyed by Social Democratic consciousness—is styled into a form of resistance. So there is no longer any need to wage genuine struggles. The war veteran Bebel describes the development as a colossal battle, a fateful struggle whose end is never in doubt. Individuals can be part of the winning side when, with a sense of discipline and duty, they join the ranks of the army of progress—an army always ready for battle, but never directly engaged. One's own individual death and life shrivel to insignificance in the face of the "common cause."[30] Some day the just rewards shall be reaped. But by whom? Bebel notes: "The future belongs to Socialism, that is, primarily, to the worker and the woman."[31]

3. *Digression: death and the future are a woman: Social
Democratic allegories*

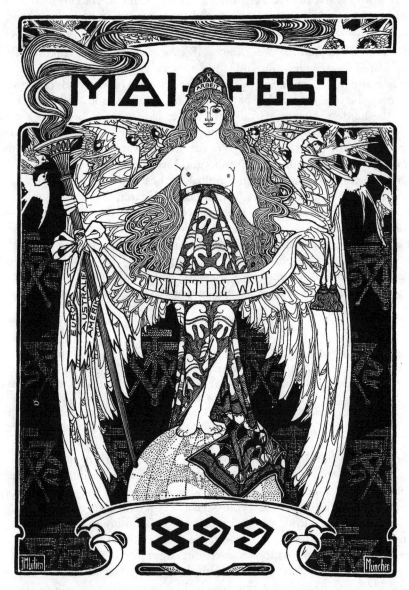

Marianne, May 1 poster, 1899

A 1978 exhibition catalog from the Historical Museum, Frankfurt contains
a collection of pictorial elements of Social Democratic agitation before World
War I.[32] The examples there reveal to us Bebel's mystery of why the socialist
future belongs to "women." Down to the turn of the century, in the alle-
gorical illustrations in the Social Democratic press, the future, freedom, and
happiness were almost always represented by a Marianne figure, a young and

aloof beauty wearing a Phrygian cap. After 1900, this figure was increasingly supplanted by the idealized image of a young and powerful hero; that representation already heralded the growing acceptance, even within Social Democracy, of the brutal allure of nationalist politics predicated on Darwinian nature symbolism. The "young beauty" of the preceding era is not a mother figure, and also lacks the realistic features of genuine young working-class women. She is a luminous figure resplendent in her superhuman virginal ideality. She often marches at the head of an endless column of workers of all ages, male and female, bearing aloft a red banner. The final goal is unknown; only concepts (eight-hour workday, socialism, etc.) mark the uncertain future. Or, like a protecting angel, she points the path to despairing workers, or consoles them about the dismal and difficult present. Yet sometimes she bears the image of an important dead leader of the workers' movement (such as Lassalle, Marx, or Engels) in her arms or stands guarding his monument.

The prototype for these figures is, of course, the goddess of liberty of the French Revolution. These female images also served as a symbol of the young nation. But another connection can also be construed: it is striking that beginning about the mid-nineteenth century, idealized erotic images of women become ever more common as decorative representations on the graves of middle-class liberals. They supplant the Christian gravestone decorations and symbolize the death of the individual as a reunification with nature, the never-ending cycle of life. We are left with the warm memory of a life lived in the fulfilment of duty. The angels of death on such graves appear just as chaste and virginal as the representations on Social Democratic decorative broadsides (such as for May Day). Untouchable and alluring, far removed from real life, they bear a certain semblance to the Social Democratic society of the future. Only later, at some date unspecified, will they consummate a union with real flesh-and-blood men and become the fecund mothers of a new generation.

It is intriguing that in the poetry of Freiligrath,[33] Georg Herwegh[34] and other writers of the nineteenth century, often recited at Social Democratic solemn occasions and festive functions, there are also links between death, the future, nature and eroticism. Here a few representative examples:

O wart in deiner tiefen Not	O do not wait in your deep distress
Auf keinen Ehebund;	For any nuptial bond;
Wer liebt, der geht in den Tod	Lovers go gladly to their death
Für eine Schäferstund';	for but an hour of sweetest dalliance;
Und wer die Ketten knirschend trug,	And whoever, in consternation, has born the shackles
Dem ist das Sterben Lust	Finds death a moment of joy
Für *einen* freien Atemzug	An instant for but *one* free breath
Aus unterdrückter Brust.[35]	From a heart so heavily oppressed.

Or:

Das Gestern ist wie eine welke Blume - Man legt sie wohl als Zeichen in ein Buch - Begrabt's mit seiner Schmach und seinem Ruhme Und webt nicht länger an dem Leichentuch! Dem Leben gilt's ein Lebehoch zu singen, Und nicht ein Lied im Dienst der Schmeichelei; Der Menschheit gilt's sein Opfer darzubringen, Der Menschheit, auf dem Altar der *Partei*![36]	Yesterday lies liked a faded flower A marker softly lain in a book Bury it with its glory and disgrace And weave no more on death's winding sheet! Sing to life a rousing chorus of cheer Not a song in the service of false flattery Bring to humanity a sacrifice To humanity, on the altar of the *party*!

And a final example:

Einstens, hört' ich, ging ein Engel durch der Herren Länder fragen, Ob ihr Boden nicht den Samen auch der Freiheit möchte tragen? Und er bat um wenig Erde, und er bat um wenig Raum, Wenig Raum und wenig Erde braucht ein solcher Freiheitsbaum.[37]	Once, I'm told, an angel went forth asking through all the world's lands Whether their soil would not like to bear the seed of freedom too? And he asked for but a bit of earth, a tiny plot of space Such a tree of freedom needs but little place, but little earth.

In these poems from the period of bourgeois revolution, the nexus between social resistance and masculine erotic fantasies also expresses a vital subjective readiness to resist. Yet the angel of male longings soon departs for the pure fields of death and the untouchable future. The angel of revolution becomes the angel of unending time. That is made clear in a text by Wilhelm Liebknecht, his funeral oration on the death of Eleanor Marx-Aveling in 1898.[38] Liebknecht was the education expert in German Social Democracy, and thus had a considerable influence on party cultural policy. In particular, his efforts to reconcile internecine differences between the Lassallians and Marxists regarding common symbols and rituals had a profound impact on official party life. It is less well known that Liebknecht's funeral orations for Marx and Engels, which were reprinted across the continent, had a key role in shaping Social Democratic forms of mourning and obituary. He was apparently quite adept at joining the feelings and political phantasies of the mourners with the respective momentous occasion of death.

That is also documented by his oration for Eleanor Marx-Aveling. Its opening sentence catches the reader by surprise: "I'll leave aside the second name she used during her final fourteen years."[39] This is all the more astonishing since Aveling was the name of the man with whom she worked together politically and also built her private life. But the riddle is solved in the text itself. In his oration, Liebknecht described an ideal personality of the kind familiar to us from the allegories mentioned earlier. Tussy, her nickname in the family, was a "great, selfless personality," she "lived only for others. And lives on for us and within us."[40] And: "The ideal of a contemporary woman [but for God's sake, not a 'modern' one—G.M.], a woman who brings all the power of her gender and its passion into the struggle, shaming men by her courage and steadfastness, a woman filled with profound love for suffering humanity, burning with a holy fury against the authors of human misery, servitude and injustice here on earth," etc., etc.[41] It is impossible that such an angel ever really lived: "And in the midst of the struggle, there was Eleanor Marx: always and ever the protector of the purest and most chaste femininity."[42] Her origins also reflect something unearthly, sublime. In any case, of course, her father was an "intellectual giant"; yet much about her mother was also ethereal, drawn from another higher sphere. She was a "highly educated woman, of noble blood, and like Iphigenia, she carried the warm gentleness of the finest and most exalted feminine decorum into the Scythian harshness of a life in exile; through the magic of her personality, she transmuted the meager household's humbleness into radiant gold."[43]

This is more than just the standard phraseology of trite obituary. It reveals underlying male fantasies that may help to explain why women had so little say in Social Democratic politics, but certainly served the "cause" in the abstraction of their idealized representation. Eleanor dead and buried served only the party's benefit, she was not even held accountable for her own suicide: "Now she is no more. In the full blossom of strength and youth— because she was one of those favored few granted eternal youth to their final hour—she departed by her own decision, her own hand. But blameless, beyond guilt." She is made a victim in order to be resurrected as an idealized figure: "her image is engraven everlastingly in the memory of those hundreds of thousands who heard her words and drank them in, imbibing them into their hearts and minds."[44]

Postscript: in memory of an older woman[45]

It was rare to find self-assured women active in Social Democracy before the turn of the century. Here too, politics was primarily a man's game. The chief ideologue of Social Democracy before World War I, Karl Kautsky, also thought it difficult to imagine otherwise.[46] His feminine ideal was not the fighter Jeanne d'Arc but the "aristocratic child, Jenny von Westphalen":[47] "quiet reserve vis-à-vis the public," "inexhaustible magnanimity," "dedication to the men's cause," "courage to confront life," and "a cheerful nature that could not be bent down, not by the most dire distress, and not by what was perhaps even worse than penury—the most vicious calumnies and curses heaped upon the cause and the man" to whom she had dedicated her life.[48]

Here too we find the sketch of an idealized image of a woman purged of all her life's internal contradictions. Yet at the time this memorial was penned, Jenny Marx was already dead 30 years. Her idealized example served to honor the passing of another woman: Julie Bebel. Evoking the spirit of Jenny Marx, the image of a woman who apparently could have been quite at home in a Protestant vicarage is made criterial:

> What he [Bebel] accomplished in those years, he (and we too) owe not only to his own efforts, his great intellect and moral strength, but also to the strong support he was given by his wife—her intelligence, the untiring effort and dedication with which she protected him from all the petty cares and worries of everyday life. And

the understanding solicitude she showed for the great problems that beset him, not merely due to a personal affection for the great man she had chosen as her mate, but also rooted in a profound faith in the majesty of our great cause, in which she believed as fervently as he. ... She never tried to put on airs, never wished to appear more than what she was. She remained the same simple modest woman she had always been. And yet, she grew apace with her husband, did not trail behind him as he pressed on.

For that reason, she was, "fortunately ... not one of those so-called emancipated women"; she was not only a housewife and the "mother of his children," but also a trusted "companion and advisor." In gratitude, she is also made immortal: "In this sense, Julie Bebel shall live on ... in the memory of all the countless fighters in the struggle for the emancipation of the proletariat."[49] It is unclear what concept of emancipation Kautsky preferred when in this same memorial he referred to the year 1911 as the "proud time of harvest."

4. The attempt to transcend life presupposes agreement with a set of higher principles. The authority of the leaders vouchsafes the truth of these principles. Their funeral rites thus serve above all to confirm the timeless truths.

Gerhard A. Ritter correctly notes: "Possibly the greatest achievement of the [German] working class has been the creation of their own highly-developed network associations. The importance of club life and club culture for the workers of the nineteenth and early twentieth century can hardly be imagined today, when numerous possibilities for entertainment exist, the radio, television, cinema, mass spectator sports, and so on."[50] Ritter reminds us that there has been far too little research to date on those diverse political organizations and clubs, and there is a paucity of source material on this complex.[51] It should be noted that on the one hand, participation in such voluntary Social Democratic associations made an important contribution to shaping workers' political identity. On the other, however, such associational culture was the matrix for indoctrination into authoritarian organizational discipline; indeed, it was the locus for building and bolstering the political passivity of the rank-and-file membership (quietism) that became a characteristic feature of the Social Democratic labor movement. Politics degenerated into club programmes and activities; individual members had a chance here to take part in decisions and engage in practical self-determination, but they were integrated into the framework of narrowly conceived forms of interaction and centrally controlled content.[52] The local and regional associations regularly organized cultural functions, such as memorial days, commemorations, memorial ceremonies for the dead. Perhaps the workers' choral society put in an appearance, tableaux vivants or poetry recitations were put on by party youth; the main speakers provided the "proper words" for the occasion.[53]

The high point of such associations were the funeral services for major leaders. They provided an opportunity to demonstrate the unity and strength of the organization and the solidarity of all members both within and without. Most particularly, the memorial services for Lassalle, Marx, Engels, and Bebel were staged as rallies against doubt and the fear of defeat. The 1879 funeral of the trade union leader August Geib brought tens of thousands into the streets in Hamburg, despite the prevailing ban on demonstrations. In 1910 in Berlin alone, the death of Wilhelm Liebknecht galvanized hundreds of thousands onto the streets of the city.[54] In 1919, the center of Bremen was thick with assembled crowds and crimson with their banners in the funeral procession of Johannes Knief, a symbolic figure of the Bremen soviet republic. In the light of the defeat already looming, the workers of Bremen demonstrated both their solidarity and their new dependence on authority.[55]

One of the original paradigms of proletarian funeral celebrations was a series of events on 19-20 March 1848 in Berlin. After the March uprising was quashed, the king was forced to bow down in deference before those who had lost their lives in the disturbances. Freiligrath has given us a striking description of this mass funeral in his poem "The Dead to the Living." Since this lyric was often recited at Social Democratic commemorations well down into the Weimar Republic, a few passages are worth quoting:[56]

Die Kugel mitten in die Brust, die Stirne breit gespalten,	A bullet in the chest, heads split wide open,
So habt ihr uns auf blut'gem Brett hoch in die Luft gehalten!	So you raised us up on bloody boards high into the air!
Hoch in der Luft mit wildem Schrei, dass unsre Schmerzgeberde	High in the air, with a wild cry that our gesture of pain
Dem der zu tödten uns befahl, ein Fluch auf ewig werde! ...	Should become a curse eternal for the man who gave the order to have us killed! ...
Und wir—wohl war der Schädel uns zerschossen und zerhauen,	And though our skulls were shattered and split asunder,
Doch lag des Siegens froher Stolz auf unsern grimmen Brauen.	Victory's joyous pride lay upon our wrathful brows
Wir dachten: Hoch zwar ist der Preis, doch ächt auch ist die Waare!	We thought: though high the price, the product yet is true!
Und legten uns in Frieden drum zurecht auf unsrer Bahre.	And so we laid down in peace upon our biers.

This is followed by an appeal to the living not to foolishly toss away what has been so bitterly gained in battle; rather, it is for the living to rekindle the hidden rage and bring the partial revolution to full fruition. The poem ends:

Oh, steht gerüstet! Seid bereit! O, schaffet, dass die Erde,	Oh, stand armed, be ready! The earth
Darin wir liegen strack und starr, ganz eine freie werde!	in which we lie so straight and stiff, oh may it be fully liberated!
Dass fürder der Gedanke nicht uns stören kann im Schlafen:	So that never in our slumber can we be disturbed by the thought:
Sie waren frei: doch wieder jetzt—und ewig! —sind sie Sklaven.[57]	Once they were free, but now—and forever more!—they are slaves once again.

This poem contains various important features of the Social Democratic cult of the dead: the gratitude of the survivors for the sacrifice made by the resistance fighters consists in their obligation to continue the struggle. The hope of having served the common goal helped the combatants to overcome their own fear of death. Death for the common cause thus creates a community that will outlast one's own finitude. Yet that passion turned hollow when instead of genuine battles, the class fate (still borne so faithfully) and the organization's rigid discipline were now what shaped the content of conceptions of common struggle. After the widespread acceptance in Social Democratic politics and the ideology of the rank-and-file of the power monopoly held by the class state, there was a need to reinvigorate the now hollow revolutionary passion with new content. Symbols of continuity supplanted the memory of the risks entailed by genuine resistance against capitalism and the nation-state. At the same time, the memory of the movement's dead was replaced by the "great dead leaders" of the movement, who had died a natural, nonviolent death.[58] The acceptance of the state's monopoly on power also points to the declining readiness among the rank-and-file to risk their own lives for the sake of the common cause. It is also worth noting that in response a new counterposed view also began to gain hold among the workers: that under certain circumstances, it might be necessary to "sacrifice" one's life for the nation-state, the "homeland."

Thus, the cult of the remembrance of the dead leaders is the product of a deepening authoritarian paralysis of the workers' movement. That is also manifested in a militarization of organizational discourse and the exaggerated representation of the celebrated dead leaders as unattainable paragons of the sense of duty, loyalty to the "cause," forcefulness, and other virtues. A few examples will suffice to illustrate this.

On the death of Friedrich Engels, Paul Lafargue stated: "The general, as his friends called him, is gone. But the battle in which he and Marx have led us as leaders of the immense army of the proletariat, that battle continues. And animated by their spirit and the common slogan, the workers of all countries have come together in unity and, until ultimate victory, will continue to labor on the great project of unification."[59] The leaders earned the prize of immortality by their achievements for the movement.[60] On the death of Marx, Wilhelm Liebknecht proclaimed with characteristic passion: "It is a hard blow. Yet we do not mourn. The deceased is not dead. He lives on in the *hearts* of the proletariat, in their *minds*. His memory shall not fade, his ideas will have an expanding impact on ever wider circles."[61]

The rank-and-file then also forget how to deal critically with the content of socialist ideas, they turn into devout followers, mere disciples. The dead leaders, ossified into monuments, also served as a bulwark protecting the common ground of the movement and its authoritarian structure. That rampart protected the organization from any unruliness and rebelliousness. As Liebknecht remarked: "Instead of mourning, let us *act* in the spirit of the great man who has passed from our midst, and strive with all our strength to assure that what he taught and aspired to achieve will soon *be made a reality*. That is the best way to celebrate his memory."[62] The valid discursive formulae of the Social Democratic cult of the leaders—in truth indeed a cult of the dead—had been well established by the funeral service for Engels, if not before. Wilhelm Liebknecht, the gifted funeral orator, played a quite key role in this. Those formulae consisted of diverse elements: the "obligation of gratitude" owed by the rank-and-file, the "duty to implement the will of the deceased leader" which he had earned by his "scientific approach," "sense of duty," his "loyalty to the cause," and "profound humanity."[63]

In a poem on the occasion of a Marx commemoration held in the Cooper Institute in New York City on 19 March 1883, Leopold Jacoby gave early expression to this new attitude toward the dead colossus among the rank-and-file; and that poem was also standard fare in Social Democratic commemorations before World War I.[64]

Im Arbeitskittel viele Tausend Sie sitzen, stehn zumal, Und Ihr Gemurmel füllet brausend den Riesensaal.	In their work aprons, many thousands Sit, others stand, Their murmurs resonate through the gigantic auditorium.

As the poem goes on, representatives come forward from the most advanced nations (England, France, and Germany):

Der Franke: 'Wie ein Weltbefreier Von Völkerhass und Krieg Focht er, und diese Totenfeier Bürgt uns den Sieg!'	The Frenchman: 'Like a world liberator Come to free us from hatred between peoples, from war He fought, and this funeral celebration Is our assurance we shall be victorious!'

The German ends the procession:

Der Deutsche sprach: 'In Liebe wollen Wir vor den Andern heut Dem Denker wie dem Kämpfer zollen Ein Grabgeläut ... Er hat für unsern Kampf auf Erden Ein scharfes Schwert verliehn, Dass eine neue Welt soll werden; Drum ehret ihn!'[65]	The German spoke: 'Today in love we wish to pay homage, standing before others Honoring the thinker and fighter with A funeral knell. ... For our struggle on earth he Lent us a sharp sword, So that a new world might arise; Therefore, honor his memory!"

Counterposed in the funeral festivities are two poles: the gray masses and the leader, living on eternally in them and through them. He has done his duty, and thus all that is necessary: he has propagated the idea that "a new world" is now a-borning. The masses stand embellished by their faith and obedience. But their own act of resistance is now no longer required. It is sufficient to abide trustingly, sheathed in the secure bosom of the organization.

5. Capitalist society itself is the author of death. The workers come to experience this directly. Yet after 1900, the life of the population was also increasingly imperiled by the mounting readiness to employ military means in economic conflicts between nation-states.—Social Democratic working-class poets and "Death for the Fatherland"

The year 1914 did not bring the proletarian revolution, it led to war between the imperialist countries. For most Social Democratic workers, the question of dying for a "cause" was now no longer a matter of resistance, but had become an "unavoidable question of national fate." It donned the cloak of "protecting the homeland" and the "struggle against Russian despotism." It now became apparent that the middle classes, unnecessarily, had entrenched themselves behind ideological and cultural ramparts to shield themselves from the workers. The "common cause" of the war revealed a long-felt yearning within the ranks of Social Democratic workers—namely to be allowed to belong, to be a part of the nation as a whole. In order to prove this, many were also prepared to even risk death "on the battlefield." It was in particular the so-called working-class poets who sang their praise and passion. Their poems appeared in the party press, which with few exceptions had been taken over by the party's right wing, and were circulated in massive numbers among the workers. In 1916, for example, the circulation of the right-wing party press still totalled a substantial 762,000.[66] Yet middle-class cultural media also discovered these poets and boosted them to sizable circulation figures. This circle included poets such as Karl Bröger (1886-1944), Heinrich Lersch (1889-1936), and Max Barthels (1893-1973). Their poems were replete with the mysticism of death and the murky mists of fate, and they venerated in them the "mother," the earth of the homeland, as a new locus of faith. Without further explanation, service in the army is declared to be a universal obligation. Death becomes a national fulfilment of duty.[67]

These views had been in the process of consolidation since about 1910. The working-class press published more and more poems that dealt with everyday working-class life and the workers' problems as a question of fate, endured for the sake of the nation. Ever more frequent were bombastic poems by workers, heavily influenced by the youth movement and subscribing to a romanticized view of nature. However, they were given little notice, overshadowed as they were by the sterile high-sounding passion of the customary Social Democratic cultural pronunciamentos. Yet as war broke out, they supplanted the internationalist socialist razzle-dazzle. What remained was the drab khaki of workers' poetry. The agitational impact of such lyrics at the war's outset was not due to their glorification of combat. Rather, their influence was based far more on the fact that they persuaded workers to accommodate to what was, in any case, "unavoidable," trying there to find something positive. Thus, Barthels in his *Vor der Schlacht / Before Battle* wrote:

| In der Freiheit der Arbeit, im Kampf um Freiheit wuchsen wir auf. | In the freedom of labor, in the struggle for freedom we grew up. |

Yet now:

Aber das Schicksal ist mächtiger als Sehnsucht und Willen, Tragisch ist unser Sterben, wir kennen den Einsatz, keiner das Ziel.[68]	But fate is mightier than longing, stronger than will, Our dying is tragic, we are pressed into service, yet none knows the goal.

Bröger adds some cheap pathos to the sense of resignation. Through the death of the soldier, the nation arises anew, as in his *Gebet zum Volke/Prayer to the People*:

Ewig junges Angesicht Kehrest Du Nach der Erde hin. Grosse Allgebärerin Du stirbst nicht	You turn a face Eternally young To the earth. Great mother of all, You do not die.

Consequently:

Tod ist Irrtum, Sterben Trug, Was da lebt Ist schon gewesen.	Death is error, Dying is deception, What lives has already been.

Because:

Mächtig schwillt das Beten, Rufen, Schrein: Geburt, Geburt![69]	Prayer swells like a mighty wave, Calls and shouting: Birth! Birth!

His most famous war poem was *Bekenntnis/Confession*:

Immer schon haben wir eine Liebe zu dir gekannt, bloss wir haben sie nie mit Namen genannt. Als man uns rief, da zogen wir schweigend fort, auf unseren Lippen nicht, aber im Herzen das Wort: Deutschland ... Immer haben wir eine Liebe zu dir gekannt, bloss wir haben sie nie bei ihrem Namen genannt. Herrlich zeigte es aber deine grösste Gefahr, dass dein ärmster Sohn auch dein getreuester war. Denke es, o Deutschland.[70]	We've always felt a love for you, But never called it such outright. When we were summoned, we left in silence, Not on our lips, yet in our hearts the word: Germany. ... We've always felt a love for you, But never called it such outright. Yet your greatest danger revealed so grandly, That your poorest son was also the most loyal. Ponder that well, oh Germany.

Franz Diederich, not a working-class poet but a university-educated editor at the publishing house Vorwärts, added his pedagogical note to this trend in 1916: "You'll soon hear the summons! Make yourselves ready!"

Berufen wir! aus Dumpfheit! zeiterwählt! Vor dem Verzweifelnde, nun lichtgestählt![71]	Summoned! From our dullness! Chosen by the times! To stand before those desperate, now steeled by light!

Or:

Volk in Waffen, Klirrende Gewalt Millionen, Blutig, blutig müsst ihr schaffen. … Tausendmassen, todumflogen, Baun dem Lande Knochenmauern.[72]	A people armed, Clanging power of millions, Bloody, bloody the work that awaits. … Mighty masses, death-encircled, Building bone-walls round the land.

The working-class poet Lersch was not a member of Social Democracy but came from the ranks of the Christian workers' movement. Yet his poems were also published regularly in the Social Democratic press during the war years. Was this perhaps because a true folk community also requires the bond of a unified belief? In his work, the figure of the suffering Christ, specifically in his capacity for self-sacrifice for the sake of others, becomes the paragon for the worker. Probably the best-known workers' poem is Lersch's *Soldatenabschied* (Soldier's Farewell). Here a few lines:

Lass mich gehen, Mutter, lass mich gehn! All das Weinen kann uns nichts mehr nützen, denn wir gehn das Vaterland zu schützen! … Nun lebt wohl! Menschen, lebet wohl! Und wenn wir für euch und unsere Zukunft fallen, soll als letzter Gruss zu euch hinüberhallen: Nun lebt wohl, ihr Menschen, lebet wohl! Ein freier Deutscher kennt kein kaltes Müssen: Deutschland muss leben, und wenn wir sterben müssen![73]	Let me leave now, mother, let me leave! All these tears are to us of no avail, Because we march off to protect the fatherland! … Farewell, o friends, a fond farewell! And if we should die for you and our future, Our final greeting will resound: Farewell, o friends, a fond farewell! A free German knows no cold 'you must': Though it cost us our lives, Germany must live!

C. Prospects

Either the triumph of imperialism and decline of all culture, as in ancient Rome, depopulation, desolation, degeneration, an immense graveyard; or the victory of socialism, i.e., the conscious class action of the international proletariat against imperialism.

Rosa Luxemburg (1916)[74]

We communists are all dead men on leave. I'm fully aware of that. I don't know whether you wish to extend my vacation leave or whether I have to join Karl Liebknecht and Rosa Luxemburg.

Eugen Leviné, in a speech to the court, 3 May 1919

As the readiness of workers to risk their lives in the struggle to advance their own interests waned, they appeared more willing to be reminded of their duty to the nation-state. Is it proper to see any linkage here?

From 1918 to 1923, bloody confrontations raged in Germany between Social Democratic workers and the forces of reaction. Erhard Lucas erected a "memorial" to the memory of the victims and the survivors, his important study on the March 1920 revolution.[75] With the decline of revolutionary hopes after 1923, old authoritarian organizational structures were reconsolidated, new authoritarian forms reinforced. Their dogmas, prescriptions, and moral views came to dominate the prospects and hopes of the social resistance. Unlike in the prewar period, the new and old leadership of the organizations had to contend with greater competition to win over the rank-and-file "followers." That was particularly manifest in the funeral services for their leaders. Ebert's burial, for example, was a state funeral in the imperial mode.[76] The memorial service for Rosa Luxemburg and Karl Liebknecht in 1932 was staged as a glorification of revolutionary party discipline under the "victorious leadership" of the Central Committee. And wasn't Lenin's interment in the Kremlin a visible demonstration to the rest of the socialist world that the center of the world revolution now lay in Moscow?

Yet all the competing organizations in the workers' movement clung to the rigid pathos and deadly dignity of the prewar cult of the leaders and of the dead. Why? In so doing, did they reveal unawares the true condition of an ever more authoritarianly ossified social movement whose reality would be so painfully exposed only later, in 1933? The party must live on—though it will cost us our lives? And nothing else ...

Notes

1. Written jointly with Petra Schwarzer.
2. Erhard Lucas, *Vom Scheitern der deutschen Arbeiterbewegung* (Basel and Frankfurt am Main: Stroemfeld-Roter Stern, 1983), p. 101.
3. Ibid., p. 97.
4. Karl Marx, "[Economic and Philosophic Manuscripts of 1844]," in: Karl Marx and Frederick Engels, *Collected Works*, vol. 3 (London: Lawrence & Wishart 1975), p. 298.
5. See the introduction in Hans Ebeling (ed.), *Der Tod in der Moderne* (Frankfurt am Main: Syndikat, 1984), p. 25.
6. Herbert Marcuse, "The Ideology of Death," in: Herman Feifel (ed.), *The Meaning of Death* (New York and Toronto: McGraw-Hill, 1959), pp. 64-76, here at 66.
7. "In the enlightened age, it [death] loses its metaphysical terror (post mortem nihil); at the same time, it becomes, as a result, truly threatening for the first time, namely as existential anxiety." See Dieter Richter, *Das fremde Kind. Zur Entstehung der Kindheitsbilder des bürgerlichen Zeitalters* (Frankfurt am Main: Fischer, 1987), p. 83. Richter points out that the enlighteners intervened with ever stronger prescriptions to try to preserve life.
8. Georg Scherer, *Das Problem des Todes in der Philosophie* (Darmstadt: Wissenschaftliche Buchgesellschaft, 1979), p. 173.

9. Ernst Bloch, *The Principle of Hope.* Trans. Neville Plaice, Stephen Plaice, and Paul Knight (Cambridge, MA: MIT Press, 1986), p. 1107.

10. Karl Marx, "Contribution to the Critique of Hegel's Philosophy of Law," (1844), in: Marx and Engels, *Collected Works,* vol. 3, p. 176.

11. Heinz-Dieter Kittsteiner, *Naturabsicht und Unsichtbare Hand. Zur Kritik des geschichtsphilosophischen Denkens* (Frankfurt am Main [etc.]: Ullstein, 1980), p. 153.

12. Ernst Haeckel, *The Riddle of the Universe.* Trans. Joseph McCabe (Buffalo: Prometheus Books, 1992), p. 212.

13. Ibid., p. 270.

14. Ernst Haeckel, *Die Lebenswunder. Gemeinverständliche Studien über Biologische Philosophie. Ergänzungsband zu dem Buche über die Welträtsel* (Stuttgart: Kröner, 1906), p. 159: "These primitive humans (such as Veddas, Australian Negroes) are mentally closer to the other mammals (apes, dogs) than to the civilized European." Because the German colonizers paid no attention to this, it led to "practical mistakes ... in the newly acquired German colonies; those mistakes could have been avoided if we had had a more thorough knowledge of the inferior mentality of the primitive peoples."

15. Ivan D. Illich, *Limits to Medicine. Medical Nemesis: The Expropriation of Health* (London: Marion Boyars, 1976), p. 197.

16. Carl Dantz, "Peter Stoll. Ein Kinderleben," in: Johannes Merkel and Dieter Richter (eds.), *Sammlung alter Kinderbücher* (Munich: Weismann, 1977).

17. Ibid., pp. 148-149.

18. Ibid., p. 48.

19. Cremation and official disaffiliation from the church did not become common practice among workers until 1919, after the church and state were separate, at least constitutionally. See Joachim-Christoph Kaiser, "Sozialdemokratie und `praktische' Religionskritik. Das Beispiel der Kirchenaustrittsbewegung 1878-1914," *Archiv für Sozialgeschichte,* 22 (1982), pp. 263-298, at 261. Kaiser shows that the entire question of leaving the church was treated in a highly contradictory manner in prewar Social Democracy, and that only after 1919 did large segments of the working class choose to disaffiliate from the church (p. 297).

20. Dantz, "Peter Stoll," p. 74.

21. Ibid.

22. Ibid.

23. Ibid.

24. See Werkkreis Literatur der Arbeitswelt (ed.), *Der rote Grossvater erzählt* (Frankfurt am Main: Fischer Taschenbuch-Verlag, 1974); Georg Bollenbeck, *Zur Theorie und Geschichte der frühen Arbeiterlebenserinnerungen* (Kronberg: Scriptor Verlag, 1976), esp. the bibliography; Wolfgang Emmerich, *Proletarische Lebensläufe. Autobiographische Dokumente zur Entstehung der Zweiten Kultur in Deutschland,* 2 volumes (Reinbek bei Hamburg: Rowohlt, 1975).

25. These savings institutions originated among middle-class craftsmen during the eighteenth and nineteenth centuries. See Ernst Vespen, *Die Sterbekassen in neuer und alter Zeit* (Berlin: Duncker & Humblot, 1966). [A brief description in English can be found in Gunnar Stollberg, "*Hilfskassen* in Nineteenth-Century Germany," in: Marcel van der Linden (ed.), *Social Security Mutualism. The Comparative History of Mutual Benefit Societies* (Berne [etc.]: Peter Lang, 1996), pp. 309-328.]

26. Otto Rühle, *Illustrierte Kultur- und Sittengeschichte des Proletariats,* vol. 2 (Giessen: Focus Verlag, 1977), p. 319.

27. August Bebel, *Woman and Socialism* (New York: Socialist Literature Co., 1910), p. 507.

28. Ibid.

29. Ibid., pp. 507ff.

30. That also becomes evident in private discourse in correspondence with Kautsky in 1913: for example, he terms his burial being "dumped into the ash bin" and calls his death a summoning to "join the great army." Karl Kautsky, Jr. (ed.), *August Bebels Briefwechsel mit Karl Kautsky* (Assen: Van Gorcum, 1971), pp. 352, 356. Or: "As far as death is concerned,

just let that be. The difference between you and me is that you can still work, I can't." Why should he still wish to continue living? (p. 357).

31. Bebel, *Woman and Socialism*, p. 508.

32. Detlev Hofmann and Victoria Schmidt-Linsenhof, "Unsere Welt trotz alledem," in: Historisches Museum Frankfurt (ed.), *100 Jahre Historisches Museum Frankfurt am Main 1878 bis 1978. Drei Ausstellungen zum Jubiläum* (Frankfurt am Main: Historisches Museum, 1978), pp. 349-384.

33. [Ferdinand Freiligrath (1810-1876), German merchant and revolutionary poet, whose poems were appeals for the struggle against absolutism. His battle song *Die Todten an die Lebenden* from July 1848 glorified the uprising in March of that year. Lived in exile in England from 1851 to 1868, where he translated works such as Longfellow's *The Song of Hiawatha* and Whitman's *Leaves of Grass*.]

34. [Georg Herwegh (1817-1875), freethinking poet, whose poetry was put to music by composers such as Franz Liszt. Lived in exile in Paris from 1843 and was president of the Paris German Legion during the February revolution of 1848. His ideas gradually came to resemble those of Karl Marx. In 1866 he became Honorary Correspondent of the International Working Men's Association (known as the First International).]

35. From the poem "O wag es doch nur einen Tag" (January 1845) by Georg Herwegh, in his *Gedichte und Prosa. Auswahl.* Edited by Peter Hasubek (Stuttgart: Reclam, 1975), p. 70.

36. Ibid., p. 51.

37. Ibid., p. 44.

38. [Wilhelm Liebknecht (1826-1900), teacher, lived in exile in London after the 1848-1849 revolution, where he befriended Karl Marx. Cofounder of German Social Democracy. Reichstag member from 1874 until his death. Eleanor Marx-Aveling (1856-1898), youngest daughter of Karl Marx and Jenny von Westphalen. Partner of the English biologist, Darwinist, and socialist writer Edward Aveling (1851-1898), whose treatment of Eleanor Marx drove her to suicide.]

39. Wilhelm Liebknecht, "Nachruf auf Eleanor Marx," in: Eleanor Marx-Aveling and Edward Aveling. *Die Frauenfrage.* Edited by Ingeborg Nödinger (Frankfurt am Main: Verlag Marxistische Blätter, 1983), p. 49.

40. Ibid., p. 55.

41. Ibid.

42. Ibid., p. 50.

43. Ibid.

44. Ibid., p. 54.

45. Karl Kautsky, "Julie Bebel," *Die Neue Zeit*, 2 December 1910, pp. 276-278. [Julie Bebel (1843-1910), born Julie Otto, daughter of a railway worker. Milliner and social democrat, married August Bebel in 1866. Little is known about her life.]

46. Thus, for example, Kautsky writes to Bebel (18 July 1913) that he has been informed "these two women [Clara Zetkin and Rosa Luxemburg] are planning an attack in Jena with their followers against all the central institutions. ... So it's necessary to be doubly alert," Kautsky, *August Bebels Briefwechsel mit Karl Kautsky*, p. 353. Bebel replies: "The masses are hungry for action, so they can be taken in by anything," Ibid., p. 359.

47. [Jenny, Baronesse von Westphalen (1814-1881), housewife, married Karl Marx in 1843, had five children, including two who died in childhood.]

48. Kautsky, "Julie Bebel," p. 276.

49. Ibid., all quotations p. 277.

50. Gerhard A. Ritter, "Workers' Culture in Imperial Germany: Problems and Points of Departure for Research," *Journal of Contemporary History*, 13 (1978), 165-89, here at 172.

51. [This was written more than a decade after Ritter's statement. Mergner and Schwarzer seem to have overlooked some important studies that had been published in the meantime, including Hartmann Wunderer, *Arbeitervereine und Arbeiterparteien. Kultur- und Massenorganisationen in der Arbeiterbewegung, 1890-1933* (Frankfurt am Main: Campus, 1980), and Vernon L. Lidtke, *The Alternative Culture. Socialist Labor in Imperial Germany* (New York: Oxford University Press, 1985).]

52. The central offices of the organization repeatedly interfered in the activities of the local and regional organizational structures whenever these threatened to become independent. But there was also central monitoring of the level of activity; see, for example, the annual *Winterprogramm des Bildungsausschusses der Sozialdemokratischen Partei*, from 1905.

53. See, for example, Brigitte Emig, *Die Veredelung des Arbeiters. Sozialdemokratie als Kulturbewegung* (Frankfurt am Main and New York: Campus, 1980); Dieter Langwiesche, "Politik — Gesellschaft — Kultur. Zur Problematik von Arbeiterkultur und kulturellen Arbeiterorganisationen in Deutschland nach dem Ersten Weltkrieg," *Archiv für Sozialgeschichte*, 21 (1982), pp. 381-402.

54. Ritter, "Workers' Culture," p. 174.

55. Modelled on the choreography of the funerals of Rosa Luxemburg and Karl Liebknecht, Knief's funeral in Bremen also became an expression of the grief of the workers mourning one of the important symbolic figures of their lost revolution, thus turning into an expression of sorrow for the revolution itself. The procession of mourners formed at the edge of the city. At its head moved the hearse, pulled by four horses and draped completely in red cloth. The hearse was surrounded by 40 marines from Wilhelmshaven, the site of the first uprising against the war. They were followed by several bands, 20 standard-bearers, more than 100 persons carrying wreaths, and delegations from many factories, unions, and communist organizations, esp. from northern Germany. Then came the funeral procession, some 10,000 mourners. The procession moved across the city and ended at the crematorium. There the guests dispersed "without incident." See Gottfried Mergner, "Johannes Knief und seine Region. Teil II," *Archiv für die Geschichte des Widerstandes und der Arbeit*, no. 2/3 (1980), pp. 45-89, at 83.

56. See, e.g., *Winterprogramm des Bildungsausschusses*, 1908, p. 18. We are grateful to Erhard Lucas for the information that at the funeral ceremonies for the victims of the March 1920 uprising in the Ruhr, this poem by Freiligrath was also recited.

57. Ferdinand Freiligrath, "Die Todten an die Lebenden," in: *Gesammelte Dichtungen* (Stuttgart: Göschen'sche Verlagshandlung, 1870), Vol. 3, pp. 172-175.

58. The simple "soldier" of the revolution was not supplanted suddenly and irrevocably by the "great dead leaders." The shift in importance was gradual. As also indicated by the cult of the dead surrounding Lassalle, which crystallized at an early juncture, the invocation of the dead leaders had submerged the memory of workers' own possibilities for resistance even earlier in various segments of the organized working class.

59. Heinrich Gemkow *et al.* (eds.), *Ihre Namen leben durch die Jahrhunderte fort — Kondolenzen und Nekrologe zum Tode von Karl Marx und Friedrich Engels* (Berlin: Dietz, 1983), p. 334.

60. Maybe that is the reason why the bodies of the most important of them were embalmed.

61. Ibid., p. 31.

62. Ibid.

63. Ibid., pp. 30-31.

64. *Winterprogramm*, ibid.

65. Ibid., p. 238.

66. Rolf Busch, "Imperialismus und Arbeiterliteratur im Ersten Weltkrieg," *Archiv für Sozialgeschichte*, 14 (1974), pp. 292-349, at 297.

67. Ibid., pp. 292-349; Günter Heintz (ed.), *Deutsche Arbeiterdichtung 1910-1933* (Stuttgart: Reclam, 1974), esp. the introduction.

68. After the war, Barthels left Social Democracy to join the Communist party (KPD) and after a phase of political abstinence, went over in 1933 to the National Socialists. Heintz, *Deutsche Arbeiterdichtung*, p. 375.

69. Ibid., p. 345. After the war, Bröger became editor of the Social Democratic *Fränkische Tagespost* in Nuremberg. He was arrested in 1933 after refusing to join the National Socialist organization. Released once again later that year, he "must" experience the fact that the Nazis have included many of his poems in their literature.

70. Ibid., p. 60.

71. Busch, "Imperialismus und Arbeiterliteratur," p. 303.

72. Ibid.

73. Heintz, *Deutsche Arbeiterdichtung*, p. 78.
74. Rosa Luxemburg, "Die Krise der Sozialdemokratie," written 1916 and signed "Junius," in: *Gesammelte Werke*, vol. 4 (Berlin: Dietz, 1974), pp. 49-164, at 62.
75. Erhard Lucas, *Märzrevolution 1920*, 3 volumes (Frankfurt am Main: Roter Stern, 1973-1978).
76. [Friedrich Ebert (1871-1925), a saddle maker, served on the board of the German Social-Democratic party from 1905 and was party chairman from 1913 to 1918. Reichstag member from 1912 to 1918 and president of the Weimar Republic from 1919 to 1925.]

CHAPTER 6

FAITHFUL FATALISM
On the Concept of "Total War" in the History of Mentality

> I ask you: do you want total war? [tumultuous applause]
> A war, if necessary, more total
> and radical than we can at all even imagine today?
> [jubilant shouts of "yes, yes"].[1]

The "total war" proclaimed by Goebbels in 1943 was only possible by first mobilizing and consolidating the "home front." What did that home front consist of? It involved a well-oiled and functioning administration, a state system of political surveillance, the planned use of terror against deviant or discriminated groups, and a population that acceded, was understanding and in tune, a popular attitude of compliance and consent.

From 1940 to 1946, that "home front" was not based on men: it was mainly women in Nazi Germany who kept the war machinery running and the state stable in the center of the Reich. There were no uprisings due to food shortages, no social disorder, no demonstrations, no refusal to serve (as there had been in World War I) that might disturb or disrupt the conduct or consequences of National Socialist warfare strategy and the totality of destruction. On the contrary: most women back home acceded like the men at the front to the demands of the "total war" and "understood" its necessities.

Given the conditions of the "total" (totalitarian) state, these facts taken alone are not enough on which to base moral critique or condemnation. Nonetheless, I hold the view that state terror in itself cannot adequately explain the abiding popular sentiment in Germany for the National Socialist regime right down to its final collapse. It seems too obvious that the regime leadership was articulating precisely what the masses felt, "speaking their heart" right down to the final debacle (and beyond).

Utilizing a document that is personally very important for me, namely the diaries of my mother, I explore here the reasons for the assent and support

---

of women for National Socialism who had come to identify with the system. The analysis intends to shed light on some aspects of how such women were integrated psychologically into the manifold of conditions underpinning the "home front" in the Nazi state.

The documents

While rummaging through my mother's attic in 1987, I stumbled across six notebooks written in a small hand bound in oilcloth that had been set aside and hidden. Each contained some 108 pages, and the entries covered the years from the end of 1940 to 1946. They were my mother's diaries from this time. Initially, I saw them mainly as authentic sources from my earliest childhood. But soon these journals also became something else for me: documents that reflected the history of the time. My parents had talked a lot about "those days." Yet now I was in a position, tapping an original source, to explore individual (and, I think, also more widespread) repressions and ideological reformulations. Unfortunately, I wasn't able to convince my mother to try to use the diaries I had uncovered to stimulate her own further recollections. But she agreed to my idea to let me work through them and evaluate their content for historical inquiry.

My mother had begun her diary as an attempt to bridge the walls of distance and censorship and communicate with her husband, who was in a prison camp in Africa. He is the person addressed, the imagined interlocutor: she informs him about her daily worries, problems, and experiences, and creates a kind of dialogue through his imagined responses and objections.

Until he was interned at the end of 1939, my father had been a mission doctor working for the Lutheran Leipzig Missionary Society in Tanganyika, and my mother was also in mission service there as a dentist. In the spring of 1940, she was able to return to Würzburg with the children without him. I was born shortly thereafter. The diary begins with my weaning. The reason my mother gave for starting the diary was that now she had more free time.

Her husband had been Locality Leader (*Ortsgruppenleiter*) of the Nazi party for the Kilimanjaro region, and she too had become a party member in 1932, though she had never entertained any ambitions for an official party function or tried to gain personal advantages by her membership. My mother and father had met as students in the "Protestant Bible Circle." Both regarded themselves all their lives as believing Christians. In Würzburg, my mother no longer practiced as a dentist but devoted all her time to being a mother for her four sons. She was helped at home by girls doing their "obligatory year of service." In 1940, her oldest son was eight years old.

Destiny dictates: the concept of "material constraint"

For understandable reasons, historiography until recently focused more on describing the well-secured spheres in the external mechanics of National

Socialist rule. Yet political power centers in advanced industrial societies cannot maintain themselves longer-term without popular assent. Without the assent and support of the German population, the National Socialist regime could not have functioned as effectively as its huge war machine required. In political administration, organization and exploitation of popular opinion, the Nazi regime had a number of quite advanced features. These should not be overlooked, despite the panoply of atavisms in which Nazi rule was decked that seem to us so strange today.

A key feature of that modernity in governance lay in the battery of statistical records the regime amassed on the population and its administrative ordering. It was also evident in its planned production of groups of outsiders in an effort to stabilize ideologies of national solidarity. And it was reflected in the successful propaganda of widely accepted constellations of so-called *Sachzwänge*. Using this propaganda, the Nazis presented their policies as "material constraints," objective necessities determined by destiny through no fault of their own, and styled themselves as interpreters, called by "Providence" to the momentous task.

I attempt here to describe this propaganda using a well-documented example that illustrates the creation of a seemingly objective, virtually already resigned but highly emotional *collective system of faith*.[2]

"Devout and faithful fatalism": the fervent belief in fate

Modern strategies of rule can and indeed must use the means for mass enthusiasm sparingly since they can lead to social instability. In politics after World War I, popular enthusiasm was increasingly supplanted by abstract, universally valid, and nontestable ideological assumptions in the form of comprehensible dogmas, doctrines which encode collective historical experience. The Nazis picked up on this development and raised it to a peak of propagandistic perfection. These tenets then serve to underpin various political, economic, scientific, and even private systems of behavior that are *rationally self-contained*. A few representative tenets or propositions:

— Communism is of the devil because it is against freedom as such and thus against God.
— The Jew is an enemy of of the German people because he is a foreign parasite within the body of the host nation where he resides.
— A "shameful dictate" was forced upon the Germans at Versailles.
— Germany must fight or go down to destruction.
— Whoever is strong must be strong, otherwise he will become weak.
— A German is a German because he is a German.[3]

These propositions are not arbitrary. They are constructions that encode historical experiences and interests, thus rendering them effective for political purposes. Through frequent repetition in propaganda, they take on a "magic life of their own" and make history, class interests, aggressions, and demarcations of Otherness appear to be arranged in some sort of ordered complex of natural and self-explanatory necessities for action. Franz Neumann gave classic expression to this construction in his *Behemoth—The Structure and Practice of National Socialism* (1942). "The emphasis on magic has even changed the language. The noun tends to supersede the verb. Things happen—they are not done. Fate, providence, objective natural forces produce things: German victories."[4]

The belief in these "necessities" unites the rulers and the ruled as long as the regime can prove that it is the true representative of history. That proof comes easily to conservative governments because they can invoke the past and their plausibility. There is no need for government propaganda and its reception to be contradiction-free or uniform. What is important is that political action retains its credibility as the logical consequence of fatalistic propositions that are accepted on faith.

National Socialism's credibility was not destroyed until its military defeat by foreign powers.[5] It is significant that the Nazis were then termed "lunatics" by their former supporters (a discourse common down to today). Precisely in order to continue to adhere to previous tenets and to be able to pursue the economic and political interests of their own that these propositions contained, the Nazi debacle made it necessary to accuse the regime in retrospect of irrationality, unreason, yes even insanity. Such a ploy did little more than to articulate the notion that an action must be insane (or so categorized) if by its own failure it threatens one's belief in the ideologies inscribed in such action.

"Faithful fatalism" documented: the example of my mother's diaries (1940-1946)

On 28 April 1945, Magda Goebbels wrote from the Führerbunker in Berlin to her son Harald Quandt:

> The world that will follow after the Führer and National Socialism are gone is not worth living in. That's why I brought the children here with me. They're too good for the life that will come after us, and a merciful God will understand why I am to give them salvation myself. You're going to go on living, and I have just one request: never forget that you are a German, never do anything dishonorable, and try by the way you live your life to make sure that our death was not in vain.[6]

Her husband Joseph added a few lines at the end of the letter:

> We are closed in down here in the Führerbunker in the Reich Chancellery and are fighting for our lives and our honor. How this battle will end only God knows. But I know that we shall only live with honor and fame or shall end here in death. ... You may perhaps be the only one who will continue our family tradition. Always do so in a way that we have no reason to be ashamed.[7]

This text is no longer cynical. The wife and husband are concerned about how they will live on after their own suicide and the murder of their children. Their own death appears here just as logical as the death of millions before. The mass agitator of "faithful fatalism" presents himself one last time as the agent of an inexorable "fate." The goal of his suicide is to relieve him of the necessity of having to look beyond the limits of his own propagated assumptions.

After the "collapse" of the Nazi state, my mother did not plan suicide. Fortunately, her faith in the National Socialist leaders did not extend to taking that drastic step. But she too was in profound desperation in 1944-1945 as "Germany's defeat" loomed. In her own mind, she too linked plans for her own life and her children's future with the *fate* of the Nazi state, this despite the ravages of total war and the Holocaust. Both Goebbels, Reich Minister of Propaganda and short-time Chancellor, and my mother risked their own life and that of others for their devout faith. Both thought "logically" in terms of "if-then" arguments *within* the limits of a self-contained National Socialist ideology. This logic of a consistent and rigorous *hostility to life* under the pretext of its *necessity for life* is among my own earliest conscious memories. The investigation and analysis of my mother's diaries from the time is an attempt to plumb the workings of a logic that in the extreme instance even sanctions suicide as a "means for life."[8]

"Faithful fatalism": letting the diaries speak

I quote from the diaries and provide only short commentaries to elucidate the historical background. My assumption is that the logic of her devout faith in fatalism will be articulated by this arrangement without changing my mother's text by manipulation.

On the Length of the War.

The diary begins on 7 November 1940: "Crushed by the feeling that the war is going to go on longer than authoritative sources assured us it would when we arrived in Berchtesgaden, I want here to write down everything for you."

The "authoritative sources" were the representatives of the National Socialist Colonial League who welcomed the Germans from abroad in the Berchtesgaden transit camp after their arrival from Africa. The unanticipated length of the war (World War II was also "conceived" as a *Blitzkrieg*) leads my mother to speculate ever anew in the diaries on the political situation: How quickly will victory over Russia come? Will the United States enter the war? Will the Japanese land in South Africa? Washington's declaration of war against Japan and by the German Reich against the United States prompt her to the following (entry of 11 December 1941):

> I feel hot and cold all over. The war once again has been forced to continue [by whom? G.M.]. There's no hope for peace now for the next ten years. The Führer himself says: "we're not afraid of time." But we who are watching our youth and happiness drain away in this "time" are indeed afraid.

Yet this "fear" does not prompt her to criticize the war and its leaders. Thus, many of her statements on the war link its length with the idea of a divine test. Typical of that thinking is an entry of 10 November 1941. After a sermon by the Lutheran pastor Wunderer on the text "Don't cast away your trust" she writes:

> Everything is going too slow for our time. The war too. How true! What feelings you have when you read expressions like the "Thirty Years' War," the "Seven Years' War." Just think of all the human suffering, pain of separation, renunciation and sacrifice these words contain. We too shall have to ... learn this patience. It seems that God wants to educate our people. Once again.— Mature individuals are to experience the glorious victory. How much suffering for mothers and families, what a burden of labor for the homeland. Oh, but may that victory be granted us! May our people be allowed to live on! May God be merciful to us sinners!

A double fatalism (God and politics) underlies her trust in the Führer (18 November 1941):

> Our situation is growing desperate. Fronts all over the world. One of our eastern neighbors, who just sits waiting like a wild, ugly monster to steal something from us in this situation, to exploit us.[9] If the entire British colonial power becomes "mandated of America,"[10] then we'll be at war with the U.S. ... Oh you poor German fatherland!! Yet if that is what our reason tells us, we also have the other side: that of faith, our great hope in the Führer's genius. He has accomplished such great things before that we are also confident he will achieve this most difficult task that now awaits us. We believe and hope in the Führer. And believe and hope that God will lead our poor, strong, capable people onto the right path and not take from us his mercy. And in all these trials, we must decease from always including our own poor, small and painful heart in these calculations. World history sweeps on over the fate of individuals.

This devout faith is even strengthened by certain signs in natural phenomena. Thus, an entry on 27 March 1941 notes:

> Now the air is filled with that tense calm before the storm, as before a very heavy thunderstorm when all living creatures grow silent and you think that nature cringes and cowers in anticipation of the first blow. Everyone knows some small bit of information they pass on in a whisper. ... The soldiers think they're going to Africa. ... Our Wehrmacht has a firm belief in final victory and we all are prepared to join together with the new hope welling up from nature. And to leave behind us all the doubts and anxieties of the winter. And join in the expectant sense of anticipation that animates our army. I think it is simply brilliant that no one, even those who at the moment are part of the preparations, knows what will happen. That's why the enemy is also so silent. ... These are truly times of greatness.

And in such "times of greatness," the individual has to accept his or her fate (24 October 1942):

> At the moment great events are transpiring in Russia. What is being accomplished there is simply enormous, its consequences unforeseeable. We are already a world

empire that dwarfs England. How wonderful it would be to live in such times if only our own small and frightened fate were not so closely bound up with that of the nation's great destiny. If we didn't have to tremble at having to risk the lives of one's children and husband as the price for the Reich. ... My dearest, when will I be allowed to have you again by my side? Must my body wither away unloved and my years pass away in longing? ... Oh, I don't want to ask this any more, even if body and soul still demand so tempestuously their due! I shall accept each day with its tasks and small joys as a gift from God, and fulfill my duty to my children and those around me loyally, cheerfully, without murmur or complaint. I shall recognize my task now at the present moment and hour, and be steadfast and true.

The belief in "fate" is represented by the Führer. The Führer stands above the base events of everyday politics and partisan strife. So he deserves love and faith. His task is to build the "new Europe" (22 November 1940): "Everything crystallizes from the centerpoint that has taken on solid shape. Such a complex of power will not be so easily threatened ever again."

And an entry on 15 September 1943:

The new Europe is in the throes of birth. It is certainly conceivable that during the greatest pangs hatred can arise for the progenitor, especially since so many had no love or affection for him. When Europe has finally formed and all can rejoice in the healthy infant, then there will be universal praise for the father. At the very least, we feel it an honor to have been allowed the chance to suffer for this new creation.

Since the Führer is an expression of the current of the times, he is ultimately a tragic figure: his fate (so closely intertwined with that of the nation) is pinned to the continuity of his victories (27 March 1941):

I long for a fatherland where tradition is enshrined in a royal house and dignified old age, in repose, can stand beside stormy youth and have its rightful say. ... Our Führer is fervently loved and venerated. So very very much!! But he must win this war. Love alone can be disappointed, can even be transformed into hate. After the catastrophe represented by a lost war, what will support and defend our dearly beloved Führer except the brute force of his praetorian troops? ... To be tough and silent in order to be loyal!

An entry on 11 November 1940:

If only we had the faith that can move mountains. We lack conviction, are of so little faith and as fearful as were the disciples of Jesus on the stormy sea while he was able to sleep. The Führer could be an example for us in this too. Once again he gave such a rousing speech, full of an absolute faith in victory! And what about us? But we should have every reason to believe. Not just in our religious life, in political life as well. Despite the great events unfolding before our eyes we are timid and frightened, oriented only to short spans of time.

That is why my mother liked to think again and again that people close to the Führer, with all their "human frailties," were to blame for the political mistakes she also saw (25 March 1941):

Some individuals are exploiting the power they think they have enormously. Oh poor Führer, your selfless ideas that are ready to give everything for Germany are often hidden strangely away in the brains of just a few who then use them for their own benefit.

Even the "Hess affair" becomes for her proof of the higher rationality guiding the Führer: Thus, in an entry dated 12 June 1941 (a month after Hess's flight to Britain), she writes:

How can a soldier desert and go over to the enemy's side in war? What kind of a slowly progressing disease does he have? Did the Führer know he suffered from paralysis? Is he surrounded only by people like that? Why did he wait so long to give someone like that the boot? They say the Führer was so furious he ripped down all the drapes in the Chancellery. Why? Because he was probably angry at himself for having been so forbearing. That must have been a terrible blow for the Führer at a time like this. Why is he so very very lonely?

Such a lonely great man deserves the love of women and children. Thus, among the first words I was taught was "Heil Hitler!" My mother felt especially responsible for nurturing the love of her children for the Führer, bringing them up for the state and in obedience to the Führer. The entry of 20 April 1941 substantiates this. First there is talk of love:

Today is the Führer's birthday. Wolfgang cut out a beautiful picture from the newspaper, pasted it on cardboard and put it on the dresser. Beneath it he put a swastika flag and some green shoots. The picture itself was also adorned with flowers and green stalks. His father's photo was next to it, decorated too. They all sang and shouted "Sieg Heil." How the Führer must sense this great love that children have for him. This love and veneration given to him by children is the most precious thing he has.

Then the reasons of state: "When are the people going to stop listening to foreign radio broadcasts and reading foreign papers! The ban on this is a wise measure of our government. They'd end up making us poor civilians completely crazy."

And finally the fruits of obedience: "Today when we were out for a walk, Dieter said very loudly in front of everybody: 'That baker's a rotten guy, he didn't even hang up a portrait of the Führer.' Enfant terrible."

Ambivalences in faith and the higher unity in divine reason.

My mother's diary indicates that toward the end of the war, the German population had an ever clearer picture of the war's consequences, the defeats at the front and the terror being used against Germany's "enemies." Perhaps most were unaware of the full extent of the Nazi policies of death, but there was increasingly enough information to lead to doubts and questioning. Yet ultimately those doubts were not strong enough to dissolve the ties to the Nazi leadership among the faithful.

The diaries contain two comments on the persecution of the Jews. The first is an entry dated 25 April 1941. My mother had gone with my brother

Wolfgang to see the movie *Carl Peters*, in which the purported failure of the "colonial hero" Peters is attributed to Jewish intrigues.[11] That same evening she wrote: "And in Germany. At least we're finally rid of the pack of Jews here. There's no threat to us any more from that quarter." Though there were still a few people around "jockeying for a cushy position."

The second entry is from 9 March 1943. She had been out shopping downtown with my brother Volker:

> A Jewish woman spoke to us while we were walking. She said she was pining for her daughter who had left four months before for southern Russia. Actually you shouldn't have even been permitted to shake her hand. In that respect I'll probably never become a good National Socialist. I feel too much pity for someone in a situation like that. I can't deny my human feeling when I'm confronted with such a story. Why does there have to be so much misery in this world?! The Jews have simply lost their war and like everywhere else, the individual has to pay. No one should be excepted.

I have given much thought to these two passages. They would appear to contradict one another. In one, my mother expresses herself in a nasty manner, after having seen a propaganda film, as a racist ("pack of Jews" we were finally "rid of"). In the other, she follows her feelings for a fellow human being and at least signals an attitude toward the crimes against the Jews that is ambivalent. Yet her justification for the Nazi crimes is alarming: wars are something "given by fate," and the individual is their defenseless victim. Did my mother also ultimately view her own children too as objects with no rights, exposed to the mercy of a history conceived as "fate" and subject to the power of interpretation of the Nazis? My mother was also aware of the consequences of the war and the mounting defeats—but that did not engender doubts in the National Socialist conduct of the war.

Already beginning in 1941, the British had virtually unrestricted access to German air space, though they did not concentrate on the bombing of civilian targets before the end of 1943. Their intention was to bomb the population into a state of weariness with the war. Yet it appears they achieved just the opposite effect. My mother's comments suggest that the fear of possible defeat grew in the population as the bombing intensified. And that appeared to rally and strengthen the "folk community," especially since the regime was able to maintain food supplies to the civilian population right down to the end. In an entry for 4 February 1943, my mother wrote:

> The sadness over Stalingrad has made captives of us all. What do you know of this, my dearest? ... What does the future now hold in store? We shall all do our duty all the more faithfully. I too intend to take on some party work. But where and how, I'm not sure yet. Time will tell. The children still need me very badly.

My mother's statements always become ambivalent and lessen the rigor of their terrible "systematic logic" at points where the church as a competing system of belief stands in contradiction with the political system. That is documented by an entry dated 11 December 1941:

Today I had a quite depressing day. The Führer's speech made a big impression on me, but I didn't like a few of his points. I'm worried about certain things. Will Christ's teachings be a permitted part of the great folk-state that is for us all the most sacred fulfillment of ancient wishes and dreams, in this great Reich—or will this stone be rejected by the builders? Oh, my people, how afraid I am for you. Shall you receive everything that you have achieved so laboriously and with such suffering robbed of its real and eternal content?

Yet what I find alarming are her comments on euthanasia (4 April 1942):

The bombs that fell on Bethel saved Bodelschwingh from arrest.[12] He refused to allow the now customary injection to be given in the institutions under his control. ... At the moment, it is a difficult decision in this question. Yet sometimes you cannot deny the definite "humane" side of this whole thing. But a Christian cannot shirk his responsibility for these poor souls too, and the burden of these so unfortunate creatures. That is the conflict. Those who don't go along will simply have to give way if this is to become a general fundamental principle in the state.

The contradiction between Christian ethics and political necessity is resolved here once again in favor of politics. Yet when personal religious hope in life after death was politically threatened, a menace that became National Socialist policy in the final months of the war, my mother "remained steadfast in her faith," at least privately. That is reflected in a number of passages in the diaries.

The contradiction between church and state naturally also involved the person of the Führer. On 18 April 1941, she described a delicate and awkward situation in educating her sons. Her children had started to wonder about the contradiction between Christian faith and state propaganda:

Wolfgang and Volker wanted today to know about the people who believe in God but don't belong to a church.[13] Do they go to heaven, things like that. What kind of a religious belief the Führer had, etc. Whether it was the will of God for the Führer to lead the German people. I said when it came to heaven, we should take care and worry only about ourselves. The decision about our fellow human beings was God's alone. Our task is only to pass on the good tidings of God's love given to us in Christ. Most certainly the Führer was sent to the German people in order to lead them from distress into a glorious freedom. I told them we shouldn't worry about the decisions in his personal life. Our only concern was that everything in our own behavior should be in order. I said it was true that the Führer was very dissatisfied with the church as it was at the moment, and in part rightfully so. But I also said the church simply could not abandon its mission.

In this way, the contradiction between religious faith and regime policy hostile to the church is bridged and resolved on a private level, in terms of individual morality. Yet wherever possible, the conflict between religious faith and political belief is harmonized. Thus, my mother commented as follows on a speech in the National Socialist Women's League (5 May 1941):

She spoke very well and persuasively. Under different circumstances, the same thing could also have been said in the church. Here too, there are only a handful who are really active and they have such a heavy load they often sigh under its crushing weight. There are not even enough women for the soldiers' socks. I see now that it is absolutely necessary to go to the local party meetings and if at all possible, you have to offer your services. Then there's automatically an increase in love and less complaining.

Ultimately, again and again, the political reasons for winning the war outweigh Christian conscience. For example, in an entry on 25 May 1942 she notes:

I think that the reason everything Christian is now being forbidden in the Reich is because at the moment the war has made it necessary to do things where one's devout Christian conscience might not be able to keep silent. They want to prevent that right from the start. … Oh, my beloved German fatherland!! But we must not lose the war, come what will!

After all, the war is even contributing to help save Christianity (26 June 1943):

All is well under His[14] guiding hand. Volunteers are coming forward to fight against Russia in Sweden, Portugal, Spain, Norway, Holland, even among the Flemish and the Walloons. Finland and Rumania see themselves as champions of Christianity in battle against the Russian style of anti-Christianity. We ourselves, we Germans, are in this way being directed toward the fulfillment of our true task. And I hope that we will be compelled in this way to decease from the previous anti-Christian actions that have been undertaken. Up to now, too, it does not appear to have been the Führer's will. So many examples speak against that.

The war against Russia thus dissolves the religious war within the Reich into a religious war on a global scale. That war justifies any and all political and military means. The alarming logic based on collective religious assumptions articulated in my mother's journals indicates the power that encoded historical experiences can acquire, extending their reach into the very heart of education within the family.

It was not mass enthusiasm that provided the mental and psychological undergirding for the Nazi crimes in the consciousness of the German population. Rather, it was the devout "faithful fatalism" with which the "necessities of history" and the nefarious deeds of their "loyal conscientious soldiers" were accepted. In her critical review of the feminist analyses of the participation of women in National Socialism, Karin Windaus-Walser has pointedly formulated the problematic: "In my view, it was not only patriarchy that showed its ugly and grotesque face in National Socialism, but the power of mothers as well. Only men and women working together were able to make such a universe of annihilation as National Socialism become a reality."[15]

In my mother's diaries, I came across a poem published in the *Fränkischer Kurier* on the Remembrance Sunday[16] 1942 written by a father to commemorate the "heroic death" of his only son. It can serve as evidence that my mother's "faithful fatalism" was no exception:

Unter den jungen Söhnen des Volkes ragt ihr, lichte Siegfriedgestalten, herrlich geraten an Körper und Seele. Nicht für die Erde—nicht für die Mütter seid ihr geboren. Ein höher Gebot heisst zu wagen, zu opfern, zu fallen, den Boden zu düngen für herrliche Saat. Herzeleid bringt ihr und Trauer den Müttern, nicht hält das Band euch liebender Arme vor der Gefahr, vor der leuchtenden Tat. Ihr seid der Trost der Männer und Väter, jener, die litten und darbten doch leben und nun mit leidgeläutertem Glauben hoffend stehen am Altar des Volkes. Ihnen den Alten leuchtet die Flamme einer Jugend und adlig Wesens, sprengt alles Dunkle auf euern Tod. Nimmer wohl zeuget ihr Söhne und Töchter, aber für immer fruchtbar dem Volke, zeugt ihr urewig den heldischen Geist. Über den Graben jungtapferer Leibe lernen die Augen der Männer zu leuchten, reichen sich all eure Väter die Hand.	Among the young sons of the people, you tower forth, radiant Siegfried-like figures, magnificent creatures in both body and soul. Not for the earth, not for your mothers were you born. A higher command is to be daring and undaunted, to sacrifice, to die in battle, to fertilize the soil for a glorious growth. You bring mothers mournful sorrow and grieving, The bond of arms held round you in love Cannot keep you from danger, or from the radiant deed. You are the solace of men and fathers, Of those who suffered and starved, yet still live and now with a faith purified in suffering stand full of hope at the altar of the people. To them, the aged, glows the flame of your youth and noble character, all that is dark is split asunder by your death. Never shall you breed sons and daughters, but forever fertile for the people you give birth in primal eternity to the spirit heroic. Over the graves of young and courageous bodies the eyes of the men learn to shine in radiance Over your graves all your fathers join hands.

My thesis of the integrative power of "faithful fatalism" cannot be documented more bombastically than in these inflated, kitschy lines.

Notes

1. Joseph Goebbels, speech, 18 February 1943, at the Sportpalast in Berlin. He goes on to conclude: "This is what the moment now demands of us. So arise, my people, and let the storm break loose!"
2. In a later study, I plan to explore the links between children's education and belief in National Socialism. [This plan was not realized.]
3. On the derivation and reasoning behind these propositions, see Rainer Rotermundt, *Verkehrte Utopien. Nationalsozialismus, Neonazismus, neue Barbarei* (Frankfurt am Main: Verlag Neue Kritik, 1980).
4. *Behemoth — The Structure and Practice of National Socialism* (London: Victor Gollancz, 1942), p. 359.
5. That also helps to explain why after 1945 it was specifically the conservative elements in the population (economic circles, churches, university teachers, civil servants, and the military) who were only able to recall their resistance to the "crazy" Nazis.
6. Joseph Goebbels, *Tagebücher 1945. Die letzten Aufzeichnungen* (Hamburg: Hoffmann und Campe, 1977), p. 549.

7. Ibid., p. 548.
8. There are some indications that my mother's outlook in this regard was no exception in conservative Protestant women's circles, see Jochen-Christoph Kaiser, *Frauen in der Kirche. Evangelische Frauenverbände im Spannungsfeld von Kirche und Gesellschaft 1890-1945. Quellen und Materialien.* Edited by Annette Kuhn (Düsseldorf: Schwann, 1985).
9. I.e., the Soviet Union.
10. In English in the original diary entry.
11. In 1941, the Bavaria Film Company made the movie "Carl Peters," starring Hans Albers and directed by Herbert Selpin. Along with its anti-Semitic tendencies this movie justified (German) colonialism and the *Lebensraum* policy of the Nazis. [Carl Peters (1856-1918), historian and philosopher, zealous supporter of German colonialism. Founded the Society for German Colonization in 1884 and initiated colonization of part of what is now Tanzania. Served as Kaiserlicher Reichskommissar for the Kilimanjaro area from 1891. His cruel policy and arbitrary application of the death penalty met with vehement criticism in the Reichstag in 1895. In 1897 Peters was dismissed from public service following a disciplinary hearing. The National Socialists regarded Peters as a great colonial pioneer and turned him into a legend in texts, documentaries, and motion pictures.]
12. Friedrich von Bodelschwingh [1877-1946] was the church leader of the Bethel mental homes and resisted attempts by the state to interfere in church institutions. There is a close link between the National Socialist war and the murder of so-called "life not worthy of life" (*lebensunwertes Leben*). The rationale for this large-scale program of murder is older and propaganda for the "policy of eradication" was initiated even before the Nazi seizure of power. Two principal reasons were given: (1) it was too costly for the "folk community" to "maintain idiots" in institutions, and funds would be better spent on loans to young married couples. (2) In war, it was mainly the "healthy and strong" who were killed. What was "pathological" was "cared for back in the homeland" and would then "infest and take over the healthy folk body." As Alfred Ploetz, an expert on racial eugenics, noted in 1935: "the contraselective effect of a war should be made up for by increasing the quota for weeding out and eradicating the weaker."

    After the beginning of the war, Hitler himself issued the order for "euthanasia" (27 August 1940). The measures for the so-called euthanasia of children had already been initiated in 1939. The plan was to introduce a legal basis for this after "final victory." The connection between the war and murder by extermination points up an additional problem: if my mother accepted the National Socialist war and its consequences as a kind of "fate," extending all the way to the "annihilation of life not worthy of life," then she must have even looked at her own children plagued by certain doubts, wondering whether they too fulfilled the demands of the dominant notions of value. Indeed, a profound inner anxiety speaks from many pages of her journals.
13. I.e., the *Gottgläubige* or "non-denominational" Christians. My mother was not *gottgläubig* in this sense, nor did she think much of the official Lutheran church of "German Christians," set up under the Reich Bishop Ludwig Müller in 1933. Along with the generally subversive contact persons of the Confessional Church, after 1945 even those counted themselves part of the Confessional Church who, like my mother, had adhered to traditional church rituals despite their loyalty to the party and state.
14. Namely God's.
15. Karin Windaus-Walser, "Gnade der weiblichen Geburt? Zum Umgang der Frauenforschung mit Nationalsozialismus und Antisemitismus," *Feministische Studien*, 6, 1 (November 1988), pp. 102-115, at 114.
16. [*Totensonntag*, the Sunday before Advent, on which the dead are traditionally commemorated.]

CHAPTER 7

SOCIAL CHANGE WITHOUT SOCIAL ACTORS?

The Continuing Legacy of the Philosophy of History

The myth of scientific prophecy

In the first volume of *Das Kapital*, Karl Marx sketches the thousand-year history of "primitive accumulation" in Europe. There he deftly manages to reduce this history to the formation of labor as a commodity: "Colonial system, public, heavy taxes, protection, commercial wars, etc., these offshoots of the period of manufacture swell to gigantic proportions during the period of infancy of large-scale industry."[1]

> What does the primitive accumulation of capital, i.e., its historical genesis, resolve itself into? In so far as it is not the direct transformation of slaves and serfs into wage-laborers, and therefore a mere change in form, it only means the expropriation of the immediate producers, i.e., the dissolution of private property based on the labor of its owner.[2]

Yet his description overlooks the numerous oppressed social movements in the past, their hopes, the ways in which the successes of their resistance were stolen from them. The history of more than a thousand years appears only as the prehistory, based on natural laws, of a process seemingly culminating in the age of industrialism.

Nonetheless, though bound to the evolutionary ideologies of the nineteenth century, Marx is at least still able to perceive the whole noneconomic "civilizing" brutality that lay beneath. In the form of wealth generated by robbery, it became a precondition for the economic development of European capitalism. That insight distinguished Marx from his Social Democratic pupils, who viewed the "process of civilization" on the European model as a

---

Notes for this section begin on page 111.

necessary, higher cultural development proceeding according to the clock-work of natural law.

Marx's Social Democratic heirs purged all doubts, contradictions, and open questions from his legacy. In blind identification with bourgeois ideas of progress, they misinterpreted Marx as the "scientist" of modern social development. As a result, they were seduced into internalizing the coercive domesticating force of civilization they had experienced themselves as children and in the workplace as a necessary ingredient in the civilizing process. They believed this was the unconditional prerequisite for humankind's advance. In so doing, they closed every window and door to other cultures, their own history, and the utopias it contained. Dazzled by their faith in progress, they forgot the ambivalent memories of the period of "primitive accumulation." In its final phase during absolutism, that "accumulation" had brought the population in Central Europe to the point of total poverty, the dissolution of all naturally evolved communities and orders, the permanent experience of dominant despotism and caprice, rape and dependence on blind fate.

At the same time, the permanent horror and experience of total helplessness inherited from this period (Thirty Years' War, witch-hunts, forced religious conversion, etc.) obliterated all memories of social resistance, hopes, and alternative cultural orientations (such as the Peasants' Wars, nascent urban cultures, dissident religious movements, and the like). The oppositional proletarian social movements reduced the complexity of this contradiction-ridden past to a monolithic "dark Middle Ages"; in so doing, they also jettisoned the memories of resistance from below, the painful losses and crushed hopes. The past was constructed as uniformly dark, full of oppression, subjugation, and despotism; in radical negation of that past, the counterposed image of the future was bright, charged with hope, intimations of the "dawn of freedom." The problems of transition were misinterpreted as the "birthpangs" of a new day, and individual identity was derived from the claim to be an heir to that new era. The upshot was that the workers' movement salvaged nothing from its history other than the unconditional readiness to accept and adopt all of modernity's putative achievements.

In the subsequent period, the neglect of the crisis-torn and violent prehistory of European capitalism and the history of social resistance in that age misled socialists of all stripes, blinded by a false Eurocentric philosophy of history, into confusing European history with modernity, the progress of humanity "as such." They also arrogantly rejected all attempts by other non-European cultures to go down their own path of development. After 1871, socialist politics were significantly shaped by a Social Democratic, future-oriented pragmatism. Socialism, degenerated into a philosophy of history, served ideologically to integrate the workers' movements into the nationalistic nation-state as social partners.[3] Moreover, today in the aftermath of the collapse of Soviet-style socialism we understand that the differences between Social Democracy and "state communism" struggled over so bloodily boiled down basically to the difference between the pragmatism of democratic state power or totalitarian state power. In the politics of the organized workers' movement, solidarity with children, women, and social outsiders was lost sight of; as was the "solidarity with the savages," i.e., with the anticolonial liberation movements throughout the world.

For example, it was not until the Second Congress of the Third International in Moscow in 1920 that the Indian "comrade" Manabendra Nath Roy was invited to speak before a "civilized" conference of workers' leaders as one of the first representatives of a colonized country. He argued with Lenin over the so "important" difference of whether insurgencies in the colonized countries necessarily had to be national-bourgeois (Lenin's view) or whether they could be permitted a modicum of indigenous autonomy and originality (Roy).[4] In this political discourse, the question of *subjective emancipation* also fell by the wayside: i.e., a form of society in which individual freedom and collective security can be combined with subjective possibilities for learning.

A further consequence of the apparent contradiction between commodity exchange and capital profit was the internalized readiness on the part of the European working classes and their leadership to take an active role in the oppression and exploitation of the world and the coercive training of their own children into "free" laborers—in the hope of profiting from the worldwide expansion and exploitation in the commodities market.[5] They were totally convinced that each individual had to earn his or her freedom by accommodating to the dominant rationality of "progress." Whoever did not wish to conform or was unable to, was justifiably "punished," suffering physical poverty, mental privation, and deprivation of rights.

Alongside the freedom to sell one's own labor power on the free market, another liberty blossomed rank after World War II: the freedom to consume. The availability of readily purchased "goods" spread the illusion of the potential gratification of all wishes. The satisfaction of needs takes place primarily via the agency of imagination. In the eyes of the subservient workers, the dazzle of the free commodities market makes the free capitalist system appear to be the agent guaranteeing the fulfillment of all their individual hopes and possibilities. Since Soviet-style socialism was unable to develop any conception of subjectivity in a socialist society beyond the shared joint heritage of the philosophy of history, its bureaucratic system of administration succumbed in sad stupidity to the Western tinsel world of consumerism—just as the productivity of its economy succumbed to old age. Down to the present, the lack of a concept of "proletarian" or even universal human subjectivity makes it impossible to overcome the bourgeois contradiction between a general promise of individual happiness and the practical gratification of the consumer, defined and dictated by the need for profit.

But the abandonment of utopian concepts for solving the question of the acting subject also led to a transfer of the authority to act to the "leadership" of the workers' movement. It now assured that the rank-and-file, in their political opportunism, supported that leadership.[6] The members at the base were not allowed to articulate their individual dissatisfactions and ambivalent feelings, and did not wish to be accused of "petty-bourgeois" thinking. The "course of history," the free circulation of goods, the (socialist or bourgeois) state and its "systemic rationality" thus retained their unchallenged power to define social reality.

Yet with the development of large factories in Germany after the 1870s, there was a growing tendency for non-organized workers (or workers active only in trade unions), especially youth and working-class women, to engage in spontaneous initiatives, insurgent reactions to state repression and the political "rationality" of the leadership. Some of those on the party's left (Rosa Luxemburg,[7] Anton Pannekoek,[8] the Bremen Left,[9] etc.) interpreted these autonomous movements at the grassroots as the proletariat's independent learning processes. Perhaps somewhat illusorily, they went so far as to dub them the "real" workers' movement (Pannekoek).[10] They believed that such autonomous movements were the matrix for the concrete "ability to learn" of the "workers' collectives," that would strike against bourgeois reality and the schemes to educate workers being organized by the authoritarian workers' organizations.

Social change without subjectivity

In the eyes of Otto Rühle, the utopias and ideas about the future in the social movements had the status of blueprints for political action. He drew the conclusion that you could evaluate and critique current social movements according to the conceptions they contained about the shape of the future. Applying that insight, I will present two designs for utopia popular in the socialist movement to elucidate my theses, interrogating their concept of how subjectivity can be realized in the socialist society they envision. My intention is to develop an archeology of the buried discussions about subjectivity at the margins of the organized workers' movement. I also draw a link to the intellectual rubble of Soviet-style socialism, this despite the (justified) criticism that my arguments are not based on history.

1. *Bebel's blueprint for a socialist future:* Woman and Socialism

The "debate on the future" in the German Reichstag in early 1893 reflected the ambivalent attitude in the Social Democratic party and its rank-and-file membership toward the utopia of subjectivity. In this debate, Bebel proudly referred to his own depiction of the nearing future in his *Die Frau und der Sozialismus/Woman and Socialism*. I will restate the key basic features of his arguments, since he elaborates there the contradiction-ridden, Social Democratic view on the issue of subjectivity. At the end of the debate, Wilhelm Liebknecht involuntarily emphasized Bebel's position in a prophetic way by equating the concepts "state" and "society" in a totally untheoretical manner, relegating utopia to a mere ideal no sensible person would be interested in championing. But the party, Liebknecht stressed, had to be guided by science and nothing else, now and in the future. Bebel also counterposes science to utopia, without noticing that his kind of science itself is transformed into dystopia. In its popularized form, the bourgeois theory of evolution became a Social Democratic theory of salvation.

Bebel called his portrait of the future, one where the state would wither away, his "private" opinion. He was dallying with the fact that his *Woman and Socialism* was at the time one of the most widely read books in Social Democracy. And he overlooked the reason for its popularity: the Social Democratic rank-and-file regarded this kind of science as a scientifically guaranteed utopia of a harmonious future in a European paradise flowing with milk and honey.

> The best-selling book was also the one most often borrowed from lending libraries! A contemporary critic of Social Democracy commented that Bebel's novel about a future state "doubtless generated more socialist conviction in the people than Marx's biting critique of bourgeois economy was ever able to." With his "unerring class instinct," Bebel captured the heart of the views of the masses, the faith in the socialist state of the future as the product of continuing advance in all areas of life.[11]

In the February 1893 Reichstag debate, Bebel describes the scientifically demonstrable course of history as follows:

> Bourgeois society was not possible until after feudal society. And socialist society will not be possible until after bourgeois society. We are its heirs. If that is the case, then you can well understand, I trust, that we do not wish (nor are we able) to artificially accelerate this entire process of development. How bourgeois society advances in the future does not depend on us. We cannot dictate to the ruling class what they should do so that we can come to power.

If Social Democracy is the "natural and necessary product of this bourgeois society,"

> then all we have to do today is to make sure the masses are enlightened about the essence and nature of bourgeois society. ... To the extent the masses suffer from the circumstances and recognize this, there is mounting awareness among the masses regarding the conditions of existing society and the need to transform them in the interest of the working class. And we should acknowledge that without any doubt, bourgeois society has created an abundance of means of culture and enlightenment unprecedented in any previous society. As a result of the stupendous means of culture and enlightenment at their disposal, the masses of workers are indeed in a position to utilize these instruments, albeit in a stunted form.[12]

You might think this was some Soviet-style socialist speaking at an officially engineered May Day rally shortly before the collapse of socialism.

The organic development of bourgeois society into socialist society based on natural laws—unfolding like an "embryo" in the womb of its bourgeois mother—also has several other important implications. Existing technology and its anticipated development within the context of capitalist profit maximalization is viewed as an important tool for solving all social questions—and thus for grappling with all vital questions in future socialist society. It can offer a solution to the problem of "lowly labor" (replaced by a "machine for polishing shoes") and overpopulation (by "making the Sahara bloom"), and compels people to cooperate (because technicians and engineers will be "indifferent toward their respective client"). Statistics will replace central state power, etc.

Bebel neglects the problem of the division of labor (and thus an important aspect of the question of the acting subject), or doesn't even regard it as a problem. In his view of the future, there is thus no discussion of subjectivity whatsoever. That was in keeping with a political "quietism" in which political will—the autonomous ability of the rank-and-file to learn and act—was considered totally irrelevant and unnecessary. As a young man, Otto Rühle formulated an educational program on this basis:

> Scientific (theoretical) socialism has the task of showing that the demands of Social Democracy are justified. The arguments for this do not derive from ethics, philosophy (ethical = aesthetic socialism), but from history and economic life in accordance with Marx's theory of economic historical socialism. ... The argumentation of scientific socialism must lead to a point where capitalism forfeits its right to exist historically and economically. And the economic foundations for socialism are derived of necessity from the historical process of development.[13]

This "necessary" development has no need of individuals who act with self-awareness; it requires only voluntarily obedient followers or loyal party servants. Friedrich Engels, the political foster-father of Bebel and Liebknecht, indicates in his 1873 essay "On Authority," written as an attack on anarchists in the party (Johann Most),[14] how the socialist organizations should "correctly" deal with the question of subjectivity:

> Modern industry with its big factories and mills, where hundreds of workers supervise complicated machines driven by steam, has superseded the small workshops of the separate producers. ... Everywhere combined action, the complication of processes dependent upon each other, displaces independent action by individuals. But whoever mentions combined action speaks of organization; now, is it possible to have organization without authority? ... The automatic machinery of a big factory is much more despotic than the small capitalists who employ workers ever have been. ... If man, by dint of his knowledge and inventive genius, has subdued the forces of nature, the latter avenge themselves upon him by subjecting him, in so far as he employs them, to a veritable despotism independent of all social organization. Wanting to abolish authority in large-scale industry is tantamount to wanting to abolish industry itself ....[15]

Authority is thus based on natural laws, the dictatorship of real existing socialism on the inherited structures of capitalist industry. Socialist progress thus consists of order, concepts of material supply and social subordination. The later bankruptcy of Social Democratic and Soviet-style socialist conceptions of the acting subject is already prefigured in this mental construction. On the soil of this thought, no social inventions and development could sprout able to compete as alternatives with the "bourgeois spirit." If the division of labor is seen as an irreversible law of nature determined by the advance of technology, the question of the nature of the socialist future is reduced to the elimination of anarchy (for example, by central state planning of production and distribution or a Social Democratic "social market economy"), increased productivity and efficiency and an acceptable distribution of goods. Capitalism was able to achieve all this in the metropolitan economies in ways far more attractive than the dominant model in Soviet-style socialism. Answers were not even sought to questions about the subjectivity of the producers, the elimination of the split between mental and manual labor, workers and management, the option to reduce and eliminate hierarchical authority, possibilities for learning through contact with other cultures, etc.

2. Bebel and the emancipation of women

A seemingly marginal problem remains intriguing: why did Bebel develop his utopia using the question of women's rights and their place in society as an armature? In addition to the hope for female suffrage and the possibility to use the growing middle-class women's movement at the time to further the goals of Social Democracy, there was another aspect to Bebel's interest in the women's issue, touched on by Engels in his book on the early history of Christianity:

> The history of early Christianity has notable points of resemblance with the modern working-class movement. Like the latter, Christianity was originally a movement of oppressed people: it first appeared as the religion of slaves and freedmen, of poor people deprived of all rights, of peoples subjugated or dispersed by Rome. Both Christianity and working-class socialism preach forthcoming salvation from bondage and misery; Christianity places this salvation in a life beyond, after death, in heaven; socialism places it in this world, in a transformation of society. Both are persecuted and subjected to harassment, their adherents are ostracized and made the objects of exceptional laws, the ones as enemies of the human race, the others as enemies of the state, enemies of religion, the family, the social order. And in spite of all persecution, nay, even spurred on by it, they forge victoriously, irresistibly ahead. Three hundred years after its appearance, Christianity was the recognized state religion in the Roman World Empire, and in barely sixty years, socialism has won itself a position which makes its victory absolutely certain.[16]

In his *Woman and Socialism*, Bebel expresses this concretely: "Christ came into the world and Christianity arose. It embodies the opposition to gross materialism that was dominant among the great and wealthy in the Roman Empire, it represented a revolt against the disdain for and oppression of the masses." Though Christianity did preach disdain for women, it preferred to remain ambiguous. But "women, like all the downtrodden, hoping for liberation and redemption from their situation, became zealous and willing devotees. Down to today, there has after all been no great and significant movement in the world where women did not play a preeminent role as fighters and martyrs."[17] Christianity owed its ultimate victory particularly to their missionary zeal. Just as Christianity drew its social-historical strength from the political community of the insulted and injured, Social Democracy will also draw on the resource of all the abject and suffering, especially women, for strength and sustenance. Bebel never inquires about the reasons for the atrophy of Christianity into an ideology of rule. Had he done so, he might have had a prophetic premonition: namely, that his concept of socialism could someday likewise degenerate into a state ideology of rule.

3. The "practical socialist" Edward Bellamy[18]

Edward Bellamy's *Looking Backward* [1888] appeared in German translation in Halle in 1888, entitled *Rückblick aus dem Jahr 2000 auf 1887*. This utopian novel was subsequently published in the cultural supplement sections of almost all Social Democratic papers. In his work, Bellamy had regarded the organized workers' movement as nothing but an impediment to development, and in the first German editions, the relevant passages were simply left out. It was not until 1890 that a complete edition in book form appeared, edited by the Conservative Georg von Gizycki.

According to Steinberg, Bellamy's utopian tale was, along with Bebel's *Die Frau und der Sozialismus*, the most widely read work of literature in the organized workers' movement down to 1914. It is thus probable that the average party member was able to identify quite well in his or her imagination with this design for the future. Two years after the German publication of this utopia that was actually anti-Social Democratic, Kautsky initiated a discussion on Bellamy that was to continue for over a decade.[19]

Kautsky accused the novel of being excessively concrete. But he was unable to completely conceal the close affinity between Bellamy's vision and Bebel's utopia. For example, Bebel and Bellamy have a similar admiration for military order and discipline. The comparison of Social Democracy with a slowly growing counterforce, an army distinguished by its discipline and commitment to a common goal, shaped not only Bebel's language, but also the ideas of Social Democracy entertained by some of its critics. For example, in his *Preussentum und Sozialismus/Prussianism and Socialism*, Oswald Spengler referred to Bebel as the "last great leader of the Social Democratic army."[20]

Yet in contrast with Bellamy, Bebel's future society is ultimately altogether civilian, although technologically overdetermined. It had more free time as contrasted with time bureaucratically administered and dominated by the system. In Bebel, the separation is maintained between the private and public spheres (the domains of freedom and necessity). The goal is private happiness, complete and developed individuality, whatever this might mean.

Bellamy, on the other hand, espouses another conception of society in *Looking Backward*. The negative consequences of industrialization are to be overcome and eliminated by a comprehensive militarization of labor and state regulation of everyday life to ensure private happiness. There is no longer any separation between working hours and leisure time. The crux of his utopia is the *total subordination of the individual to the rationality of increased productivity under national-state supervision in an economy organized along military lines*. These ideas were later implemented during World War I by large capital in cooperation with the military high command as "wartime socialism"—though of course without holding out any promise of happiness for the individual. Bolshevik policies under Lenin and Trotsky down to 1923 also have conceptual similarities. Fascism was later to perfect the total militarization of society.

"But you have not told me how you have settled the labor problem," asks the narrator from 1887, who has been mysteriously transported to an America anno 2000. His interlocutor Dr. Leete replies:

> "After the nation had assumed conduct of the mills, machinery, railroads, farms, mines and capital in general in the country, the labor question still remained. In assuming the responsibilities of capital the nation had assumed the difficulties of the capitalist's position. ... When the nation became the sole employer all the citizens, by virtue of their citizenship, became employees, to be distributed according to the needs of industry."
>
> "That is," I suggested, "you have merely applied the principle of universal military service as it was understood in our day, to the labor question."[21]

Bellamy regards capitalist anarchism, proletarian terrorism and the symbols of the workers' movement equally as symptomatic of a primitive period in which individual interest confounds the common interest. He even goes so far as to speculate that the stupid and wild mob of Social Democrats has actually been subsidized by the capitalists, though he retracts that in a note.[22] The party that had brought about the fortunate turn to utopia was not a workers' party, but a so-called *national* one. Doctor Leete:

> "The labor parties, as such, could never have accomplished anything on a large or permanent scale. For purposes of national scope, their basis as merely class organizations was too narrow. It was not until a rearrangement of the industrial and social system on a higher ethical basis, and for the more efficient production of wealth, was recognized as the interest, not of one class, but equally of all classes, of rich and poor, cultured and ignorant, old and young, weak and strong, men and women, that there was any prospect that it would be achieved."[23]

The national party, with a program to "nationalize the functions of production and distribution," made the nation into "a family, a vital union, a common life, a mighty heaven-touching tree whose leaves are its people, fed from its veins, and feeding it in turn."[24] The goal of social utopia is to enforce world peace, the creation of a national community on the basis of technocratic rationality and a quasi-military hierarchical order that unites the individual with the community in a smooth-functioning bond of utility. Of course, the existing (class and biological) division of roles in society (wife, doctor, scholar, officer, etc.) should be maintained and further developed, along with the division of labor and the separation between manual and intellectual labor, "brawn and brain."[25] Bellamy formulates the ideology of a "folk community" which even gives proper regard to racial hygiene: "for the first time in human history the principle of sexual selection, with its tendency to preserve and transmit the better types of the race, and let the inferior types drop out, has unhindered operation."[26]

In looking at this social utopia conceived in 1888, two facts seem astounding today:

— The readiness on the part of Social Democratic editors to popularize this book and the enthusiastic rank-and-file response in the workers' movement to Bellamy's ideas, their readiness to accept his ideas as a blueprint for their own conceptions of the future. The broad popularity this work enjoyed within Social Democracy points up the mentality that underlay the relatively smooth integration of the Social Democratic and trade union majority into the state policy of a temporary "truce" between opposed class interests during World War I, whose aim was indeed to create a "folk community" capable of defending itself if necessary on the battlefield.

— The author's downright "prophetic" ability to eclectically meld the various authoritarian strategies of the most important political currents in the twentieth century (nationalism, Social Democracy, socialism, and National Socialism) within a uniform conception. In that utopian design for America 2000, he weaves the state and social suspicions regarding subjective diversity ("service before self"), authoritarian-technical solutions for social problems and crises into a common denominator, conjoining a concept of unity which confuses collectivity with order. Instead of autonomous learning and collective steps in learning, Bellamy espouses a bureaucratic, technical-scientific rationality which has to be imposed by the wise leaders on the "masses" for their own good.[27]

In the historical reality that followed, these ideologies resulted in the adapting of the nonconformed to the dominant rationality of profit or utility as defined by the state. But it also led to the destruction of countless "uneducable," "unmanageable" individuals (and thus *lebensunwert*, with no "right to live") through brutal methods of upbringing, schooling, and coercion. In the Nazi concentration camps and Soviet labor camps, the victims were literally "reeducated" to death. The customary practices of the bourgeois nursery escalated in the camp slogans ("Labor Makes You Free" [Dachau], "To Each His Own"), the beatings, the discipline and drill to the point of final liquidation of the outsiders. Bellamy develops a model of the militarization of labor, the subordination of the individual to the rationality of national interests. Like Bebel, he conceals the dispossession of the population's subjectivity by means of a "utopian" depiction of petty-bourgeois dreams, which were necessarily deficient for the workers of his time.

In conclusion

The utopias produced and consumed by social movements point to unmastered past problems, unresolved current questions and contradictions—and to possible past concepts and answers to tomorrow's questions. A research focus on utopias in social history would also have to look at the trivial utopias, and the utopian images, symbols, and metaphors of social organization contained in political forms and discourse. In addition to the question of *empirical reception*, such inquiry should also investigate the history of the *impact* of specific blueprints for the future. One aim in my brief exploration here of two of the most popular such utopian books in socialist history has been to point up the nexus between imagination and political ability.

The lack of social fantasy, the conceptual poverty of Social Democracy and Eastern European socialism can no longer be covered up by strategies of force. The consequence of this deficiency has been most conspicuous in the collapse of Soviet-style socialism. Yet the impotence of Social Democracy in the parliamentary democracies in the industrial nations can also be seen as one product of this dearth of imagination. The prohibition on political fantasy and nonutilitarian dreaming is closely bound up with the authoritarian control of individuals by the machinery of conformity, denying them their autonomy. Down to the present, the history of the organized workers' movement has been unable to break free from its authoritarian beginnings.

Notes

1. Karl Marx, *Capital*, vol. 1. Trans. Ben Fowkes (Harmondsworth: Penguin, 1976), p. 922.
2. Ibid., p. 927.
3. See Heinz-Dieter Kittsteiner, *Naturabsicht und unsichtbare Hand. Zur Kritik geschichtsphilosophischen Denkens* (Frankfurt am Main [etc.]: Ullstein, 1980).
4. See Max Perthus, *Henk Sneevliet. Revolutionair-socialist in Europa en Azië* (Nijmegen: SUN, 1976), pp. 220ff. [John Riddell (ed.), *Workers of the World and Oppressed Peoples, Unite! Proceedings and Documents of the Second Congress, 1920 (The Communist International in Lenin's Time*, vol. 4), 2 volumes (New York: Pathfinder Press, 1991), Vol. 1, pp. 211-290.]
5. See Norbert Elias, *The Civilizing Process*. Trans. Edmund Jephcott (New York: Pantheon Books, 1982), 2 volumes; Michel Foucault, *Discipline and Punish. The Birth of the Prison*. Trans. Alan Sheridan (New York: Pantheon Books, 1977).
6. See Gottfried Mergner, *Arbeiterbewegung und Intelligenz. Die politische Pädagogik Otto Rühles* (Starnberg: Raith Verlag, 1973).
7. [Rosa Luxemburg (1870-1919), socialist theoretician of Polish-Jewish heritage. In 1898 she settled in Germany, where she was initially part of the left wing of the SPD. In prison she wrote *Die Krise der Sozialdemokratie*, which became known as the Junius pamphlet. She later cofounded the Spartacists and the German Communist Party (KPD). She was murdered by right-wing paramilitary troops soon after the November revolution in 1918.]
8. [Anton Pannekoek (1873-1960), Dutch astronomer, social democrat since 1899, was active in the German party from 1906 to 1914 and joined forces with Rosa Luxemburg in a struggle against "reformism" from about 1910. Later became a founding father of Council Communism and was a professor at the University of Amsterdam.]
9. [Bremen Left: radical wing of the German social-democratic party concentrated in the port city of Bremen since about 1905. The key figure in this movement was the schoolteacher Johannes Knief (1880-1919).]
10. [See Serge Bricianer (ed.), *Pannekoek and the Workers' Councils* (St. Louis: Telos Press, 1978); D.A. Smart (ed.), *Pannekoek and Gorter's Marxism* (London: Pluto Press, 1978).]

11. See Hans-Josef Steinberg, *Sozialismus und deutsche Sozialdemokratie. Zur Ideologie der Partei vor dem I. Weltkrieg* (Hannover: Verlag für Literatur und Zeitgeschehen, 1967), p. 138.

12. Minutes, Reichstag, 3 February 1893, p. 817.

13. Mergner, *Arbeiterbewegung und Intelligenz*, p. 42.

14. [Joh(an)n Most (1846-1906), German social democrat, Reichstag member 1874-1878, later anarchist. Emigrated to England in 1878 and to the United States in 1881.]

15. Friedrich Engels, "On Authority," (1873), in: Karl Marx and Frederick Engels, *Collected Works*, vol. 23 (Moscow: Progress Publishers, 1988), pp. 422-425, here at 422-424. Spelling adapted.

16. Friedrich Engels, "On the History of Early Christianity," (1894), in: Karl Marx and Frederick Engels, *Collected Works*, vol. 27 (Moscow: Progress Publishers, 1990), pp. 445-469, here at 447. Spelling adapted.

17. Bebel, *Die Frau und der Sozialismus* (Frankfurt am Main, 1985), pp. 83f.

18. [Edward Bellamy (1850-1898), US-American author, became widely known for *Looking Backward: 2000-1887* (1888), a narrative account in which the author advocates a society where the state owns all means of production, pursuit of profit is totally lacking, and each person receives an equal share in the affluence. The doctrine gave rise to an international Bellamy movement.]

19. K. [Karl Kautsky], "Der jüngste Zukunftsroman," *Die Neue Zeit*, 7 (1889), pp. 268-276.

20. Oswald Spengler, *Preussentum und Sozialismus* (Munich: Beck, 1920). [Oswald Spengler (1880-1936), right-wing philosopher, became well-known for *Der Untergang des Abendlandes*, 2 volumes (Munich: Beck, 1918-1922); American edition *The Decline of the West* (New York: A.A. Knopf, 1934).]

21. Edward Bellamy, *Looking Backward* (New York: New American Library, 1960), pp. 56-57.

22. Ibid., p. 170.

23. Ibid., p. 171.

24. Ibid.

25. Ibid., p. 64.

26. Ibid., p. 179.

27. See Erich Fromm's comments on Bellamy in his 1960 "Foreword": "Bellamy did not see the dangers of a managerial society and of bureaucratization." Ibid., pp. xi-xii. Note also his remarks on the current relevance of "Bellamy's vision" (pp. xviii-xx) in the light of twentieth-century history, though his is a view of Bellamy I do not share.

CHAPTER 8

RACISM AS A DISTINCTIVELY EUROPEAN SPECIES OF XENOPHOBIA

"What can he do if he's not white like you? ..."

Every culture has forms and rituals to guard against what is unknown and alien, as well as instrumentalities to help come nearer to what is Other. Yet comparison remains highly problematic due to the historically conditioned, differing social patterns and life circumstances in any given society. This can ultimately be accounted for by the fact that human beings are parochial, culturally blinkered. We have great difficulty in opening up to what is unfamiliar and unaccustomed. Yet basically we could learn a great deal from the existing variety of forms developed in other cultures for stepping out of one's cultural skin and approaching alterity: i.e., how they grapple with, ritualize, and work through their fears of the alien.[1]

An analysis of the determinant conditions in European history that give rise to the specifically European form of xenophobia is absolutely essential for explaining the social consequences of contemporary hatred toward foreigners in Europe. That xenophobia had excessive consequences for the production of outsiders, the "destruction of aliens," and the elimination of human beings thought to have "no right to live," what Nazi discourse termed *lebensunwertes Leben*.

I would like to illustrate the difference between being frightened of strangers, a fear we all suffer from to a greater or lesser degree, and the politics of xenophobia in our culture by referring to one of the stories in the classic collection of cautionary tales *Struwwelpeter*.[2] We all are familiar with the touching tale of the three bad boys who make fun of an African because he's black, the story called "Inky Boys." Big Nicolas then punishes them for this by painting them all black. At first glance, this popular story by Hoffmann, first published in 1847, would seem to be a plea for tolerance. Yet lurking beneath this tolerance lies a deeper layer: namely, the systematic defense against what is alien in ourselves and the alien Other as part of the European history of education that dovetails into the history of European expansionism across the planet.[3]

The tale about the African in *Struwwelpeter* indicates that there is something systemic in the history of European education about the transformation of childish fears of strangers into social downgrading, racist exclusion and the removal of the alien; it is a part of the middle-class, bourgeois form of rule. The label "alien" was slapped onto anything that appeared to the system and its representatives to be useless either for the moment or permanently, whether that be the unruly proletariat, the workers, "hysterical" women, "lazy Negroes," "naughty" children or, in the most current form, "economic asylum-seekers."[4]

Nicolas punishes three bad boys

In the children's story, the three white boys encounter a "Negro" out for a peaceful stroll outside the city walls, and thus external to the boundaries of the bourgeois life-world, and ridicule his black skin. Children everywhere will do that when they experience something "funny," i.e., unaccustomed, "ridiculous." Making fun collectively of someone is a ritual of the so-called fear of strangers and what is strange. At this point, "big Nicolas" appears as a symbol of patriarchy. And now this everyday story of children's prejudice toward someone outside the standard fold turns into European educational history. His warning alone speaks volumes: "Hey kids, you listen to me. Just leave that African be!" The figure of authority here does not help the children make contact and become better acquainted with the stranger, but rather cautions them to keep their distance. And Nicolas continues: "This Negro can't help it. What can he do if he's not white like you?" The stranger is defined by the external characteristic of his skin color, regarded as inferior. A reference is made from a standpoint of superiority to the inferiority of the man with the black skin. This blemish or "stigma" of an inferior status is an unerasable part of the natural order of things. It is only too understandable that the children are unwilling to obey this command to keep their distance and show some sympathy: after all, Nicolas's words merely confirm them in their contempt and arrogance, since they tell them only not to *show* openly how they feel. The appropriate emotion vis-à-vis the strange "Negro" is pity which precedes contempt—just as long as the African remains on external turf, outside the perimeter of the dominant interests (i.e., on a stroll outside the city gate).

But the boys do not heed Nicolas's patriarchical advice: "But the boys don't obey. They laugh in his face and then laugh even nastier than before at the poor black Negro." Now the patriarch becomes "angry and wild," because disobedience has to be dealt with consistently and punished accordingly. The nature of the punishment: whoever does not obey the authority figure completely and fully will himself be changed into a "Negro." The children are put into an "enormous ink-well": "You see them here, how black they are, much blacker than the Negro child." Only someone who obeyed, is sensible and normal, has a right to the unblemished color white, to the dignity of the norm, to recognition by the dominant system. The disobedient and unruly are blackened and thus equated with the "poor black Negro." And like him, they are excluded.

Now what does this patent overinterpretation of a nice and harmless children's cautionary tale have to do with the specifically European form of xenophobia? In our monographic investigation of racial stereotypes in German children's literature from the Enlightenment to the Nazi era,[5] we have been able to show, using the example of the "image of the Negro," that there is a close and strategic link between pedagogical coercion against European children and European expansionism across (and against) the rest of the planet. Children's books are quite eloquent sources for illuminating this nexus, and emerge as not so very charming on closer inspection. Bourgeois, middle-class education repeatedly reveals the consequences inherent in its makeup in the way it treats the naughty and ungovernable children, so-called "difficult kids," outsiders, and the disobedient.[6] The alien Other becomes an object, a training ground and example held up for schooling children into the ways of utility or for excluding the useless.[7] Disobedience toward industrial rationality is branded a regress into unreason and irrationality, rattlebrained refusal and recalcitrance; it leads ineluctably backward into the lawless state of nature of the "Negro." The children learn that here, the alien Others here and back home.[8]

Individual constitutive factors shaping prejudice toward those who are different

The child psychologist William Stern[9] defines "judgment" as follows: "Any perception or perceptual association only becomes a judgment when the self assumes a positive or negative attitude to it, i.e., recognizes or rejects it as actual fact." He continues: "At first every act of judgment is accompanied by absolute conviction of its correctness; thus thought in the individual, as in the race, begins with dogmatism."[10]

Caught up in the blinkered confines of Eurocentric evolutionary ideology, Stern believed that doubt, the ability to see things in relative terms, and intellectual openness as a permanent feature of learning were the normal traits of the advanced, mature human being and of European culture as a whole. In other words: childish dogmatism is nothing but an immature, naive, and dogmatic judgment that serves only to convince the person that they are right. By contrast, the adult's mature ability to judge is perfectly able to overcome all dogmatism by a probing relativization and the constant readiness to exercise self-criticism.

His protégé Jean Piaget developed this position into a theory of general character development. In contrast with psychoanalysis, which developed the notion of "object selection," he prefers the more normative concept of "object constitution." From this perspective, "judgment" refers to the capacity individuals can acquire to create a web of reasonable relations between themselves and the world of objects, utilizing all possible and necessary information. This, Piaget argued, led to harmony between the individual and his life-world. Individuals would thus not be surprised by errors, they would become able to come to grips with reality and act. They would also be in a position to process and arrange new and alien information and to cope successfully with this information. Piaget apparently overlooks the fact that this ability to deal with objects in the world by no means precludes the formation of a biased and partial view of them.

Psychoanalysis probes the human predisposition to prejudice more deeply and inquires into possible motives for dogmatic, infantile judgments. In its view, the infant develops preferences and interests in the infantile tension between desire and its lack, and tries to achieve these aims even contra reality. From the psychoanalytic perspective, adults view the world the way they have learned to wish it should be, or the way their life history constrains them to wish it might be.

Naturally, there are other theories that attempt to explain the genesis of prejudice. They all more or less concur that individuals have an innate readiness to acquire prejudices and that they must overcome this in order to be able to function properly in reality. In their shortsightedness, they overlook the close ligature between the predominant form of rationality, modern education and the dominant interests in "primitive" and undifferentiated judgments. Similar to various educational and psychological theories, they tend to derive general phenomena, such as racism, xenophobia, and ideologies, from the plane of the acting subject. They blame individuals for what is wrong and false. They then either go on to view society idealistically and subject to change by transforming individuals, a view especially popular among educators, or attempt to justify the basic unchangeability of society, a perspective particularly common among politicians.

Peter Brückner,[11] by contrast, sees the close nexus between the individual and society as the product of modernity:

> Homogeneity of the population, governability, "law and order" and individual freedoms find a modus vivendi together in urban-industrial Europe. Finally, socialization and individualization derive from one and the same source. What shapes the genesis of the subject also regulates the forms of middle-class intercourse. The "ego" now becomes the internalized state.[12]

One consequence from this is that society and individuals must be investigated on the basis of their common, sociohistorical conditioning factors. Yet that should not lead to the mistaken view that individuals and the bourgeois order are identical, that there are no ambivalences in the life histories of individuals, no contradictions in society. Brückner inquires into the agencies that mediate between the individual predisposition for "primitive" judgment and the political and social impact of a "primitive," hostile view of the alien Other, or one that is reduced to mere bureaucratic rationality.[13]

Important in this regard are the "infantile structures of prejudice," because crucial social conditioning factors that shape xenophobia are based on exploiting such structures.

Four theses on the social factors conditioning xenophobia in industrial society

1. A move to retreat to prejudices that simplify the complex is closely bound up with the difficulties experienced by individuals in developed industrial societies based on a division of labor to grasp their own life-world and the social relations they live in, to comprehend them adequately and process the available information.

It is therefore necessary to investigate the social preconditions that cast a veil over sociohistorical relations, turning them so opaque and incomprehensible for various groups and strata in society, who then retreat to or rely on simplified and inadequate solutions, whether by choice or its lack.

In situations of cultural upheaval when traditional forms of communication break down or are destroyed by internal or external processes, one can observe an increase in the public readiness to embrace and disseminate simplified and aggressive solutions to social problems. One example for this are the witch hunts in Central Europe at the end of the crisis of feudal society and during the transition to the absolutist state. Another was the upsurge in popularity of images of the enemy, domestic and foreign, a development in the context of industrialization and the centralization of capital in Central Europe in the late nineteenth and early twentieth century.

The increase in fascist social movements, particularly the growth of National Socialism in Germany, as agents of politically simplified structures of prejudice and rabid xenophobia, instances of witch hunting in certain large cities in Africa, the increasingly more simplified images of the enemy in the Arab world, the burgeoning of evangelical-fundamentalist churches in Latin America—these are all the product of modernization processes accompanied by a crisis in social differentiation and the collapse of traditional and culturally established forms of communication and living. Under the impact of the irreversible and crisis-ridden global spread of modern forms of governance and bureaucracy, industry and dependency on global markets, shared features turn into means for control and dominance.

Traditional tribal and community loyalties are invoked in the political arena and transformed into fetishes by the impoverished masses. Thus, one can see today a worldwide rebirth of chauvinism and nationalism, most specifically wherever modern forms of governance, industrialization, and dependency on global markets try to consolidate their hold, buffeted by continuing crisis, or are attempting to maintain their position and weather out the storms. The new movements and initiatives for ethnic, racial, or national identity thus necessarily meet with exclusion and animosity, and are countered by violence and terror against outsiders. If we can no longer even discuss the point of a common bond, because community has been drained of its original meaning, coherence, and context of consent, then there is a fundamental threat to the basic rights of the Others, or anyone in our midst perceived and categorized as alien. The obsession with feelings of identity and tribalism is but the flip side of modern individualization, isolation, and cultural insecurity.

2. The more abstract, i.e., rationalized the essential interests of people become and the more impersonal the causes for social deficiencies, poverty, repression, and exploitation, the stronger the longing to find conceivable causes for the plight, persons who can be blamed— individuals or groups whose attitudes, behavior, and characteristics can be used to give an explanation for circumstances, events and anxieties that elude rational understanding.

Just as children attribute moral capacity to inanimate objects—"ouch, you nasty stone, you hurt me!"—thus stripping them of their anonymity and turning them into animate agents who can be blamed for their own unhappiness, failure, or illness, anti-Semitism springs from an analogous attempt to personalize and concretize abstract relations, underlying sets of causes and problems, i.e., to render them comprehensible. The hunger for leaders, a personal authority, also has its origin here.

But a singular contradiction arises, namely the fact that these attempts to make abstractions concrete does not work. Why? Because the images required must be *general* and *unspecific* so that they can engender political agreement, catalyzing distinctions between insiders and outsiders that are fortified against emotional onslaught. Simultaneously, however, it has to be possible to make these conceptions concrete in *individual* terms: they have to be able to become a kind of "black box" where everyone can unload their own attitudes about just who to blame, seek their own strategies for relief, assuage anxieties about trying to reach some understanding with the Other. The political danger here lies in this contradiction between insufficient concreteness and inadequate abstraction. The bogus generality and counterfeit graphicness of these images inoculate bias against experience, inspection and rationality. Thus, they prevent communication with the Other represented in them, hermetically sealing off those who adhere to these images of bias from reality.

3. There has always been a specific tendency in European history to develop rational and expedient, one-dimensional generalized solutions for one and all, and then to implement these politically by any means necessary.

The more centralistic and bureaucratically rationalized rule became, the more violent, simplistic, and brutal were the "cultural" strategies for solving problems that were imposed on all. The politics of simple solutions and violent bureaucratic rationality meld in an attempt to destroy intercultural and social communication, leading to the social production of outsiders. The most important means in the production of outsiders is to correlate prejudices and defined hegemonial knowledge with describable and alien Others. In this process of ascription, those who live inside the perimeters of normalcy gain the ostensible albeit spurious collective certainty that they know who and how they are: e.g., that all "good Germans" are hardworking, clean, loyal, and conscientious. Those outside the pale of the dominant norms are stamped as outsiders.

The problem of the outsider is not his or her alterity but rather the familiarity of the constructed image that has been cast to represent them. Outsiders must perforce be transformed in this process into objects that are associated with a set of generally familiar negative attributes. Racism is always ascriptive, hatred of Others always grounded on transposed "knowledge." Thus, Jews in Germany were not "unknown strangers" of some sort: before their destruction, they were quite "familiar" to the bureaucracy or were made so as a result of work by bureaucrats and scientists. In their speeches politicians disseminated their "knowledge" about them. And so every "good German" knew then exactly "what a Jew was," why they were dangerous and had to be liquidated.

It is not just our government that thinks most refugees today are "economic refugees." The biggest problem faced by Turks, Roma, or Africans in Germany is that we "know" so much about them. The "good, normal" Germans know far too much about "the" stereotyped foreigners: they're all lazy, driven by physical urges, criminals, drug smugglers, or have AIDS. This stereotypical knowledge is permanently reproduced and amplified by the foreigners themselves, who are powerless to elude its net: after all, each and every outsider stands for all the others if you can find even a modicum of those features and familiar characteristics represented in him or her that brand the outsider in the public mind—and thus confirm the stereotype. As a rule, official cultural contacts tend to augment the general knowledge about the specific foreign group and thus serve to complement the image into which the outsiders have been forcibly cast: they construct them as typical representatives of defined cultures, groups, or races, rather than as individuals with their own subjective properties and possibilities.[14]

The extraordinary ability exhibited by administrative officials, police officers, educators, scholars, and self-styled experts down at the local bar to classify, excluding and including whom they will, should give us pause for thought. We should be careful not to blame xenophobia of some purported lack of knowledge. On the contrary: the narrow-minded certainty that one "knows" about Others as a collective, the lack of curiosity about difference, exceptions, and other people's subjectivity—and the fear of new unsettling information that might not jibe with preconceptions—conserve prejudice and guarantee its political misuse.

4. There is hope in the midst of hopelessness. It springs from the fears, longings, and biographical ambivalences contained in the dominant imagery of bias. These must be brought to the surface and articulated in relations and contacts with Others. So that individuals can begin to speak to one another, subject to subject.

Any person can be born into any given culture. Learning how to describe a given person as belonging to one or another culture, especially when we are young, is a process that is linked primarily to our personal relations. Thus, a close nexus develops with enculturated orientations. Yet these initial experiences in childhood can also lead to the internalization or incorporation of authoritarian attitudes, masochistic self-hatred, and violent inability to communicate. Such internalized cultural patterns are a valuable vital aid for individuals in assisting them to cope with life by resorting to these traditional orientations and to solve individual problems using collectively developed solutions. They become a burden when they harden into a prejudiced imagery of hate, preventing individuals from working out necessary revamped solutions and creatively shaping new open situations to advance their own vital interests. Political catastrophe looms wherever these earlier acquired biases against alterity come to be directed against concrete human beings.

Individuals' bonds to the objects of their memories, the social and cultural elements through whose agency they have acquired the hope for security and value in their own lives, are a part of their biography. They are integral to their own unmistakable identity and self-esteem. Their loss or devaluation compel the isolated individual to neutralize memory by means of simple, simplistic explanations and collective organizations that confirm the sense of self. Ideologies of one's homeland, ethnic cultural associations for German expellees from the East and nationalistic political parties also serve as instrumentalities of compensation for memory and experience that has been devalued or lost. Hope lies beyond the circumscription of these exclusive associations: namely, in the frozen subjective experiences submerged beneath. Bringing them to the surface and communicating them could dissolve the power of a desperate and blind battery of defenses. Banishment from a person's familiar environment, the loss of one's native place, destructive external coercion and constraint, cultural losses, and the insecurities that are generated in the struggle to survive give rise to debilitating crises—and these in turn lead to collective counterreactions. Yet they also catalyze personal crises which harbor prospects for reorientation, reflection on one's own real needs, and new directions in and for society. The subjective quest for homeland, which must precede conscious mourning over what has been personally lost, provides the basis for a mode of communication with Others that is open to perceiving and appreciating the rich diversity and possibilities immanent in the other, unknown individual.

An appeal for subjectivizing our relations with the Other

As a result of the preconditioning in their own biography, individuals find it extremely difficult to open themselves up to what is unfamiliar and alien. Any learning experience is bound up with the surrender of previously acquired secure moorings and the risk of insecurity. In industrial society, where the utilization of human labor power in the interest of profit is most advanced, there is an especially powerful political temptation to exploit this "constitutional human weakness" for political ends. It leads to the production of outsiders, the elimination of the useless, and the intimidation of those who refuse to conform and obey. Yet the ambivalences embodied in prejudice, anxieties, and objectified wishes can be once again brought to the level of articulation through communication between acting subjects on the basis of solidarity and trust. This can only come about if we relativize ethnic, national, and cultural forced communities and thus subjectivize our relations to Otherness and Others.

Notes

1. See Marcel Mauss, *The Gift: Forms and Functions of Exchange in Archaic Societies* (Glencoe, IL: Free Press, 1954).
2. [Lit. "Shock-Headed Peter."] Heinrich Hoffmann, *Struwwelpeter, oder lustige Geschichten und drollige Bilder,* first edition 1845, several hundred later editions. [See also the recent American edition, *Struwwelpeter* (New York: Dover Publications, 1995).]
3. Peter Gstettner, *Die Eroberung des Kindes durch die Wissenschaft. Aus der Geschichte der Disziplinierung* (Reinbek bei Hamburg: Rowohlt, 1981).
4. Hans Mayer, *Aussenseiter* (Frankfurt am Main: Suhrkamp, 1975); see also the American edition: *Outsiders. A Study of Life and Letters* (Cambridge, MA: MIT Press, 1982).
5. Gottfried Mergner and Ansgar Häfner (eds.), *Der Afrikaner im deutschen Kinder- und Jugendbuch.* Second, revised edition (Hamburg: Ergebnisse, 1989).
6. Mayer, *Aussenseiter,* pp. 9-29; Ernst Köhler, *Arme und Irre. Die liberale Fürsorgepolitik des Bürgertums* (Berlin: Wagenbach, 1977).
7. What is Other is categorized a priori as useless in modern industrial society: utilizing science and technology, and with the aid of bureaucracy and the factory, it is either rendered useful or relegated to the scrap heap. Nature, foreign cultures, or social resistance movements all succumb to this force from without.
8. The German Law on Foreigners also distinguishes between the useful, serviceable foreigner and those who are useless.
9. [William Stern (1871-1938), German philosopher and psychologist. Founder of the "personalism" concept in psychology and inventor of the intelligence quotient. He based his socialization research in part on daily observation of his own children.]
10. William Stern, *Psychology of Early Childhood up to the Sixth Year of Age.* Translated from the Third Edition by Anna Barwell (New York: Henry Holt & Co., 1924), pp. 385 and 389. Spelling adapted.
11. [Peter Brückner (1922-1982), was a Psychology professor at the university of Hannover from 1967. Suspended in 1972 and 1977, the first time for suspected contacts with the Rote Armee Fraktion (RAF) and the second time for his responsibility for an underground publication. His writings include *Zur Sozialpsychologie des Kapitalismus* (Frankfurt am Main: Europäische Verlagsanstalt, 1972) and, together with Johannes Agnoli, *Die Transformation der Demokratie* (Frankfurt am Main: Europäische Verlagsanstalt, 1968).]
12. Peter Brückner, *Psychologie und Geschichte. Vorlesungen im "Club Voltaire" 1980/81* (Berlin: Wagenbach, 1982), p. 134.

13. The amendment to the Law on Foreigners in the German Federal Republic differs from the primitive hatred of foreigners among neo-Nazis in that it wishes to reserve for itself the possible utility of foreigners and the utilization of their labor power and skills. The neo-Nazis only want (or are able) to see the uselessness and worthlessness of the foreigner, so as to boost their own self-esteem.

14. By official cultural contacts I mean functions such as cultural festivals, gastronomy, media reporting or visits to ethnological museums. The example where Africans are reduced to drum-beating folklorists shows that in such cultural events, the distinction between positive and negative discrimination is often blurred.

CHAPTER 9

INCULCATED NORMALITY
AND EXCLUSION

Six Theses on the History of European Xenophobia

The fanciful notion still prevails among scholars that xenophobia is a global phenomenon identical in all societies beset by insecurity as a result of cultural crisis. Scholarship thus "explains" xenophobia by recourse to "universal human traits," and in so doing denies the existence of the distinctively European historical reasons underlying hatred for foreigners, or more generally, of all those stigmatized as outsiders. In this blinkered approach, science fails to see the bond between European power expanding externally and the internal violence directed against all stigmatized pariah elements in society.

Yet even those of us who have for years struggled to combat and reduce prejudice toward those from the periphery are sadly deluding ourselves when it comes to our own historical, ideological shackles. We take refuge in idealizing generalizations about "other cultures," in an undifferentiated sympathy with the "victims of colonialism and imperialism" that tends to devalue and disparage them. We are rarely able to shed the gestures of a basically belittling compassion for the "poor and persecuted" that strips them of their dignity and selfhood. Consequently, we have a deepseated fear of the contradictions and differences in our "wards," their subjectivity and distinctive character. That is why we prefer to speak in general and undifferentiating terms about the so-called rights of other cultures, other *Völker*,[1] especially common in discourse on the "multicultural society"—and not about the right of each individual to their own self-selected culture, lifestyle, and outlook.

In this paper, I will explore the close link I perceive between inculcated normality and exclusion, presenting my argument in the form of six succinct theses.

Notes for this section can be found on page 130.

1. European history demonstrates that the heirs of the cutthroats who murdered and plundered in the past later reap rewards in the very name of the nation-state. We too are their direct beneficiaries, and continue to profit from the state crimes of the past.

In power and violence, Europe's expansion over the planet during the last millennium has been unprecedented. That expansionism was rooted in the matrix of the Europe-wide crisis of feudal rule that erupted around the year 1000. It generated an increasingly dynamic spiral of force both internally and externally, giving rise to ideologies, forms of communication and self-representation whose lethal brutality is unparalleled in human history. In the name of the Christian deity, the nation or the "race," "Occidental" violence escalated, culminating in the bureaucratic and technological perfection of industrial mass murder. The history of the German states points up the especially close nexus between internal authoritarian force and the dutiful readiness on the part of submissive subjects to do the merciless dirty work of expansion. They were faithful and willing executioners, obeisant to authority, to carry out the genocidal slaughter of resistant fighters in East and Southern Africa around the turn of the century,[2] the crimes against Belgian forced laborers in World War I, the unimaginable mass murder of Jews, Roma, and Sinti and numerous others labelled "inferior, unworthy to live." Just as nowadays, the cold calculations of so-called development aid can rely on its "sensible" and complying agents.

After the liberation of Nazi Germany by the Allies at the end of World War II, the fledgling West German democracy was marked by a massive repressing of the recent shared crimes, the cultural continuity of fascist views, and the preemptive rush by the state's submissive subjects, new and old, to conform and obey. The successes of this "democracy" flourished; our mothers' and fathers' submissiveness has continued to pay dividends down to the present, even for us. Good old "common sense" (appropriated by the Nazis in the guise of a modern technological vision) remains in Germany only too willing to leap to identifying "inferior" and "worthless" life and excising it from the body politic. It is no accident that the categories "worthless" and "socially and politically harmful" were written into legislation on foreigners still valid in the Federal Republic as yardsticks to be applied in their expulsion. In addition, the law states that civil servants can be required, under threat of punishment, to inform against such aliens.

The political opposition also finds itself hard put to shake loose from the benevolent and solicitous embrace of our national politics of success. Our own rank prosperity, our ever so sophisticated, free and eminently sensible ideas—yes, all emancipatory goals and works of art—are in danger of being swept up into the triumphal procession of power celebrating victory over the vanquished on the margins. The conventional wisdom in politics is stamped by insight into the purported necessities of the prevailing relations of power and force. Even the organizations of the workers' movement, the women's movement, and Eurosocialism continue to profit from the successes of European expansion, and integrate into its luring logic: we have everything, we can do anything, we can judge one and all. Of course, collective guilt does not exist—the children cannot be implicated in the deeds of the execution-ers. Yet there is a continuity in dividend from these crimes. We are inheritors of the benefits accruing from the misdeeds. The more we wish to distance ourselves from the crimes, the more we seem dependent on the boons and benefits they have bequeathed. To augment their freedoms, the freedom-lov-ing subjects need the patrimony of assets, prosperity, and rights those deeds have passed on to succeeding generations.

Then there is the flip side of the racialist disk: Africans are still held in uni-versal contempt as an "inferior race," objects at best for compassion and scorn—because in our perception, they still continue to be branded by the stigmata of the crimes perpetrated against them, the stripping of their dignity, slavery, colonialism, the laws of uneven exchange. In our discursive concepts and metaphors, they have degenerated into stereotypes of inferiority.[3] A clear proof of that is our inability to see their lands and towns on the "periphery" as anything but disaster zones, devoid of the patina of ordinary normal life.

2. Our own biographies are part and parcel of a European history of upbringing, an annal of docility, the domestication of loyal subjects for world conquest.

When Habermas views "subjectivity" as a product of modernity, our modernity, he is idealizing European history, at the same time masking over its internal violence. European history is not the history of the evolution of subjectivity, it is the chronicle of socially conditioned crises of the acting subject. When we deny persons from other cultures and ways of life their subjectivity (and Habermas is not the only party guilty in this regard), that is tantamount to a bid to enshrine our own pathology as the general norm for health.

The normality pounded into us, our subjectivity, is profoundly neurotic. Already as small children, we experience in our society the individual loneli-ness of persons caught up in a general competitive system, we perceive the public sphere as threatening and thus cling in neurotic reversion to our mothers and (if lucky to have one) our fathers, and later to their surrogates.[4] Our insatiable greed for things, ground into us in early childhood, clogs our ability to experience meaning, self-understanding, and certainty. At an early age, we learn how impotent we are in the face of those who are stronger or more powerful. Early on we learn that those classified as "useless," "worth-less," "not worthy to live" have no basic rights. As adults, we then go about propagating the neurotic world view engendered by these early experiences, styling it as a general and valid rationality, the conventional wisdom.

Upbringing today is changing from corporeal compulsion to psychological-structural force, from an authoritarian manipulation to the mute might of cir-cumstances. Yet the result remains the same: training for efficiency nurtures neurosis, turning us into mercenaries and agents of European expansionism, or at least into its ready rationalizers. Only now do we seem to be growing painfully aware that it will cost enormous effort to cast off these inculcated European patterns for social life, the neurotic normalcy of our society.

*3. Collective and individual experiences are shaped by long-term
continuities and short-phased events. If analytical inquiry neglects the
long-term continuities, it becomes impossible to account for the motives
and driving forces behind the individual events.*

In the history of societies and individuals, nothing is ever really past—it is
merely repressed, covered over, forgotten. Other societies appear to be more
clearly aware of this fact than our own. This is because they are able to
"process" the past in serviceable rituals and customs, in myth, folktale and
parable, and even long conversations. The cafe, the village well, the traditional parley, the courtroom, and the schools can become sites for subjective
and collective memory-processing, loci where the day's events can be spliced
with the past.

But in our culture it is amply evident that evanescent topicality dominates.
We appear to live only within the envelope of our life's daily unfolding; our
few remembrances lack the dignity of historical significance and continuity.
Like senile octogenarians, we babble on, repeating a few incoherent fragments of memory, bits of narcissistic vanities and self-pitying sentimentalities:
that is historical consciousness on the level of friendly banter down at the
local bar. Yet these events of our daily lives are also molded in part by long-
term, historical continuities. We are only rarely aware of their violent genesis
and underlying rationale.

Take one example: on 9 March 1990 in Bonn, the French minister of
defense Chevènement (a member of the Socialist Party)[5] justified his government's determination to retain atomic weaponry by reference inter alia to
the security tasks facing his nation in Africa. France had to act to guarantee
"stability" and "democratic" development, and it was therefore imperative
that Paris retain atomic weapons at its sovereign disposal.[6] He also expressed
support for French guarantees for the Oder-Neisse border.[7]

This foreign-policy stance of the French Social Democratic administration
reflects the presence of the past in three aspects:

1. In the process of European union, the previous nationalist and
   imperialist history of individual states (here French colonialism) is
   not being jettisoned but rather further elaborated.
2. The imperial, national goals and interests of the various nation-states
   are constantly reblending into new combinations. History's
   continuity encompasses the past victories and defeats.
3. The traditional political means (military force, geographical spheres
   of influence and national power politics) are being further developed
   in dynamic form by new instruments, especially technological and
   economic (e.g., atomic weaponry, technologies of communication
   and control, the internal European market).

4. Europe's relations with the periphery bear the imprint of the long-term continuity of humiliation, violation and violent interference in the vital interests and affairs of those economically and militarily weaker. That history colors all personal contacts we have with people from these areas.

There is no naive, friendly cooperation between the beneficiaries of the history of European expansionism and those who bear its burden, between us and the Others. As long as we repress the origins of our prosperity, we will, in neurotic anxiety about the possible loss of our privileges, inject either our pity (in the form of the so-called bad conscience) or our arrogance (i.e., internalized violence) into relations with the underprivileged Others. And vice versa: our "partners" retain many diverse memories of the humiliations they have been subjected to. We must learn to see the history of our ostensible sovereignty, our monstrous and masterly efficiency as managers, our apparently smooth-functioning recipes for communication for what they truly are: a history of violence. And we must supplant these with our own insecurity, the attempt to be open, to be curious in newfound impotence.

But the building blocks for a bridge of understanding to the Others can only be provided by conscious recollection of the injuries, deformations, and experiences of violence we endured as children in our own society. However, the greed ground into us for ever more things, ever better commodities, the daily hectic race for novelty submerges and blocks out these experiences of suffering in early childhood. My concern here is less with "individual therapy" and more with political consciousness: what was inflicted in our society on children in molding them into "rational, reasonable, capable" Europeans, in the past and today.

Imagine the following scenario: as automobile drivers, full of zest, ready and restless, we associate technologically mediated, collective fantasies of power with social orders of discipline and the need individuals have for momentary escape. The automobile is both a product and the symbol of European history. Neurotically addicted to car traffic, how can we ever succeed in communicating in and with societies that travel basically by bicycle, on foot, and on horseback? How can they communicate with us? Were we to venture off on foot and experience the planet more as wanderers on the open road, then we would become vulnerable: we would open ourselves up to the Others, be at the grace of their friendliness or hostility, their experiences and problems, on their turf—discovering in the process our own historical limitations.

5. *The fear of the powerful Other and the defenses erected against him may perhaps be something universal. But the need to guard against alterity, the "weak and inferior" outsider, springs only from a fear of losing one's own privileges and the special prerogatives unjustly acquired in the past. It is also driven by the sense of isolation and loneliness pounded into us as individuals in the process of growing up.*

Our mode of xenophobia is European in origin and is spreading around the globe hand-in-glove with the aggressive, industrial achievement-oriented society we have created. Inherent in this form of hatred for what is alien and Other is an element of *self*-rejection, the self-hatred with which we have been inoculated. In downgrading and rejecting the Other, we struggle against our own defeats, our own weaknesses, our lack of nonconformism, drilled out of us at an early age, our loneliness, our sense of inferiority mediated by the marketplace. The greater the social isolation for individuals and its authoritarian consolidation, the more intense their collective hatred of foreigners. The critique advanced by forgotten critics of bourgeois society such as Ernst Bloch, Peter Brückner, Hans Mayer, Otto Rühle, Agnes Heller, Ernst Jouhy, and others must be reintroduced anew into analytical inquiry on the cold, lonely, and lethal tawdriness at the dark heart of industrial societies. "Real-socialism, acting on a global plane" is historically to blame for having blocked the path for these (self-)critical utopias. The pedestrian opportunism of the "real-socialists" vis-à-vis their capitalist competitors, and the silencing of any and all independent criticism and autonomous initiative in their own sphere of power, spawned the police-state dictatorships of the senile old men who were then rightfully swept from power and the stage of history.

Today we can see the enormous extent of the damage when the old xenophobia—and even the beginnings of a renewed push to annihilate life labelled "useless"—resurface from beneath the tattered cloak of glib and facile slogans. Little time remains for humankind to turn utopias for survival into reality. We can feel nothing but sorrow and rage in the face of the utopian designs that were wasted and destroyed, the time and possibilities squandered. Yet the blind hopes placed in the resistance movements and the idealization of simple agrarian cultures on the periphery also are deceptive, deluding us about our own responsibilities in the metropolitan nerve centers. Hans-Jürgen Krahl is correct in placing the politicization of our own needs at the very center of processes of political consciousness.[8] In our own neuroses, deformations, and history lie the prospects for an international politics that can shatter the armature of the old system.

6. European history will remain hopelessly shackled to past and present injustice should we lose our memories of resistance, of the suppressed dreams of the excluded outsiders—and the courage to look squarely at our own neuroses, forced upon us by society.

In the face of National Socialism, Walter Benjamin formulated the following thesis:

> The class struggle ... is a fight for the crude and material things without which no refined and spiritual things could exist. Nevertheless it is not in the form of the spoils which fall to the victor that the latter make their presence felt in the class struggle. They manifest themselves in this struggle as courage, humor, cunning and fortitude. They have retroactive force and will constantly call in question every victory, past and present, of the rulers.[9]

For us today, class struggle signifies more than just the history of the workers' movement. The memory of our own unruliness and that submerged in the annals of history, the resistance erupting within the all-powerful triumphal procession of European expansionism, the recollections that flash up in moments of danger—these link us with the resistance of all outsiders, the stigmatized everywhere. The bond is biographical: our many privileges notwithstanding, we were all once, at least in childhood, ourselves victimized by upbringing. In the confrontation with our own history and the history of European expansionism, we can experience the existential contradiction between conformity and resistance. Despite our dubious inheritance, the consciousness of this ambivalence—our double life— allows us to stand in solidarity with the resistance movements throughout the world without forfeiting our own identity. Within that ambivalence, our own personal subjective childhood history links up with collective history, our own life prospects join with the vital interests of the discriminated outsiders and aliens.

Notes

1. Concepts are freighted with politics: "We're the people!" articulates the contradiction between the rulers and the ruled. "We're the German people" distinguishes one's "own people" from the "others" — "the" Poles, "the" Russians, etc. The pluralized concept of *Volk* or nation always raises the question of belongingness and non-belonging. And violence against those excluded also often marks the postrevolutionary history of "national" liberation struggles.
2. See Gottfried Mergner, "Solidarity with the Savages?" in this volume.
3. See Gottfried Mergner and Ansgar Häfner (eds.), *Der Afrikaner im deutschen Kinder- und Jugendbuch. Untersuchungen zur rassistischen Stereotypenbildung im deutschen Kinder- und Jugendbuch von der Aufklärung bis zum Nationalsozialismus.* Second, revised edition (Hamburg: Ergebnisse, 1989).
4. See Gottfried Mergner and Peter Gottwald (eds.), *Liebe Mutter — Böse Mutter. Angstmachende Mutterbilder im Kinder- und Jugendbuch* (Oldenburg: Bibliotheks- und Informationssystem der Universität Oldenburg, 1989).
5. [Jean-Pierre Chevènement (1939) was active in the French socialist party (SFIO/PSF) from 1964. From 1988 to 1991 he was minister of defense in the second Rocard administration. In 1993 he left the Parti Socialiste to establish the Mouvement des Citoyens.]
6. Proceedings of the Conference "Von der Spaltung zum Gemeinsamen Haus? Die Deutschen, die West- und die Osteuropäer," Forum der Historischen Kommission der SPD, 8-9 March 1990.
7. [Oder-Neisse border: border effectively established between Poland and Germany in 1945 along the Oder and the Neisse rivers. East Germany (the GDR) recognized this border in 1950, West Germany in 1970.]
8. Hans-Jürgen Krahl, *Konstitution und Klassenkampf: Zur historischen Dialektik von bürgerlicher Emanzipation und proletarischer Revolution. Schriften, Reden und Entwürfe aus den Jahren 1966-1970* (Frankfurt am Main: Verlag Neue Kritik, 1971).
9. Walter Benjamin, *Illuminations*. Edited with an introduction by Hannah Arendt (New York: Schocken Books, 1969), pp. 254-255 (Thesis IV).

CHAPTER 10

SOLIDARITY IN A WORLD OF GROWING INTERCONNECTIVITY

> No, I'm neither a martyr nor a hero; just a quite selfish man who's
> not ashamed of it. It's better to be proud of one's vices, my dear
> (then you'll have lovely children), than play up to the goody-goodies
> in order to get ahead in life. Pity the poor fool who sensibly takes
> the side of right-thinking people. When you're no longer ashamed of
> being ugly and identify proudly as ugly, you become handsome.
> Then you taste all the vibrancy of life—even if you've taken
> the wrong road.[1]

I would like to forge a communicative link between two thinkers, the Congolese writer Henri Lopes and the Jewish philosopher Hannah Arendt. Both try to provide answers to the question of solidarity from the standpoint of the "rebellious individual" in a world ever more interconnected. They differ in the way they view technology and the state. The African Lopes believes technological and political development is possible without the negative and murderous consequences of the past. He grounds his reason for optimism on the potential for development that accompanied destructive violence in the history of European expansion across the globe. For him, the causes of its misuse and abuse should be sought in an incompetent and corrupt elite and a passive population submissive to authority. Hannah Arendt is more pessimistic, fearing that the technology and bureaucracy develop by a kind of automatism into ever more embracive systems of destruction.

In his epistolary novel *Sans Tam-Tam*, Lopes describes the contradictions in the post-revolutionary situation in the People's Republic of the Congo from the perspective of a teacher who has been transferred for disciplinary reasons to a small village. In Lopes's narrative, the teacher formulates his faith in the future of Africa from the ambivalences of the past.

Notes for this section begin on page 137.

In hating our enemies, we mustn't despise what gives them their strength. These tyrants had a love of work, a pioneering energy and a loyalty to their flag that were not inherently the characteristics of oppressors.[2]

Colonialism is a perversion, but a perversion that only countries whose people had a special fund of energy and dynamism were capable of. Nazism was born in Germany, but Mozart, Beethoven, Kant, Hegel and Marx, Germany's son, also sprung up there. The people who crushed Hitler never stopped listening to and studying these musicians and philosophers. I'm deliberately citing non-African events and names, because our history and our redemption must stretch beyond this continent. We are linked to humanity, and in solidarity with its past.[3]

He thus views European individualism "less a characteristic of civilization than like a historical conquest."[4] Lopes seeks prospects for the future for the formerly colonized and thus psychologically still handicapped countries of the South wherever people can learn to work and live for themselves. And he sees the North's potential solidarity with Africa manifested in the respect accorded this will to life and these achievements.

We too have built works that are bigger than human-size—but as slaves, under the cat-o'-nine-tails! Now the moment is coming while we will do it on our own, for ourselves …. I never stop telling myself that our independence is the refutation of colonialism. I would like us not only to defeat it, but even to win the approval of the old colonists if they happened to revisit our land. In this sense, I am not sure that we have won yet. Much of the work remains to be done.[5]

In stark contrast, Hannah Arendt sees a failure of individualism in the totalitarian systems of socialism and fascism. In her view, the logic of production and bureaucratic rationality have taken on an independent existence in the highly industrialized countries, destroying the diversity of individual and collective aims here and across the globe. Profit for the sake of profit, growth for growth's sake, multiplication of the means of power as an answer to the means of power. Again and again, the rationality of the means has, like some gigantic megamachine, sucked up individuals, groups, entire cultures, disruptive concepts, and domains of nature and disgorged them useless, drained them of value, or exploited and then excluded them. In Arendt's view, modernity has destroyed all human solidarity and any viable form of individualism.

For Arendt, the extermination camp was thus the product of a machine of rationality liberated from all ambivalences and disruptive ends. It became a paradigm for the way in which the means take on a sinister life of their own in modernity. Yet she too retains a sliver of hope. Ambivalent, obstinate ends keep emerging on the peripheries of the dominant discourses across the planet, devalued but nonetheless pregnant with hope. The weak, wretched, derided margins and peripheries of the industrial centers were and are repeatedly persecuted or annihilated, analogous to outsiders within their own societies. Why? Because they were turned into stereotypes of excluded, "useless" ends. Or because they continue(d) to cling, rebellious and hungry for life, to their own aims and purposes.

But in Arendt's view, there is hope for a viable human future: if the diversity of human ends and goals can be made a solid political reality. The struggle of the industrial rationality against the diversity of people's real interests and aims repeatedly led to the destruction of what was deemed disruptive or branded useless—setting society in order by bureaucratic means. Yet are there still possibilities for acting in solidarity with others? How can individual morality and human solidarity exist in a world where, time and time again, violence by the state and industry breeds systems based on the use of force?[6]For Arendt, the question of morality and thus of solidarity under the sway of modern rule by rationality actually consists of two questions:

> first, in what way were those few different who, in all walks of life, did not collaborate and refused to participate in public life, though they could not and did not rise in rebellion? Second, if we agree that those who did serve on whatever level and in whatever capacity are not simply monsters, what was it that made them behave as they did ...?[7]

She advocates a morality grounded in the individual and thus able to operate without general moral rules and norms. As Arendt sees it, in general systems of ethical rules individual conscience only functions in an "automatic way."[8] Perpetrators can justify their actions morally in terms of obedience to the state, the constitution, or the dominant reality, thus becoming willing tools of modernity's lethal orders and systems of order.[9] Colonialism, National Socialism, Soviet-style socialism, and the atomic bomb[10] were always also systems of destruction, powerfully buttressed by an extreme moral and rational foundation. They required obedient and well-functioning human cogs to serve as integral components in their machinery of terror and crime, repeatedly reproducing such persons with the aid of their moral systems. But Arendt argues that a morality of solidarity *between* individuals can only come into being by refusing to be obedient, by withholding one's readiness to function. Here her view is similar to that of Lopes.

> The non-participants, called irresponsible by the majority ... asked themselves to what an extent they would still be able to live in peace with themselves after having committed certain deeds; and they decided that it would be better to do nothing, not because the world would then be changed for the better, but because only on this condition could they go on living with themselves. ... To put it crudely, they refused to murder, not so much because they held fast to the command "Thou shalt not kill," as because they were unwilling to live together with a murderer—themselves. ... In this respect, the total moral collapse of respectable society during the Hitler regime may teach us that those who are reliable in such circumstances are not those who cherish values and hold fast to moral norms and standards; ... Much more reliable will be the doubters and sceptics, not because scepticism is good or doubting wholesome, but because they are used to examine things and to make up their own minds. Best of all will be those who know that, whatever else happens, as long as we live, we are condemned to live together with ourselves.[11]

Thus, Arendt sees the political perspectives for solidarity in an individualized and decentralized world. "Eurocentrically," she overlooks here the dependency of the countries of the South on the technologically advanced North. The African novelist Lopes, by contrast, asks what conditions of development could make it possible for the South to achieve equal rights with the North in a postcolonial world. He thus raises the question of colonialism's devastating consequences and the indigenous sources of strength. Lopes arrives at a surprising conclusion: despite colonialism, Western individualism constituted a step forward for Africa; therefore, it should be fused with Africa's traditional vital forces into a new composite of promise. Africans, he counsels, must bring themselves psychologically, organizationally, and technologically to the point where they can shape their own lives themselves. In individual and social terms, this means reducing dependencies and replenishing the resulting liberated zones with self-responsibility. Taking a cue from Arendt, one could say that here too, what is central is the possibility for the individual to be able to live in dignity and self-respect.

In letters to a friend in the government in Brazzaville, who wants to persuade him to take a government post, the fictive teacher ponders the reasons why he prefers living in the remote village to life in the metropolitan center as "a frail flower in a land of illusions."[12] The return to himself and his village roots first leads the narrator back to a consciousness of self deformed by colonialism. The refractory personality that can weld Western individualism and African identity can only be born in the confrontation with one's own history and that of the collectivity:

> Putting an end to alienation in our country means decolonizing people's minds. But we can't do this by throwing the whole history and civilization of our old oppressors onto the trash heap. We have to show the contradictions between the best of their history and civilization and the reality of what they have done (and are still doing) in Africa.[13]

> My family wanted me to be a good "civilized native," an assimilated, flag-waving French citizen. And as with most children, I took everything my parents said as gospel truth. So to begin with I wanted to create myself in the image of their dreams. This means that what I am today, my reason for living and dying, is the outcome of an inner struggle. I have sworn never to adopt an idea and never to do anything just because it's in fashion. ... When the enemy is someone you were taught to love before you could even think for yourself, an honest, self-respecting person does not want to be inferior to this enemy in any way. You want to imitate all his good qualities. Faithful to one of your master thinkers, I am searching our past and the whole past of humanity for everything that can be "put back on its feet," so as to build a solid future. I am not looking back at the past with regret, but I am hunting for every scrap that I can recover from the mess of this heritage, with all the meticulousness of a common miser.[14]

From his father, the "faithful servant" of a colonialist, he imbibed the contradictions between Western individualism and the colonialized African personality. His father impressed on him:

> "Today it's no longer the law of the village that counts, but the customs of the whites. To live the happy life that white people lead, follow their law." I need not stress how sharply his words broke with tradition.[15]

While his father tended to represent the Western principle, his mother was for him the symbol of oppressed Africa. She died of a strangulated hernia. The doctor treating her, a Frenchman, is surprised that in Africa only women seemed to get this disease:

> It's because he hadn't seen who inhabits our manioc fields. He hadn't seen the burdens that our peasant women bear. Without cattle, horses or donkeys, they are laborers and beasts of burden themselves. The day she died I didn't just shed tears for this part of me that was being lowered into the earth, but also for her life, which flashed by like a bolt of lightning and was no more than a hyphen between childhood and death. She spent her life bent over, as I said, sometimes over her children, sometimes over the nourishing earth, sometimes over the fire in the hearth, and never had the time to stand up to look at the sun or the stars. She spoke of politics as well as *Dongolo-miso* [a bogeyman], and lived and died a symbol of the country, of Africa itself. She was a symbol of our history, of our account—and she never knew it.[16]

For Lopes, there are two consequences for the education of African youth flowing from the contradiction-ridden history of Africa, strung between oppression and thwarted self-determined development. First, African youth must learn to grapple critically and confidently with the achievements of the industrial cultures. And learn to accept itself: "Education in our country must take care above all to transmit to our young people the messages of all those who have risen up against oppressive conformism, and who have opened up new vistas to humanity by trampling the rack underfoot."[17]

Lopes formulates here a humanistic and enlightened perspective that looks to concrete social relations and their intrinsic contradictions. Latitude for individual and social action opens up by this dissolving of what is "unambiguous" in the perception and interpretation of reality. The insight into such possibilities contributes to the creation of a material basis on which the postmodern, resigned view[18] of the often postulated "unavoidable" catastrophe of modernity can be overcome. For example, African countries are not some sort of reservation preserving untouched fragile nature or primordial cultures either. As in the industrial nations, Africans too must learn to grapple with the contradiction between the means and the ends. There too, the individual multiplicity of ends is threatened by the "rationality" of the means and the centralization of state power. Efforts to forge a sense of self under common global conditions of industrial force and violence tend to create common problems—despite and by dint of the pluralism of people's diverse goals in life. Thus, we need exploratory conceptions that can recognize the general conditions under which human beings are constrained to act and, simultaneously, their multifarious unruliness, their deviant peculiarities—conceptions able to respect and interconnect these in a sense of solidarity.

I proceed from a basic assumption: everyone as a child learns anew the conditions under which they must live. Children learn this "by necessity" via the affection and discourse of loving individuals in a nurturant environment, and respond with the variety of their many needs, ingrained in their bodies and souls. This is why children everywhere embody the newly born possibilities for society. The child's capacity for learning generates and reproduces the prerequisite for social diversity anew, even under the dominant social relations of power. However, their education acts again and again as a source for social limitation. In enculturation, the children's vital needs and openness are pitted against the rigid cultural norms and ways of behavior in their society. The memories, identificational patterns, and experiences of individuals thus contain two dimensions: both conforming behavior and unruly, resistant learning. Collective situations and communal experiences can either strengthen individual learning behavior or act to smother it.

Mario Erdheim has pointed out that childlike openness repeats itself in puberty and can be tapped and recovered again and again throughout one's life by means of reflection. That is also the shared pedagogical message of both Lopes and Arendt. An interest in the Other, in alterity, develops through insight into one's own strangeness, otherness. And one's own sense of being a stranger is rooted in the estrangement imposed by force from above.

Yet we repress this basic estrangement, transforming it into xenophobia. We are thus "ethnocentric" and easily integrated into "patriotic" systems based on a sense of "homeland." We react to the loss of a communal frame to our lives either by retreating into a well-armored, hedonistic solitude and/or by submitting to abstract communities of faith, rigid codes. Nor is this a phenomenon limited just to the so-called developed world.

"Many hanker to live in the security of a village, but moved long ago to the periphery of the metropolis."[19] The yearning for an idyllic community, reflected in all attempts to create a forced, hermetically sealed existence within folk, cultural or religious communities or in the fetishism of possession, is a product of modernity, global in its spread. At the same time, we are integrated objectively into worldwide networks that turn the distant foreigner into a close neighbor—although we are unable to directly recognize this, let alone experience it. The global web of interconnectivity being woven through the destruction of the environment, poverty, coercive enculturation, or wars is hard for the individual to comprehend. It drives people back again and again toward the illusory comfort of the imagined idyll. Not only are the means of remedy developed and propagated by the industrial centers no longer attuned to our aims and ends, they have also slipped from the grasp of our conceptual and controlling rationality. (This despite the fact that the populations in the centers of industrial production retain a bigger slice of the profit pie than those on the peripheries.) They weld myriad connections without connective experiences and communicative structures. Across the globe, the wildly expanding possibilities of the means hamstring any thought about the purposes being served, relegating it to the limbo of a vague "maybe later."

If we are to survive on this planet, it is imperative that we think through the universal impact of the process of civilization. This common purpose unites us all objectively, compelling global cooperation and communication. Egon Becker has spoken of the need for a critical theory of regionalization.[20] Although there is increased global networking, Becker believes the workable prospects for genuine solutions lie in multiplying options for

regional self-determination and conceptions of living that can enter into dialogue with one another by surmounting common structures of coercion,
force, and exploitation.

This rather idealistic critical concept can be made more concrete by infus-
ing it with reflections and images from Lopes's novel. Yet there is a strange
contradiction within the development of the necessarily universal unruliness
of the human subject. Cooperative contemplation on these questions is possible only if at the same time, an individual's own site can be explored and
accepted. The ability to grieve over the thwarted perspectives for existence
and deformations where I live, in my existential *hic et nunc*, is the first step
toward solidarity with the Other. Without the need for home—*Heimat*, that
place I still hope to arrive in (Ernst Bloch)—I only wander aimlessly from one
fata morgana to the next.

This I where I see the task for an education that builds solidarity with the
stranger. The methods and skills for *self-reflection* become here a necessary
prerequisite for communication and cooperation. In this way, the philosophy
of individual unruliness takes on global importance. Here the discourses of
Lopes and Arendt meld.

In conclusion, a passage from Lopes's novel:

> I'd rather have time turn my flesh and sweat into compost first; have roots push
> deep down into my soil and pump up the rejuvenating sap of this unhappy world.
> Let this region's reddish *poto-poto* [mud] knead my character well for many seasons
> of rain.[21]

Formulated more generally: "I don't see democracy as a resigned return
to the bleating, stinking herd, but as opening up a path for them to forbidden riches."[22]

Notes

1. Henri Lopes, *Sans Tam-Tam (roman)* (Yaoundé: Editions CLE, 1977), p. 9. [Henri
   Lopes, born 1937 in Léopoldville (now Kinshasha, Zaïre), was one of the founding members of the Socialist Workers Party in the Congo and served as Prime Minister of the People's Republic of the Congo from 1973 to 1975. His epistolary novel *Sans Tam-Tam*,
   written in 1976-1977, consists of five long letters by the history teacher Gatsé to his friend
   in Brazzaville, and contains a probing critique of the regime of N'Gouabi, assassinated in
   1977. Lopes's first novel, *Le Pleurer-Rire* (1962), a biting satire on African power politics,
   is available in English as *The Laughing Cry: an African Cock and Bull Story*. Trans. Gerald
   Moore (New York: Readers International, 1987). *Tribaliks: Contemporary Congolese stories*, an English translation by Andrea Leskes of *Tribaliques* (Yaoundé: Editions CLE,
   1971), appeared in 1987 in the series Heinemann African Writers. Lopes has been
   awarded the prestigious Grand Prix Littéraire de l'Afrique Noire. See also Ange-Séverin

Malanda, *Henri Lopes et l'impératif romanesque* (Paris: Silex, 1987), and André-Patient Bokiba and Antoine Yila (eds.), *Henri Lopes: une écriture d'enracinement et d'universalité* (Paris: L'Harmattan, 2002).]

2. Ibid., p. 39.
3. Ibid., pp. 39-40.
4. Ibid., p. 40.
5. Ibid.
6. Many European countries have denied the right to asylum to conscientious objectors from the former Yugoslavia and its successor states. In so doing, they demonstrate they have more sympathy for than opposition to the rationality of the state.
7. Hannah Arendt, "Personal Responsibility under Dictatorship," *The Listener*, 6 August 1964, pp. 185-187 and 205, here at 205.
8. Ibid.
9. On the concept of modernity, see Zygmunt Bauman, *Modernity and Ambivalence* (Ithaca, NY: Cornell University Press, 1991), pp. 3-14.
10. It was astonishing how quickly the leading industrial countries achieved a moral consensus during the 1991 Gulf War.
11. Arendt, "Personal Responsibility," p. 205.
12. Lopes, *Sans Tam-Tam*, p. 9.
13. Ibid., p. 63.
14. Ibid., p. 79.
15. Ibid., p. 34.
16. Ibid., p. 26.
17. Ibid., p. 83.
18. The postmodern, resigned outlook is a reaction to the shattered hopes and utopias of the modern faith in progress. In that postmodern stance, there is a resigned reversal of the faith in redemptive certainties — as materialized and embodied pragmatically in the dominant form of industrial capitalism and as utopia in the so-called real-socialist systems of the former Soviet bloc — transposed into cynical visions of apocalyptic scenarios of downfall and destruction that negate human beings qua subjects, denying them the ability to act and assume responsibility. This too is a form of "collective exculpation," because only human beings can be responsible. Systems, bureaucracies, and institutions cannot.
19. Timazio Diallo, in comments at a conference of the Protestant Academy Bad Boll in 1993 (personal transcription).
20. Egon Becker, "Diskurs-Verwirrungen: Ökologisches Lernen im Entwicklungsprozess — Umrisse einer Theorie des praktischen Überlebenswissens," in: idem (ed.), *Umwelt und Entwicklung* (Frankfurt am Main: Verlag für Interkulturelle Kommunikation, 1992), pp. 51f.
21. Lopes, *Sans Tam-Tam*, pp. 9-10.
22. Ibid., p. 70.

CHAPTER 11

COMPULSIVE AND COERCED IDENTITIES

Once More on the Theory of Social Limits to Learning

What do I have in common with myself?

Confident of ourselves, we are always defining our own identity and that of others by resorting to the attributes of profession, personal and social history, culture, family, religion, or even a person's passport or ID. As we assign self-hood and otherness, we are busy processing body signals, forms of expression, and encoded social knowledge.[1] To maintain our image of self, we block out disruptive characteristics and memories; we draw a sharp defining line between our "selves" and other human beings, their patterns of living, codes, and norms. All this we do mobilizing a battery of seemingly secure and solid perceptions and prejudices—biases and prejudices we have adopted and assimilated over the years, attitudes we identify with because we want in turn to be identified by them. In appropriating these forms, we also represent patterns of living and thinking that are basically recognized by our society, enacting them in public and private space in identifiable roles.

Our secure sense of self is grounded on the continuity of our perceptions of Self and the Other and on our abiding faith in the validity of social roles, social boundaries, and normative definitions. We have been schooled in how to deal with them, have practised their application: we are well aware how to behave and react in a wide array of socially defined sitiations. I term this continuity of certainty and conviction "identity in process." That notion underscores the fluid character of this identification of self and other: it is not control over something that remains literally identical and unchanging, but rather involves a semblance of security, a shadowy and illusive hunt for certainty, a manufacture of ideas about ourselves and others and a process of exploratory "trial-and-error," repeated gropings and forays toward a Self that remains ever-elusive.

In empirical experience, our accurate identifications of the Self and Others are also accompanied by recurrent error: we are uncertain, become entan-

---

gled in misunderstandings, mistakes, and arbitrary distinctions between our selves and the rest. Our assumptions regarding others and our own selves are at best conjectural; thus, we are repeatedly obliged to test them anew. On closer inspection, we discover that our own self-images contain a bewildering multitude of very different "identities" banded together in the confederacy of our Self. That confederation is not always voluntary: we sometimes are also coerced into its seeming unity, and others "read" putative "identities" into our persons. Our "identities" are thus always a reflection of the successes and defeats we have experienced. In their genesis, painful events are masked, concrete experiences constantly reinterpreted.

This entire contradictory multiplicity of seemingly secure and well-anchored identities only becomes evident in social and personal crises: when control over the exchange relations of recognized and understood forms of communication crumbles, revealing the lack of identity lurking beneath such presumed homogeneous unities. Thus, the people of the poets and philosophers[2] was also the nation of the robbers and murderers. The peacemakers blessed the bombs, the meek in spirit obeyed the militant dictator. Yet the external shell of our individual habitus can be shattered even by events as minor as infatuation or illness, psychological distress and solitude. What remains of professional identity after retirement, of the theologian's integrity in the throes of Alzheimer's syndrome, of pastoral dignity in a nursing home for the elderly?

Anxiety in the face of non-identity

Human life repeatedly leads to the usually painful insight that we are estranged from ourselves. Children already are plagued by this harrowing experience and adults cannot elude its unsettling grip. I am estranged from myself whenever new needs or unresolved problems pry me from my set ways. The "angels of Paradise"[3] that can drive us from the comfort of our familiar frame are psychological and physical: love, passion, ambition, curiosity, illnesses, crises in your career or in social dealings with others, the list continues. In order to assuage the anxiety we feel in the face of possible dependency on what is Unknown, exposure to the mercy of the Strange and Other, we try hard to habituate the uncustomary, transmuting whatever is strange within and around us into something familiar and unthreatening; we attempt to tame it, get it under our control. We seek to incorporate what is unusual into the commonplace, what is unknown into the everyday, what is novel into our traditional tales and templates. We only succeed by enormous effort, usually availing ourselves of crazy and bizarre constructions.[4] If that does not help, we resort to force. In this process, we constantly draw a defining line around ourselves: others are excluded beyond this perimeter, or absorbed into our constructed identity.

Our cultural life unfolds between the experiences of alterity and our efforts to bolster our self and its ramparts. But the greater the anxiety, the weaker our sense of ego or group—and the more neurotic and compulsive our efforts become to flee from threatening experiences with Otherness. The small child admonishes the stone it has stumbled over: "You nasty stone, you hurt me!" and in fury strikes out at the mute object. In this way, the stone is rendered animate, made into something ostensibly known and familiar—and thus amenable to the child's factitious control. The Non-Identical is seemingly assimilated into one's own identity, open to explanation and control. The objective cultures thus constitute collective and individual museums of memory, storehouses of experiences with Otherness we have acquired or which were forced upon us, and our attempts either to domesticate or exclude that Otherness.

However, the human facility to question, and thus to communicate and learn, is grounded on the insight that Otherness begins in my own being, it is rooted in me and must therefore be accepted as a primal part of my existence. Yet all social and cultural reality is subject to change in the swirl of the historical process, and is thus itself dependent on our ability, predicated on this insight, to grasp and learn.

Human culture and its constructedness

Anybody can be born into any culture. But children do not enter the community of their family and culture "voluntarily." Each community is founded initially on coercion and exclusion; in the best instance this entails the constraining force of shared interests and the exclusion of noncomparable experiences. In their earliest phase of life, individuals from one or another culture are described by reference to personal ties, love relations, utilizing their mechanisms of imitation and identification. This cements a close and lasting link to our earliest cultural orientations. Hidden here too are the conundrums of our continuity.

Since relatively few individuals participate in our cultural "description" during childhood, we remain culturally circumscribed and must learn the onerous task of overstepping inculcated limits and boundaries in a kind of "border traffic."[5] As culturally limited persons, we find it extremely difficult to expose ourselves to anything unfamiliar, unknown (to us). From the persons we love and cherish, we learn both the forms and rituals for fending off the unknown and the practiced patterns for approaching the unfamiliar: the code of traffic regulations between "us" and "them." We need these border regulations because of our limitations, and we must buttress and defend these boundaries lest we dissolve into the void of relativity. In the protective bosom of the family community, we thus first learn how to deal with and interpret the available cultural objects in which the cultural boundaries and border regulations have taken on solid form.

Individuals reify themselves in their activities, in the circumscribed spaces and times in which they play out their lives. Their ideas, concepts, thoughts and wishes appear—in an historically shaped and adapted form—in the objects and institutions they have created. Cultures are immeasurable, vast unordered lumberyards containing the residues and slag of the reifications of past and present human endeavors. Each cultural pattern also places a certain limitation on possible human diversity, it adapts the individuals under its sway to the respective dominant powers of definition. Family socialization acts like a filter, restricting the unbounded pleasure and curiosity of average individuals to the defined social frame into which they were born. Under repressive conditions, the cultural patterning that has been inculcated into us becomes a burden, preventing us from learning necessary new solutions. Paralysis and ossification under repressive conditions prevent us from coming to creative grips with new open situations in our own vital interest. Authoritarian orientations, masochistic self-hatred, and violent inabilities to communicate can also be internalized via our first experiences of dependency in childhood. They are subjective forms for processing the suffering we have experienced under the heel of repression.

Dissolving cultural forced communities

There is a broad array of options for coming to grips with life's problems. It is this multitude of developed possibilities to shape life and approach its vital problems that constitutes the wealth we all share. Today it is increasingly obvious that there can no longer be societies with a cultural monopoly on definitions—only cultural diversity will be able to guarantee our species' future, not one-sided narrow "truths." But socialization and education repeatedly act to narrow down the great diversity and wealth of human possibilities for the individual. As individuals, our enculturation acquaints us with but a tiny portion of the total range of human options and possibilities. That limitation is evident particularly in the objects we surround ourselves and live with, to which we are fixated. The limitedness, fixation, and fossilization of human cultural boundaries, concepts and objects lead cultures again and again into deadends, turning them false: i.e., they can no longer provide adequate solutions for pressing social problems. They harden into forced communities, serving primarily to anneal and consolidate existing systems of rule, exploitation, and destruction.

This is one dimension of cultural determination. Yet the lifelong tie of individuals to their childhood memories, the social and cultural entities in and with which they have imbibed hope and security and nurtured a sense of self-esteem, are an integral part of their unmistakable individual biography, their personal dignity and worth. Their loss or degrading force the human being to grapple with and work through these painful memories.[6] To be shaped culturally by loved persons is a unique possession: it is a valuable vital adjunct for individuals that can help them to master their lives utilizing traditional orientations, to solve their individual problems using collectively developed and traditional solutions, and to tackle new experiences, bringing to bear the reservoir of past knowledge accumulated in the community. We become historical persons only in and through cultural limitations and our sovereign interaction with these defining limits. Although such limitations circumscribe our scope for action, they make it possible for us to act altogether.

These products of culture and their use are a vast pool: they contain the vital hopes of the society, the vitality of subjects, strategies for survival and their opposite—patterns of dominance hostile and destructive to life, oppression and the strangling of all vitality. The material reality of life humans create shackles them to the systems of their reification and makes possible their orientation. Reification can only be overcome and transformed into a guidepost for orientation when we learn to recognize the tyranny of the compulsively frozen patterns of culture in which we are embedded. But the close ties we acquire in early childhood to our own culture and its configurations and the threats and fears of loss that plague us throughout our lives block our insight into that tyranny, cloud its recognition.

Consequently, the common prerequisites for intercultural learning are (a) reflection on ethnocentrism, i.e., thinking in ambivalence on our own cultural ties and rootedness and (b) our need for the Other. Only when we ponder the consequences of the ossification of our own daily life do we open a window to other "foreign" patterns of living and cultural solutions. That does not bring us to disparage our own roots, it energizes their vitalization.

Identity in industrial cultures

There are hardly any "idylls" left, any garden-like sites of circular patterns of living. The "idyllic" life of the small towns and "peaceful" villages has been supplanted almost everywhere by the dynamism of the industrial centers. Since the formation of a small number of power centers during the European age of absolutism and the feverish turmoil of the bourgeois revolutions, the world has been changing, irreversibly and at an ever-faster pace, a process spreading from the European core to the world's four corners. Power has been centralized, spawning numerous conflicting peripheries. The history of Europe's expansion to the rest of the world is a triumphal chronicle of destruction that has relegated virtually all the previously viable cultures on our planet to the storerooms of ethnological museums and libraries.

The triumphal procession of capitalist civilizations led to the dangerous illusion entertained by the men of the bourgeois Enlightenment that for the sake of the "pure concept" and thus "Pure Reason," they could liberate themselves from nature and unreason. Along with being a means to implement economic interests (force against the workers *and* the native populations in the colonies) and buttress political power, the definitional force of the Concept was an attempt to overcome the insurmountable dependence of human beings on their own creaturely nature, on birth, life and death.

That "liberation" was doomed to fail. But the repressed anxiety it was driven and simultaneously repressed by promoted the violent subjugation of nonconforming thought and unconformed individuals. The liquidation of outsiders and women found its subjective correlate in the eradication of one's own ambivalent childhood memories. In devaluing and downgrading the "savages" on the peripheries and the enormous diversity of human cultures, there was a compulsive restriction to one's own culture: it was now elevated perforce to a position far above all other cultures. The bourgeois male individual banished whatever was excluded and suppressed into the putrid cellars of his unconscious, the underworld of his repressed thoughts, wishes, and dreams, so as to advance and implement the discourse of his economic and political interests.[7] Over the dungeons of his repressed ambivalences, he constructed his "impressively" rational conceptual edifices and the systems of his economic, political, and ideological force.

Systematic, institutionalized education was (and remains) a tool helping to crank out functional individuals for the ruling system of rationality. The education of one's own children was concentrated instrumentally on its utility for society. This cultural identity thus produced the ambivalence between the ability to orient oneself and blinkered vision, the capacity to understand and limited simplemindedness, presumption and melancholy.

In European history, there has been a recurrent tendency to make the instrumental-rational solutions, truths, and norms concocted by Europeans binding on others and to implement them by all necessary means, including force. The more centralistic and rational-instrumental dominance becomes in industrial systems, the more violent, simpleminded, and brutal are the "cultural" strategies and truths it imposes on itself and others. Even in the dynamic industrial states, the longing for security, community, and identity is constantly reproduced via personal experiences and relations in early childhood. Yet at the same time, the industrial division of labor and the concomitant individualization and atomization of society ravage the social foundations for the warm security so fervently desired.[8]

All communities and associations (societies)[9] are constituted in the tension between the social compulsion to conformity and individual assistance for life, the interests for security on the part of the individual and their basic lack of empowerment as adults. Individuals experience the limitations on their ego abstractly and anonymously via the marketplace, especially the labor market and the educational institutions that imitate it. The upshot is that individuals are ultimately isolated in their conflicts on the boundaries and their attempts to assert themselves. They achieve a flimsy sense of security only by internalizing a readiness to adapt and conform to an abstract normality. Throughout their lives, they suck sustenance from the few warming experiences of their cultural-personal shaping in childhood, to which they cling with a kind of neurotic compulsiveness.[10]

Consequently, the concrete now shrinking communities remaining in capitalism, such as dyadic relationships, mother-child relationships, and peer groups, are overloaded to the point of breaking with the never gratified, childlike longings of isolated individuals for community. Since these are no longer functional, pseudo-erotic ideologies of folk and fatherland dangle sham quasi-familial securities and guarantees of identity on the national plane before the eyes of a hungry and deranged citizenry. Lonely individuals try to find psychological solace in the warming bosom of an imagined extensive family, in delusive ideas such as culture, personal achievement motivation, health, yes, even religion and folk custom. The nation-state has exploited the crisis of the longing for homeland in capitalism emotionally, fashioning from pseudo-communal ideologies a psychological crutch for isolated, atomized lonely and estranged individuals to hobble on. Via the false "solidarity" of a fictive "shared organic community" of the "truly" useful and usable citizenry, the vital interests of those "inside" are played off against everything categorized as foreign and "external." The ideological boundaries fossilize into rigid dogmatic truths; in this ossified form, they are then defended, using any means necessary, as the protective sheath of one's own imagined identity.

This easily manipulated voracity for feelings of identity and the addictions of specious solidarity are but the flip side of modern individualization, isolation and cultural insecurity. No productive political prospects for the future or feelings of solidarity can be grounded on this rickety foundation. Because in democracy, political bonds of shared conviction and solidarity are grounded on conscious and articulated needs and openly formulated interests[11] expressed by individuals conscious of their selfhood and ego.

The ideologically ever so shrewd and violent xenophobia endemic in industrial societies grants the "foreigner" "free" entry into society via the gateway of the marketplace. It then leaves their fate to the workings of the marketplace and the fear of foreigners that haunts the hearts of the "native" citizens. The market's dynamism spawns an insatiable, systematic hunger for new and unknown spaces, topics, realms, and objects; commodities from all corners of the globe are gathered in and amassed for consumption. Expansion, increased productivity, and evolution are concepts which combine with colonialism, imperialism, the New World Order, and the destructive "control of nature"[12] on the basis of an unquenchable thirst for whatever is foreign and unfamiliar. Otherness is firmly anchored in industrial life in the form of commodities from abroad, including the commodity labor power, and its use-value is repeatedly exploited anew.

In industrial societies, what is recognized as foreign is utilized chiefly as a "means for disciplining and education." The industrial systems of socialization and education require readily available, submissive and obedient individuals within the system's perimeters—and groups that are readily stigmatized outside the ambit of utility to be exploited as a useful foil. Via this duality, the boundary between "them" and "us" is demonstrated and, if need be, is forcibly enforced.[13] This repeatedly leads to force against unproductive, useless outsiders.[14] There is thus no naive friendly coexistence of some kind between the beneficiaries and the victims of the European history of expansion, between those within and without. But even the citizens within the walls are justifiably afraid they themselves may be banished, labelled as "foreign" and ousted: the disabled, vagabonds, the elderly and, as strange as it may sound, even children. The anxiety that they may no longer be a part of the community often engenders in them an aggressive rage against other outsiders, catalyzing an excessive identification with the fictive promises for community held out by industrialized society.

The modern school

The modern school is the most important institution of transformation mediating between the culture of the family and the demands of industrial society. There the curriculum no longer concentrates mainly on imparting patterns of behavior to children that can be experienced and reflect traditional values and norms. Now the focus is on a multitude of skills and attitudes geared to one overriding aim: to make learners usable for the demands of a (market) situation that cannot be gauged in advance, available when needed, and prepared to prove their exchange-value again and again. The schoolchild does not learn dignity and identity but freedom from value, insecurity, relativity, perseverance, and a readiness to fight against any and all competition. Anxiety and insecurity, especially in the face of the threat of worthlessness, have to be compensated by conforming, learning how to function efficiently, obeying one's superiors, ever-ready to fight against competitors. In this way, everyday life becomes a constant struggle against the threat of being turned into an outsider.

The construction of my abstract, individual potential worth and its concrete social realization are separate processes in my biographical trajectory. School prepares me as a child for society, i.e., the market; only later as an adult must I be able to realize the value of the education invested in me via the marketplace.[15] This is why children learn at an early age to subject themselves to abstract demands and, in their young imaginations, to picture their future "wages" in an array of imagery full of longing and invention. This virtually unlimited ability children have to project the fulfillment of their own longings and needs onto the cornucopia of available commodities could help to explain the frenzied desire to buy more and more and the aesthetics of consumerism that shape the daily round of the masses in industrial societies.

Four aspects of school education contribute to the constant renewal of the readiness among Europeans, in a ceaseless process, to subjugate the rest of the world to their control and destroy everything that is alien to their own value systems.

1. The educational process geared to churning out children who are readily available when needed is often torturous, bound up with injuries, insults, and insecurities. The child learns here that an abstract grade means everything; its own concrete abilities in a given instance are worthless.
2. An attempt is made to compensate the injuries this process inflicts by devaluing what society denigrates and identifying with what society holds up as worthy of esteem.
3. My own strivings and longings, i.e., my own emotions, are necessarily neurotic because from the time I was a small child, I have been conditioned to subject myself to utility—to means-ends relations—to identify with them emotionally and integrate myself prudently into their instrumental ordering.

4. In the quest for buttressing their sense of self-esteem, individuals strive for just such an education, an undertaking that can only be successful in and through the marketplace. Thus, in each and every confrontation with alterity, that confronts them as a real or imaginary threat to their own individual sense of self-worth, they will first attempt to devalue this Otherness in ways similar to the self-devaluations they have personally experienced while growing up.

The sons of the bourgeois strata were the first to experience the consequences of this mode of education. Their education was designed to train them to take over their father's place in a society stamped by competition and economic struggle. Later these educational functions were transferred to the basic school for the masses, which mutated from an academy for drill and discipline to a national primary school system. As Europe expanded, that became a global educational commodity for export to the peripheries. In the form of the Christian mission school, it was adapted to the demands of the so-called underdeveloped countries.

The methods of education in industrial society have undergone substantial further elaboration in recent decades. Education changed from physical compulsion to psychological-structural force, from authoritarian manipulation to the nameless power of the prevailing circumstances. But the results remained the same: education for instrumental efficiency breeds neurosis, educating children into being "agents" for the European "way," or at least its apologists. Only now are some of us slowly to realize that we have to liberate ourselves from the European designs for living that have been drummed into us, the neurotic normalcy of our society.

Collective compulsive neurosis

The European self-image and its conjunct xenophobia are grounded on the same contradiction-ridden mélange of conformity, anxiety, and utopia. This mix of narrow-minded ethnocentrism, existential anxiety, and longing for a change in society harbors within its depths, however hidden, an enduring hope. In his 1980 book *Verkehrte Utopien. Nationalismus, Neonazismus, Neue Barbarei*, Rainer Rotermundt injected this complex of issues into educational discussion.[16]

He points out that the arguments of the neo-Nazis contain values actually analogous to the ingrained values of the middle classes, but which have lost their potency and meaning in the everyday reality of urban industrial society: e.g., solidarity, reliability, a sense of duty, decency, courage, loyalty. Rotermundt raises the question why individuals who feel the magnetic pull of neo-Nazi propaganda seem caught in a cage of faulty reasoning:

— The current political and social conditions and the ruling elites who manage them do not correspond to our ideals.

— The blame must be put on foreign influences, racially and ethnically alien (*artfremd*).

— Every means is permitted in the struggle against the enemies of our ideals, against "alien" individuals. Our "own" ideals have no validity in their case.

Rotermundt hypothesizes that persons prone to such notions are actually perverted idealists: they have a contradictory longing for translating ideals into reality. In order to realize their utopia of an "ideal" society, they claim a license to carry out non-ideal, immoral acts in a bid to achieve that goal.

What would happen, asks Rotermundt, if the utopian longings of the neo-Nazis for an ideal society, a society in which ideals are possible and workable, were to be taken seriously in political education? If, in the very core of neurosis, we discerned a desire for health?[17] Wouldn't this be a way for those "infected" by the contagion—to continue the metaphor—to free themselves from the reactionary quack doctors? Rotermundt calls such a pedagogy restorative: a means to "gain (back) the ability to reflect."[18] In this way, the real, individual, and social causes underlying the social crisis could be articulated anew, regain discursivity.

In order to substantiate his thesis, Rotermundt went out to speak directly with young neo-Nazis. He took their confused statements seriously: as utopian wishes for an identity of their own and the bonds of social solidarity. He noted that reflected within them was "in perverted forms ... the knowledge that those social conditions which once made National Socialism possible had not been overcome."[19] By this, Rotermundt refers to the lack of a prospect for the future among young people aside from their use-value and exploitation in a system of production determined by others. These young people viewed Hitler as the leader who "cut the Gordian knot of hopelessness, resignation, anxiety and loneliness at one fell and violent swoop."[20]

As Rotermundt sees it, the decision made by such people to opt for xenophobia, backward-looking nationalism, and neo-Nazi politics was preceded by an experience both individual and shared. What was it? "Society made clear to them in a thousand ways that they were not needed, that they were even some kind of burden, and the future seemed more tightly closed than ever."[21] "Alcoholism, drugs, 'flipping out,' mounting suicide rates, criminality—and ultimately even neo-Nazi groups—can be seen as specific means used by the young to overcome their collective identity crisis."[22]

He concludes that as long as the production of our wealth remains based on the devaluing of self-worth and personal relations, on utilization of a person's use-value instead of meaningfulness, the political power inherent in "perverted" utopias, i.e., utopian blueprints hostile to life, will remain a virulent menace. "There is 'within us' the latent possibility of a new barbarism in the same way that National Socialism was latently 'inside' our parents and grandparents: namely as a conceptional form of perverted social praxis, as ideology."[23]

The wellspring of this lies in the contradiction between the insatiable hunger for cultural security and individual conformity to the industrial destruction of culture. In other words: we can only attempt to deal effectively on a "pedagogical level" with the susceptibility, particularly among the young, for being seduced into xenophobia, the cult of the Führer, and excessive German nationalism if there is a basis in society for alternative perspectives on behavior, alternative avenues for action that would restore to them their dignity, human relations grounded on solidarity and individual prospects for a future, for hope.

This is why all successful concrete relations with foreigners are more effective "pedagogically" than abstract appeals to compassion and morality. But another prerequisite is that the victims of xenophobia in our society must come to be viewed once more in the media and the speeches of politicians in all their diverse humanness, individuals with whom discourse is possible, with whom we can build a life together. Genuine human relations are not possible with labeled categories: "Negroes," "Gypsies," "asylum-seekers," refugees, and "foreign cultures." There can be no real compassion with and sensitivity for stereotyped, anonymous groups or abstract, foreign cultures. And no basis for building practical solidarity.

These assumptions pose a number of questions for educational discussion. What social hopes, yearnings, and expectations for the future flow into these xenophobic ideas? How are these hopes then perverted against themselves? And why is Intercultural Education stymied, does it seem to be getting almost nowhere? Is perhaps the principal reason that the reality in industrial societies does not generate any concrete models and convincing potential solutions for maintaining and buttressing individual dignity?

To phrase it differently: educational models must develop alternative counterexperiences and emancipatory learning situations to counter the force in our society that nearly eludes subjective grasp and the abstract channeling and control of our experience. The work of intercultural translation will not end up in resignation and empty drill only if concrete learning experiences can be worked through on an interpersonal plane—both conceptually and in terms of lived experience. There can be no emancipatory learning unless it is triggered and galvanized by discontent, by the abiding ambivalences intrinsic to living individual and social reality themselves.

Learning through concepts

> Human beings make their own history, but they do not make it just as they please in circumstances they choose for themselves; rather they make it in present circumstances, given and inherited. Tradition from all the dead generations weighs like a nightmare on the brain of the living.
>
> Karl Marx[24]

Social experiences, institutions, and solutions to problems become individualized in the field of tension between the social conditions individuals adapt to in the search for personal blueprints for living on the one hand, and their subjective desire for freedom on the other.[25] Society is repeatedly confirmed

through language, but is also brought into flux. Language encloses the contradictions of individuals within itself and thus conforms them to their surroundings. In this manner we learn to deal ambivalently with society in the
form of concepts, codes, rules, myths, and symbols. The systemic discourses
reproduce themselves via rituals and the significations individuals engage in
in everyday discourse, blending there with their wishes and desires. Here too
are preserved the temptations, dreams, and utopias handed down from the
past. But the realized, reified compromises between wish and reality lead to
social limits to learning that lock wishes into historical boundaries. To overcome social limits to learning presupposes a doubting mind, a sense of dis-
satisfaction with the existing states of affairs, the given social circumstances;
it also presupposes vital needs of one's own. Not until we are able to communicate with other like-minded interlocutors can we develop historical
prospects for action, and thus the ability to engage in dialogue with alterity,
with what is strange and unfamiliar.

The effort to consciously change one's own historical reality is what I
understand "learning" to be. Such learning can be groping and provisional,
hesitatingly halfhearted or consistent to the point of self-sacrifice. Our ability
to take history itself into our own hands begins with this kind of learning. It
begins with your own body, with your own history inscribed in its synapses.
The necessary beginning of all genuine learning is the voyage of discovery to
your own self, to the strange and distant places in your own wishes and longings, the repressed suffering and memories of suppressed resistance.

In this vein, Michele Borelli[26] has advanced the thesis that a nonreified concept of culture today is principally a critical *concept*, geared to one overriding
aim: *conceptual comprehension* (*Begreifen*). Such a concept of culture does not
refer to a defined or existing reality, to defined and specific cultures, but rather
is oriented to the prospects for a society yet to be created: one in which there
will no longer be any need for a cultural industry or cultural defined forced
communities—a society which will enable human beings to develop their subjective options for living to the full, tapping the prodigious expanse of human
diversity. Such a concept of culture is predicated on an epistemic precondition:
namely, that existence has been conceptually grasped, is *begriffene Existenz*.
Only a thinking and acting subject can have "culture," and then only their
own.[27] The arduous and anxiety-ridden work of comprehension encompasses
the existing collective (historical) learning experiences *and* curiosity regarding
the multiplicity of human possibilities. Comprehension of cultures (one's own
and foreign) thus entails a self-critical perspective on a reality that is worthy of
transformation (and thus specifically nonidentical).

In Borelli's view, *conceptual learning* and communication are conjunctive.
Only where I am capable of comprehending, where I am prepared to view
my own uncomprehended variety in the frame of an open and differentiated
conceptuality (*Begrifflichkeit*) am I able to enter into possible communication with the Other. And vice versa: only where I expect to be confronted
with what is unregulated, strange and foreign, undefined, am I capable of
grasping the world conceptually, can I expect something "graspable" (*begreif-
bar*), comprehensible from a communication. Cultural self-understanding

and understanding of Otherness becomes possible where humans communicate with one another on a conceptual level, beyond the respective boundaries and limits into which they have been socialized and enculturated. Seen from this angle, cultural boundaries are at the disposition of acting subjects and their comprehended interests, they can be confronted and crossed. In Borelli's view, this also leads to a new concept of education, since education either serves to assist in "overstepping boundaries and limits" (emphatic concept of learning) or it remains a method designed for the social buttressing and defense of boundaries in the interest of the ruling powers. It either builds bridges or bolsters bulwarks.

The difficulty in developing another mode of education lies in the fact that such learning requires encouragement to negotiate the path to nonidentity, to be curious, ready, and able to criticize. That is only possible in a social environment that has been liberated as much as possible from subjective, institutional, and social impediments to learning. Such a learning is communicative in that it thematizes our individualization inculcated from outside and above. Such a learning is conceptual in that it makes subjective and collective perspectives for action a focus for learning and discussion. Through communication, collective and subjective interests are interlinked and articulated. Such an education becomes conceptual by confronting these interests with the dominant constraints in society—in order to develop practical resistance against them.

This form of education thus aims at reducing authority and promoting a free unfolding of subjective and collective abilities for learning and a cooperative praxis between teachers and learners in a learning community founded on solidarity. It also tries to bring to open articulation the manifold of ambivalences, contradictions, and hidden needs lurking beneath the surfaces of social discourse. Paulo Freire has attempted to employ this didactic conception in his literacy campaign work. He found the paradigms for his "pedagogy of liberation" in the traditions of European progressive education. But the varying history of his learning experiments also illustrates that the longer-term success of his learning methods is only possible in conjunction with changes in the living conditions of the learners.[28]

Learning through your own ambivalences

Reflection shows us that our image of happiness is thoroughly colored by the time to which the course of our own existence has assigned us. The kind of happiness that could arouse envy in us exists only in the air we have breathed, among people we could have talked to, women [and men, GM] who could have given themselves to us. In other words, our image of happiness is indissolubly bound up with the image of redemption. ... The past carries with it a temporal index by which it is referred to redemption. There is a secret agreement between past generations and the present one. Our coming was expected on earth. Like every generation that preceded us, we have been endowed with a *weak* Messianic power, a power to which the past has a claim.

Walter Benjamin[29]

Along with the ravaging of communication and the destruction of communication, the dynamism of European expansionism has repeatedly spawned its own contradiction in its "borderlands" in the form of human beings capable of conceptual understanding and conceptuality (*Begrifflichkeit*, learning's results).[30] Yet what had been comprehended was repeatedly in danger of congealing into something set, defined and thus false—of ossifying into a knowledge at the disposal of power. Moreover, what people failed to grasp or what was still unknown was again and again shut out of consciousness—or forcibly simplified and whittled down to fit in with strategic needs. Enlightenment did not founder on the lack of curiosity or its distinctive forms of thought. It failed because, utilizing its power of definition, it chose to exclude alterity in the interest of male power and capitalist and socialist exploitation. What was unconformed and unfamiliar was banished beyond the pale. It silenced Otherness, suppressed it, denying it any right to exist. In the competitive fray, concepts hardened into weapons and were integrated into the gearwork of existing power by dint of their participation in the dominant discourse. The systems of power repeatedly restricted the scope of conceptual learning of individuals by the "mustering" of key concepts into their discursive ranks.

So the concept of "learning" encompasses more than just the comprehension (*Begreifen*) of our own limits and their judicious overstepping. It also embraces the exhilarated "dance" upon enticing, seductive boundaries behind which uncertain historical opportunities lie hidden. Human vitality encompasses far more than just the regulated and comprehended "border traffic" alluded to earlier. Faith, love, and hope cannot be locked in the constraining perimeters of reason and conceptuality. Nor in the confines of dogmatism. We are not organized in terms of a straight and unswerving line, unambiguous and clearly oriented—we are diverse, undefined and ambivalent, *das noch nicht festgestellte Tier* (Nietzsche). Learning is also impeded by blindness for the ambivalences within us and our blindness for what is workable, both socially and historically. Infatuation, ardor and ambition, the readiness to sacrifice and the itch for adventure, dedication and heroism—these all demonstrate that we are capable of "exceeding ourselves," that we have "unimagined capacities" and are in rapport with forces that go beyond our mere powers to grasp and understand.

Consequently, understanding and insight into the objective necessities of our situation are usually not enough to motivate people to learn[31]—although without an anchoring in conceptual understanding, learning situations are swept up into the vortex of the ambivalences that inform them.

Learning needs trust in your own powers (and especially your own imagination) *and* the conceptual perception of your own ambivalences. Otherwise it can issue in subjugation to authoritarian systems of hope. The hope for possible changes in collective and subjective conditions then ends up in communal authoritarianism, individual surrender or collective resignation.

Notes

1. Social knowledge is encoded via language. Language constitutes a virtually infinite reservoir of signs for making the buzzing multiplicity of reality accessible to humans and thus amenable to communication.
2. [That is the German people (*Das Volk der Dichter und Denker*).]
3. The "angels of Paradise" have driven us from our Garden of Eden. This mythological image contains the fundamental experiences of both estrangement and banishment. The "angel of Paradise" here is not merely external, but can also appear as an internal power: in one instance, I become an object to its externality, in the other I remain an acting subject.
4. Thus, for example, the advertising campaign in Germany "My friend's a foreigner" tries to incorporate the foreigner, constructing a positive counterpole to his or her stigmatization by suggesting that foreigners are really our friends and thus familiar to us. In this process, what is strange and other is "included by exclusion," so to speak — a construction whose flimsiness is patent.
5. Munasu Duala-M'bedy points up the distinction between fear of the foreigner and xenophobia, see his *Xenologie. Die Wissenschaft vom Fremden und die Verdrängung der Humanität in der Anthropologie* (Freiburg and Munich: Alber, 1977).
6. Alexander and Margarete Mitscherlich call this the ability to mourn. See their *Inability to Mourn. Principles of Collective Behavior*. Preface Robert Jay Lifton. Trans. Beverly R. Placzek (New York: Grove Press, 1975).
7. Erdheim terms this process of dominance the "social production of unconsciousness," see Mario Erdheim, *Die gesellschaftliche Produktion von Unbewusstheit. Eine Einführung in den ethnopsychoanalytischen Prozess* (Frankfurt am Main: Suhrkamp, 1983).
8. Ernst Bloch, *The Principle of Hope*. Trans. Neville Plaice, Stephen Plaice, and Paul Knight, vol. 3. (Cambridge, MA: MIT Press, 1986), see the concept of "homeland" (*Heimat*), pp. 1320ff.
9. The distinction between the ideal types *Gemeinschaft* and *Gesellschaft* derives from the folkish-conservative social philosopher Ferdinand Toennies, see his *Gemeinschaft und Gesellschaft. Abhandlung des Communismus und des Socialismus als empirischer Kulturformen* (Leipzig: Fues, 1887), English ed. *Community and Association*. Trans. Charles P. Loomis (London: Routledge & Kegan Paul, 1955). On implications for education, see Paul Natorp, *Sozialpädagogik: Theorie der Willensbildung auf der Grundlage der Gemeinschaft*, 6th ed. (Stuttgart: Frommann, 1925). I consider this distinction to be of critical value.
10. Gottfried Mergner and Peter Gottwald (eds.), *Liebe Mutter — Böse Mutter. Angstmachende Bilder von der Mutter in Kinder- und Jugendbüchern* (Oldenburg: Bibliotheks- und Informationssystem der Universität Oldenburg, 1989).
11. George L. Mosse, *Toward the Final Solution. A History of European Racism* (New York: H. Fertig, 1978); idem, *Nationalism and Sexuality. Middle-Class Morality and Sexual Norms in Modern Europe* (New York: H. Fertig, 1985).
12. A new theoretical approach to these problems is presented in Thomas Mitschein, *Die Dritte Welt als Gegenstand gewerkschaftlicher Theorie und Praxis. Zur Analyse internationaler Politik metropolitanischer Gewerkschaften* (Frankfurt am Main: Campus, 1981), esp. pp. 51ff.
13. Michel Foucault, *Discipline and Punish. The Birth of the Prison*. Trans. Alan Sheridan (New York: Pantheon Books, 1977). Foucault points out that "power" constitutes an unceasing machine for the production of knowledge. As what is unknown is transformed into definite knowledge in a constant and uninterrupted process, power extends its reach to all "previously unknown" spaces and niches, all persons everywhere. The unknown is power's material.
14. On the one hand, these are the external "enemies," on the other the useless and unusable persons inside the system, see Hans Mayer, *Outsiders. A Study of Life and Letters* (Cambridge, MA: MIT Press, 1982).

15. Siegfried Bernfeld, *Sisyphus. Or The Limits of Education*. Trans. Frederic Lilge. Foreword Anna Freud. Preface Peter Paret (Berkeley, CA: University of California Press, 1973), pp. 31f.

16. Rainer Rotermundt, *Verkehrte Utopien. Nationalismus, Neonazismus, Neue Barbarei. Argumente und Materialien* (Frankfurt am Main: Verlag Neue Kritik, 1980), p. 129.

17. It goes without saying, of course, that the prerequisite would be a society in which criminality and violation of the law would be properly punished.

18. Ibid.

19. Ibid., p. 123.

20. Ibid., p. 125.

21. Ibid.

22. Ibid.

23. Ibid., p. 129.

24. "The Eighteenth Brumaire of Louis Bonaparte [1852]," in: Marx, *Later Political Writings*. Trans. Terrell Carver (Cambridge [etc.]: Cambridge University Press, 1996), pp. 31-127, at 32.

25. See inter alia Alfred Adler, *The Practice and Theory of Individual Psychology* (London: Kegan, Paul, 1925); see also Ernest Jouhy, *Bleiche Herrschaft — Dunkle Kulturen. Essais zur Bildung in Nord und Süd* (Frankfurt am Main: Verlag für Interkulturelle Kommunikation, 1985).

26. Michele Borelli (ed.), *Interkulturelle Pädagogik: Positionen, Kontroversen, Perspektiven* (Baltmannsweiler: Pädagogischer Verlag Burgbücherei Schneider, 1986). [Borelli's distinctive discourse here hinges on variations on the thematic German verb *begreifen* (grasp, comprehend) and is somewhat problematic to render systematically in English.]

27. Non-identity as subjective identity. See Theodor W. Adorno, *Negative Dialectics*. Trans. E.B. Ashton (New York: Continuum, 1983) and idem, *The Jargon of Authenticity*. Trans. Knut Tarnowski and Frederic Will (Evanston, IL: Northwestern University Press, 1973).

28. [Paulo Freire (1921-1997), Brazilian philosopher and educationalist, supervised a massive literacy campaign in Brazil in 1963, based on a method named after him. Following the military coup in 1964, he moved to Chile, where education programs based on his method were launched as well. Like Ivan Illich, Freire is considered one of the founders of a revolutionary educational theory based on the practice in poor countries. His best-known book is *Pedagogy of the Oppressed* (1970).]

29. "Theses on the Philosophy of History," in Benjamin, *Illuminations*, edited with an introduction by Hannah Arendt (New York: Schocken Books, 1969), pp. 253-4 (Thesis II).

30. The biographies and works of critical European (especially Jewish) intellectuals such as Heinrich Heine, Ernest Jouhy, Walter Benjamin and others are an expression of this anomie.

31. Jean Piaget viewed himself as a sociologist, a fact often overlooked in his reception. The reason for regarding himself in this way is partially bound up with the sociocultural significance he accorded the process of the transition from imitative learning through identificational learning (identity formation) on to conceptual learning (formal operational learning) in the development of childhood. The unfolding of the concept is repeated in the history of each and every individual (epigenetic sequence) as their own history of learning and development.

ACKNOWLEDGEMENTS

Manuel Mergner (Amsterdam) made the project possible by authorizing publication of his father's writings. Petra Schwarzer (Oldenburg), Gottfried Mergner's companion, supported the publication with unabated enthusiasm and provided many helpful instructions. Bill Templer (Tel Aviv/Dresden) translated all of Mergner's writings reproduced here from German, including the passages quoted in the introductory chapter. Lee Mitzman (Amsterdam) translated the introduction from Dutch. Peter Drucker (Amsterdam) translated the sections quoted from Henri Lopes in Chapter 10 from French. Thomas Geisen (Trier) advised in the selection of texts, and Irfan Ahmad and Alice Mul reviewed sections of the anthology.

The original references to the writings of Mergner published here are as follows:

Chapter 2 ("The Theory of Social Limits to Learning. On Social History as a Method"): "Theorie der sozialen Lerngrenzen. Zur Sozialgeschichte als Methode," in: Gottfried Mergner, *Ausgewählte Schriften*, Vol. 2: *Lernfähigkeit der Subjekte und gesellschaftliche Anpassungsgewalt. Kritischer Dialog über Erziehung und Subjektivität*. Herausgegeben und eingeleitet von Thomas Geisen (Hamburg: Das Argument Verlag, 1999), pp. 13-26.

Chapter 3 ("The 'National Heritage' of German Colonialism"): "Das 'Nationale Erbe' des deutschen Kolonialismus. Rassistische Bilder—Mitleid mit den Opfern—die Unschuld der Erben," in: Andreas Foitzik *et al.* (eds.), *Ein Herrenvolk von Untertanen. Rassismus—Nationalismus—Sexismus* (Duisburg: Duisburger Institut für Sprach- und Sozialforschung, 1992), pp. 143-162.

Chapter 4 ("Solidarity With the Savages?" German Social Democracy and the African Resistance Struggle in the Former German Colonies): "Solidarität mit den 'Wilden'? Das Verhältnis der deutschen Sozialdemokratie zu den afrikanischen Widerstandskämpfen in den ehemaligen deutschen Kolonien um die Jahrhundertwende," in: Frits L. van Holthoon and Marcel van der Linden (eds.), *Internationalism in the Labour Movement, 1830-1940*. Leiden [etc.]: Brill, 1988, Vol. 1, pp. 68-86.

Chapter 5 ("Death and Social Democracy"): "Der Tod und die Sozial-demokratie," *Psychologie und Gesellschaftskritik*, 12, no. 45-46 (1988), pp. 59-86.

Chapter 6 ("Faithful Fatalism. On the Concept of 'Total War' in the History of Mentality"): "Gläubiger Fatalismus. Zur Mentalitätsgeschichte des 'totalen Krieges' am Beispiel der Kriegstagebücher meiner Mutter, 1940-1946," in: Marcel van der Linden and Gottfried Mergner (eds.), *Kriegsbegeisterung und mentale Kriegsvorbereitung. Interdisziplinäre Studien* (Berlin: Duncker & Humblot, 1991), pp. 179-92.

Chapter 7 ("Social Change Without Social Actors? The Continuing Legacy of the Philosophy of History"): "Gesellschaftlicher Wandel ohne Subjekte? Die fortwirkende Erbschaft der Geschichtsphilosophie," in: Wolfgang Frindte and Heinz Pätzold (eds.), *Mythen der Deutschen. Deutsche Befindlichkeiten zwischen Geschichten und Geschichte* (Opladen: Leske+Budrich, 1994).

Chapter 8 ("Racism as a Distinctively European Species of Xenophobia"): "Rassismus als spezifisch europäische Form der Fremdenfeindlichkeit," in: Gottfried Mergner, *Ausgewählte Schriften* , Vol. 1: *Dominanz, Gewalt und Widerstand. Fragmente und Brüche europäischer Mentalitätsgeschichte*. Herausgegeben und eingeleitet von Thomas Geisen (Hamburg: Das Argument Verlag, 1998), pp. 45-54.

Chapter 9 ("Inculcated Normality and Exclusion. Six Theses on the History of European Xenophobia"): "Erzwungene Normalität und Ausgrenzung: Sechs Thesen zur Geschichte der europäischen Fremdenfeindlichkeit," *Forum Wissenschaft*, 8 (1991), pp. 42-44.

Chapter 10 ("Solidarity in a World of Growing Interconnectivity"): "Lernen von Solidarität in einer Welt wachsender Zusammenhänge," *Zeitschrift für internationale Bildungsforschung und Entwicklungspädagogik*, 17, 3 (1994), pp. 19-23.

Chapter 11 ("Compulsive and Coerced Identities. Once More on the Theory of Social Limits to Learning"): "Zwanghafte und erzwungene Identitäten. Zur Theorie sozialer Lerngrenzen," in: Gottfried Mergner, *Ausgewählte Schriften*, Vol. 2: *Lernfähigkeit der Subjekte und gesellschaftliche Anpassungsgewalt. Kritischer Dialog über Erziehung und Subjektivität*. Herausgegeben und eingeleitet von Thomas Geisen (Hamburg: Das Argument Verlag, 1999), pp. 136-52.

INDEX

A

Abendroth, Wolfgang 3
absolutism 22, 26, 102, 143
Adler, Alfred 10, 16n14
Adorno, Theodor W. 3
Africa 8, 29, 32, 34-37, 39, 42, 43,
44n11, 49, 52, 54-57, 89, 92, 93,
117, 124, 126, 131, 132, 134, 135
Africans 9, 33, 37-43, 47-49, 51-53,
113-115, 118, 119, 125, 134, 135
Arendt, Hannah 131-138
Algeria 57
alterity 11-13, 29, 33, 34, 39, 43, 48,
64, 113-120, 121n7, 127, 128, 136,
137, 139, 140, 143, 146-148, 150,
152
ambivalence 7-10, 12, 21, 129, 143, 144
anticolonialism 31n9
anti-Semitism 118
Arabs 37, 38
atomic bomb 133
authoritarianism 3, 152
authority 4, 64, 71, 76, 77, 103, 106,
107, 114, 115, 118, 124, 131, 151
Aveling, Edward 74

B

Barthels, Max 80, 86n68
Bebel, August 47, 51, 52, 54, 58, 60n7,
66, 71, 75-77, 85n45, 85n46, 104-
108, 110
Bebel, Julie 75, 76
Becker, Egon 136
Bellamy, Edward 108-110
Benjamin, Walter 20, 28, 29, 31n11,
129, 151, 154n30

Berlin Conference (1884-85) 35, 46,
59n2
Bernfeld, Siegfried 26
Bismarck, Otto von 36, 37, 43n6, 61n20
Bloch, Ernst 14, 29, 128, 137
Bodelschwingh, Friedrich von 97,
100n12
Borelli, Michele 150, 154n26
Bremen Left 104, 111n9
Bröger, Karl 80, 81, 86n69
Brückner, Peter 116, 121n11, 128

C

Cameroon 49, 54, 60n8
Caprivi, Georg Leo von 44n13
chauvinism 117
Chevènement, Jean-Pierre 126, 130n5
children 8, 9, 11-13, 22, 25, 30, 33, 34,
37, 38, 40, 41, 47-49, 76, 89, 91,
92, 94-97, 102, 103, 114, 115, 118,
125, 127, 131, 134, 135, 140, 141,
144-147
Christianity 98, 107, 108
church 34, 35, 38, 64, 65, 70, 96, 97
civilization 12, 39, 41, 43, 47, 48, 53,
54, 58, 71, 101-103, 132, 134, 136
Colletti, Lucio 14
colonialism 23, 32-40, 46, 47, 49, 51-
53, 55-58, 123, 125, 126, 132, 133,
134, 143, 145, 153
community 11, 13, 22, 24, 27, 46, 48,
49, 53, 57, 64, 65, 67, 68, 78, 82,
96, 107, 109, 110, 117, 118, 136,
141, 142, 144, 145, 151
compassion 38, 55, 57, 123, 125, 149
conceptual learning 150, 152
Congo 35, 57, 131
cremation 69, 70

D

Dantz, Carl 68, 69
Darwinism 66
David, Eduard 57, 62n43
death 8, 9, 13, 25, 63-74, 77, 78, 80-82, 91, 92, 95, 97-99, 107, 110, 135, 143
Deutsche Demokratische Partei (DDP) 58, 62n45
Deutschnationale Volkspartei (DNVP) 58, 62n45
Deutsche Volkspartei (DVP) 58, 62n45
dialectics 10
Diederich, Franz 81
discipline 9, 12, 26, 71, 76, 78, 83, 108, 110, 127, 147

E

Ebert, Friedrich 57, 87n76
education 5, 9, 12, 23, 25-28, 30, 33, 38, 40, 41, 43, 48-50, 70, 74, 98, 114-116, 135-137, 142, 144-149, 151
Elias, Norbert 48
Engels, Friedrich 73, 74, 77, 78, 79, 106, 107
Enlightenment 3, 4, 6, 7, 23, 25, 27, 30, 64, 68, 105, 115, 143, 152
Erdheim, Mario 19n82, 136, 153n7
Eurocentrism 33
euthanasia 97, 100n12

F

Fabri, Friedrich 36, 37, 44n13
fascism 2, 13, 46, 57, 88-92, 95, 96,98, 109, 110, 113, 115, 117, 124, 128, 132, 133, 147, 148
fathers 34, 99, 125
Feuerbach, Ludwig 3, 66
Flaubert, Gustave 7
Foucault, Michel 153n13
Frankfurter Schule 3
Freiligrath, Ferdinand 73, 77, 85n33
Freire, Paulo 151, 154n28
Fromm, Erich 112n27
funerals 8, 68, 70

G

Geib, August 77
Germany 2, 32, 37, 40, 42, 46, 47, 49, 50, 53, 56, 57, 65, 79, 83, 88, 90, 95, 96, 104, 117, 119, 124, 132
Gerstäcker, Friedrich 56

Gizycki, Georg von 108
Goebbels, Joseph 88, 91, 92
Goebbels, Magda 91
Gorter, Herman 4

H

Habermas, Jürgen 125
Haeckel, Ernst 48, 60n18, 66, 67
Heidegger, Martin 64
Heine, Heinrich 154n30
Heller, Agnes 128
Herero 54, 55, 62n39
Hervé, Gustave 58, 62n47
Herwegh, Georg 73, 85n34
Hitler, Adolf 91-95, 97, 100n12, 132, 133, 148, 149
Hoffmann, Heinrich 113
Holocaust 92
homosexuals 7
hope 9, 10, 12, 13, 24, 29, 30, 64, 65, 68, 70, 78, 92, 93, 97-99, 102, 103, 107, 119, 120, 132, 133, 137, 142, 147, 149, 152
Horkheimer, Max 3

I

identity 7-9, 11-13, 29, 47, 51, 76, 102, 118, 120, 129, 134, 139-141, 143-146, 148
individualization 11, 116, 118, 144, 145, 151
insecurity 11, 118, 120, 123, 127, 145, 146
intellectuals 4, 5, 7

J

Jacoby, Leopold 79
Jews 7, 12, 95, 96, 119, 124
Jouhy, Ernest 9, 10, 31n3, 128, 154n30

K

Kautsky, Karl 54, 61n37, 66, 75, 76, 85n46, 108
Knief, Johannes 8, 77, 86n55, 111n9
Kollontai, Alexandra 4
Kommunistische Partei Deutschlands (KPD) 86n68, 111n7
Korsch, Karl 6
Krahl, Hans-Jürgen 3, 4, 128
Kulturkampf 35, 36, 44n9

L

Lafargue, Paul 78
language 13, 27, 53, 91, 108, 150
Lassalle, Ferdinand 73, 77Latin America 117
Law on Socialists 49, 61n20
Ledebour, Georg 51, 52, 61n26
Lersch, Heinrich 80, 82
Leviné, Eugen 82
Lewin, Moshe 1
liberals 35, 36, 37, 73
Liebknecht, Karl 82, 83, 86n55
Liebknecht, Wilhelm 74, 77-79, 85n38, 104, 106
Lopes, Henri 131-138
Lucas, Erhard 47, 63, 64, 83, 86n56
Lukács, Georg (György) 6
Lumumba, Patrice 42
Luxemburg, Rosa 82, 83, 85n46, 86n55, 104, 111n7

M

Marenga, Jacob 55, 60n6
Marianne 72, 73
Marx, Karl 3, 5, 6, 20, 28, 63, 64, 66, 73-75, 77-79, 85n34, 85n38, 101, 102, 132, 149
Marxism 4, 13, 66
Marx-Aveling, Eleanor 74, 85n38
May Day 73, 105
Mayer, Hans 7, 128
Mehringer, Hartmut 3
memory 14, 22, 23, 29, 30, 47, 73, 75, 76, 78, 79, 83, 120, 126, 128, 141
Merkel, Johannes 69
military 23, 24, 36, 66, 80, 91, 98, 108, 109, 126
Mitschein, Thomas 61n36
monism 66
Most, Joh(an)n 106, 112n14
mothers 8, 9, 34, 73, 93, 98, 99, 125
Müller, Paul 50

N

Namibia (German Southwest Africa) 9, 40, 52, 54-56
nationalism 67, 110, 117, 148, 149
neo-Nazis 122n13, 147, 148
Neumann, Franz 91
nonconformism 128
Norddeutsches Volksblatt 9, 53-56, 58
Noske, Gustav 51, 52, 57, 60n8

O

outsiders 7, 11, 14, 90, 103, 110, 113, 115, 118, 119, 121, 123, 129, 132, 143, 145

P

Pannekoek, Anton 4, 104, 111n8
patriarchy 98, 114
Peters, Carl 96, 100n11
Piaget, Jean 116, 154n31
Pippert, Richard 5, 30
pity 34, 96, 114, 127, 131
police 22, 24, 55, 119, 128
prejudice 27, 114-117, 119, 121, 123
proletariat 22, 25, 47, 48, 68, 76, 78, 82, 114
property 22-27, 63, 101
Protestantism 35, 36, 69, 75, 89, 117
psychoanalysis 7, 116

Q

Quandt, Harald 91

R

Reichstag 36, 37, 47, 51-55, 104, 105
reification 6, 143
religion 2, 11, 23, 65, 66, 90, 91, 93, 97, 107, 139, 144
resistance 28, 31n5, 47, 64, 71, 74
revolution 1, 3, 4, 22, 23-25, 27-29, 31n4, 47, 73, 74, 77, 80, 83, 143
    Chinese Cultural Revolution (1966-69) 29
    French Revolution (1789) 1, 22, 31n6, 73
    German Revolution (1918-19) 4, 8
    Russian Revolution (1917) 1, 31n4
Richter, Dieter 69
Roma 119, 124
Roman Catholicism 35, 36, 70
Roman Empire 107
Rotermundt, Rainer 31n5, 147-149
Roy, Manabendra Nath 103
Rühle, Otto 4, 5, 10, 14, 50, 104, 106, 128

S

Sartre, Jean-Paul 7
scapegoat 12
schools 27, 39, 126